Updated & Enlarged 3rd Edition!

RX-7

Mazda's rotary engine sports car

Brian Long
Foreword by Takaharu 'Koby' Kobayakawa

VELOCE PUBLISHING
THE PUBLISHER OF FINE AUTOMOTIVE BOOKS

Also from Veloce Publishing –

This page is a publisher's catalog listing hundreds of book titles organized into series. The full listing is omitted here for brevity, but includes the following categories:

Speedpro Series — titles on engine building and performance tuning (4-Cylinder Engine Short Block, Alfa Romeo DOHC, Alfa Romeo V6, BMC 998cc A-series, 1275cc A-series, Camshafts, Competition Car Datalogging, Cylinder Heads, Distributor-type Ignition Systems, Fast Road Car, Ford SOHC 'Pinto' & Sierra Cosworth DOHC, Ford V8, Holley Carburetors, Honda Civic Type R, Jaguar XK Engines, Land Rover Discovery/Defender/Range Rover, MG Midget & Austin-Healey Sprite, MGB 4-cylinder Engine, MGB V8 Power, MGB/MGC/MGB V8, Mini Engines, Motorsport Getting Started In, Nissan GT-R, Nitrous Oxide, Race & Trackday Driving Techniques, Retro or classic car for high performance, Rover V8 Engines, Secrets of Speed, Sportscar & Kitcar Suspension & Brakes, SU Carburettor, Successful Low-Cost Rally Car, Suzuki 4x4, Tiger Avon Sportscar, TR2/3/4/4A, TR5/250 & TR6, TR7 & TR8, V8 Engine, Volkswagen Beetle Suspension, Volkswagen Bus Suspension, Weber DCOE, & Dellorto DHLA Carburetors)

Enthusiast's Restoration Manual Series — Classic Large Frame Vespa Scooters, Classic Car Bodywork, Classic British Car Electrical Systems, Classic Car Electrics, Jaguar E-type, Reliant Regal, Triumph TR2/3/3A/4/4A, Triumph TR5/250 & 6, Triumph TR7/TR8, Ultimate Mini Restoration Manual, Volkswagen Beetle, VW Bay Window Bus

Expert Guides — Land Rover Series I-III, MG Midget & A-H Sprite

Essential Buyer's Guide Series — Alfa Romeo Giulia GT Coupé, Alfa Romeo Giulia Spider, Audi TT, Austin Seven, Big Healeys, BMW E21 3 Series (1975-1983), BMW E30 3 Series (1981 to 1994), BMW GS, BMW X5, Citroën 2CV, Citroën ID & DS, Cobra Replicas, Corvette C2 Sting Ray 1963-1967, Choosing/Using & Maintaining Your Electric Bicycle, Fiat 500 & 600, Ford Capri, Ford Escort Mk1 & Mk2, Ford Mustang First Generation 1964 to 1973, Ford Mustang Fifth generation/S197, Ford RS Cosworth Sierra & Escort, Harley-Davidson Big Twins, Hinckley Triumph triples & fours 750/900/955/1000/1050/1200–1991-2009, Honda CBR FireBlade, Honda CBR600 Hurricane, Honda SOHC Fours 1969-1984, Jaguar E-type 3.8 & 4.2-litre, Jaguar E-type V12 5.3-litre, Jaguar Mark 1 & 2, Jaguar 2.5-litre V8 1955 to 1969, Jaguar S-Type 1999 to 2007, Jaguar X-Type 2001 to 2009, Jaguar XJ-S, Jaguar XJ6/XJ8 & XJR, Jaguar XK 120/140 & 150, Jaguar XK8 & XKR (1996-2005), Jaguar/Daimler XJ 1994-2003, Jaguar/Daimler XJ40, Jaguar/Daimler XJ6/XJ12 & Sovereign, Kawasaki Z1 & Z900, Land Rover Series I/II & IIA, Land Rover Series III, Lotus Seven replicas & Caterham 7: 1973-2013, Mazda MX-5 Miata (Mk1 1989-97 & Mk2 98-2001), Mazda RX-8 all models 2003 to 2012, Mercedes Benz Pagoda 230SL/250SL & 280SL roadsters & coupés, Mercedes-Benz 280-560SL & SLC, Mercedes-Benz R129 Series, Mercedes-Benz W124 All models 1984-1997, MG Midget & A-H Sprite, MG TD/TF & TF1500, MGA 1955-1962, MGB & MGB GT, MGF & MG TF, Mini, Morris Minor & 1000, Moto Guzzi 2-valve big twins, New Mini, Norton Commando, Peugeot 205 GTI, Porsche 911 (964), Porsche 911 (993), Porsche 911 (996), Porsche 911 (997) 1st generation 2004 to 2009, Porsche 911 (997) Second generation models 2009 to 2012, Porsche 911 Carrera 3.2, Porsche 911SC, Porsche 924 All models 1976 to 1988, Porsche 928, Porsche 930 Turbo & 911 (930) Turbo, Porsche 944, Porsche 986 Boxster, Porsche 987 Boxster & Cayman, Rolls-Royce Silver Shadow & Bentley T-Series, Royal Enfield Bullet, Subaru Impreza, Sunbeam Alpine, Triumph 350 & 500 Twins, Triumph Bonneville, Triumph Herald & Vitesse, Triumph Spitfire & GT6, Triumph Stag, Triumph Thunderbird/Trophy & Tiger, Triumph TR6, Triumph TR7 & TR8, Velocette 350 & 500 Singles, Vespa Scooters Classic 2-stroke models 1960-2008, Volvo 700/900 Series, VW Beetle, VW Bus, VW Golf GTI

Those Were The Days ... Series — Alpine Trials & Rallies 1910-1973, American 'Independent' Automakers – AMC to Willys 1945 to 1960, American Station Wagons – The Golden Era 1950-1975, American Trucks of the 1950s, American Trucks of the 1960s, American Woodies 1928-1953, Anglo-American Cars from the 1930s to the 1970s, Austerity Motoring, Austins the last real, Brighton National Speed Trials, British and European Trucks of the 1970s, British Drag Racing The early years, British Lorries of the 1950s, British Lorries of the 1960s, British Touring Car Racing, British Police Cars, Café Racer Phenomenon, Don Hayter's MGB Story, Drag Bike Racing in Britain, Dune Buggy Phenomenon, Dune Buggy Phenomenon Volume 2, Endurance Racing at Silverstone in the 1970s & 1980s, Hot Rod & Stock Car Racing in Britain in the 1980s, Last Real Austins 1946-1959, Mercedes-Benz Trucks, MG's Abingdon Factory, Motor Racing at Brands Hatch in the Seventies, Motor Racing at Brands Hatch in the Eighties, Motor Racing at Crystal Palace, Motor Racing at Goodwood in the Sixties, Motor Racing at Nassau in the 1950s & 1960s, Motor Racing at Oulton Park in the 1960s, Motor Racing at Oulton Park in the 1970s, Motor Racing at Thruxton in the 1970s, Motor Racing at Thruxton in the 1980s, Superprix The Story of Birmingham Motor Race, Three Wheelers

Rally Giants Series — Audi Quattro, Austin Healey 100-6 & 3000, Fiat 131 Abarth, Ford Escort RS Cosworth & World Rally Car, Ford Escort MkI, Ford Escort RS1800, Lancia Delta 4WD/Integrale, Lancia Stratos, Mini Cooper/Mini Cooper S, Peugeot 205 T16, Saab 96 & V4, Subaru Impreza, Toyota Celica GT4

WSC Giants — Audi R8, Ferrari 312P & 312PB, Gulf-Mirage 1967 to 1982, Matra Sports Cars – MS620/630/650/660 & 670 – 1966 to 1974

General — (extensive list including titles on Alfa Romeo, Alpine, BMC, BMW, Bugatti, Caravans, Ferrari, Ford, Jaguar, Lamborghini, Lancia, Land Rover, Lotus, Maserati, Mazda, Mercedes-Benz, MG, Mini, Morgan, Motor Racing, Nissan, Porsche, Rolls-Royce, Rover, Toyota, Triumph, Volkswagen, and many others)

---

www.veloce.co.uk

First published in 2001 by Veloce Publishing Limited, Veloce House, Parkway Farm Business Park, Middle Farm Way, Poundbury, Dorchester, Dorset, DT1 3AR, England. Updated & revised second edition published 2004. Third paperback edition published August 2016, reprinted February 2017.
Fax 01305 250479/e-mail info@veloce.co.uk/web www.veloce.co.uk or www.velocebooks.com.
ISBN: 978-1-787111-33-2 UPC: 6-36847-01133-8
© Brian Long and Veloce Publishing 2001, 2004, 2016 & 2017. All rights reserved. With the exception of quoting brief passages for the purpose of review, no part of this publication may be recorded, reproduced or transmitted by any means, including photocopying, without the written permission of Veloce Publishing Ltd. Throughout this book logos, model names and designations, etc, have been used for the purposes of identification, illustration and decoration. Such names are the property of the trademark holder as this is not an official publication.
Readers with ideas for automotive books, or books on other transport or related hobby subjects, are invited to write to the editorial director of Veloce Publishing at the above address.
British Library Cataloguing in Publication Data – A catalogue record for this book is available from the British Library. Typesetting, design and page make-up all by Veloce Publishing Ltd on Apple Mac.
Printed by CPI Group (UK) Ltd, Croydon, CR0 4YY.

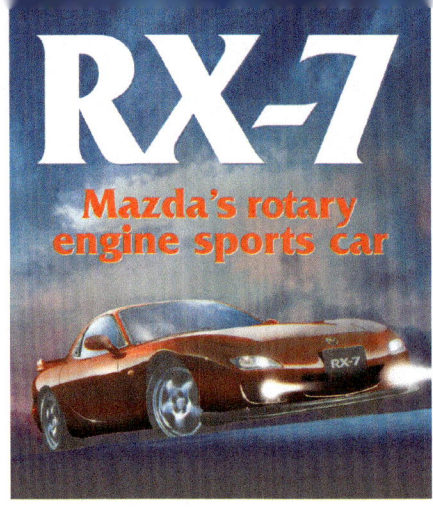

Foreword by Takaharu 'Koby' Kobayakawa

It is virtually impossible not to include the story of the rotary engine at Mazda when one discusses the situation of Japan's automobile industry in the late-50s and early-60s. It was a significant development, and one that perfectly reflects the mentality and spirit of the Hiroshima-based company, then known as Toyo Kogyo.

The history of the internal combustion engine stretches back well over 100 years. It is no exaggeration to say that, during this time, almost every automotive engineer in the world has tried to tackle and refine this form of motive power.

Thus, compared with conventional reciprocating engines, the development of the rotary unit was still in its infancy when it made its public debut. Over the years that followed, Mazda made a virtually single-handed attempt to make it viable – a period of challenge and discovery that could be likened to a sea voyage without the aid of navigation.

One of the key lessons we learnt whilst developing the rotary was that conviction and passion can overcome almost all difficulties. Without a doubt, the RE project forged a strong company spirit.

Looking back, Mazda obtained the necessary licences to develop Felix Wankel's rotary engine because of Tsuneji Matsuda's vision. As a Hiroshima-based businessman with a strong independent spirit and technical background, he could see the unit's charm and merit, and decided to bet Mazda's future independence in the Japanese auto industry on this new technology.

On the other hand, I can still remember the number of scholars and scientists who said it couldn't be made into a practical engine. Needless to say, when we first started working on it, it was blindingly obvious that the RE was still in need of a great deal of development.

Durability and reliability were essential issues that had to be tackled. Sealing the combustion chambers to make them airtight, and developing oil seals that wouldn't leak were tasks given priority, but these turned out to be only the tip of the iceberg. Many more challenges would face us, with another problem occurring the minute one had been cured.

Eventually, in 1967, when we were at last happy with the results achieved by the engine, it appeared in a brand new sports car – the first generation Cosmo Sport (110S).

Just at that moment, air pollution became a serious matter in the USA, especially in California, and the US was the very place we were expecting to take a large proportion of production. We decided to tackle this latest problem head-on and duly opened up the American market, defying the pundits who said it would be impossible for anyone to make the RE clean enough to meet the strict new standards. With this latest episode behind us, and the introduction of the R100, RX-2, RX-3 and RX-4, we felt the marketing possibilities for the rotary were infinite.

But then fate dealt us yet another cruel hand. Although we had reduced the engine's emissions, and there was no question of its ample reserves of smooth power, the 1973 Oil Crisis highlighted fuel consumption. The American Environmental Protection Agency labelled the RE a 'Gas Guzzler' and, overnight, our sales dropped to disastrous levels. Indeed, the situation became so severe, certain members of the media were predicting that Mazda would have to withdraw from the US market.

If we had given up on the RE at this point, the history of the rotary would almost certainly have ended there. It would also have left a clear message for future generations: "Do not try and attempt to harness unproven technology."

Fortunately, the wisdom of our management prevailed, and the rotary project was allowed to continue. However, this was on the proviso that outrageous new targets were met, for which we had to cut fuel consumption by 40% within two years.

This was a time of mixed emotions for the engineers who had devoted their lives to the rotary. On the one hand they were glad not to see their endless toil go to waste, whilst on the other hand it was a truly daunting prospect. Anyway, the programme was given a symbolic name – the so-called 'Phoenix Plan' – and would hopefully enable Mazda to rise from the ashes just like this legendary bird.

This bold scheme incorporated plans to produce a new vehicle in which the rotary engine's advantages could be maximized. The unit's unique characteristics led to the development of the original RX-7, intended primarily for export markets. This was a brave and inspired move.

Thankfully, the first RX-7 was a great success. It allowed the company to recover from the flurry of body blows, and the injured fighter to return to the centre of the ring to give the next round his best shot. Consequently, the second and third generation models followed, of which I have very fond memories. However, before concluding this Foreword I would like to add a few words regarding the insatiable challenge of Le Mans.

Mazda's history at this famous French event dates back to 1974. At that time though, it was privateers who represented the marque, the main entries coming from a dealership's motorsport division, better known as Mazdaspeed. The first generation RX-7 provided the basis for the early racers but, at least as far as Le Mans campaigns were concerned, it was obvious that the model's development was limited.

In 1984, Mazdaspeed became a subsidiary of Mazda and, as such, an all-out works assault on the 24-hour classic was accelerated. The two-rotor

engine gave way to a three-rotor unit in 1986, with a four-rotor RE following in the 1988 season.

A car powered by the latter engine finished seventh in the 1989 event, the best achievement in Mazda's Le Mans challenge history, though as a works effort, a higher finish would have certainly been preferable. Furthermore, time was running out for the rotary, as FISA announced that only 3.5 litre reciprocating units would be eligible after 1990. This change in the regulations made us face up to a number of facts: if we were to win with an RE, we needed at least 100bhp more, and a vast improvement in fuel consumption in just one year. The gauntlet had been thrown down!

The targets were finally achieved at the last minute, with 700bhp being developed by the R26B unit. Unfortunately, however, there had not been the time to make it reliable enough for the rigours of the 24-hour race so, apart from a Class win, we came away humiliated, assuming this to be our last chance for an outright victory.

After our return to Japan, though, we learnt that FISA had amended the rules, meaning that our RE had one more season in which it could compete. This was great news, prompting a concerted effort from everyone involved in the project. We re-evaluated the car in no less than 80 different areas until confident we could mount a serious challenge.

In June 1991 the 787B duly won, becoming not only the first Japanese car to take an outright victory at Le Mans, but also the first to be powered by anything other than a conventional piston engine. One month later, the powerplant was stripped down in front of a group of journalists in Japan, leaving all those present with little doubt that the same unit could have covered the race distance at least a couple of more times!

Winning at Le Mans, the world's toughest race, was undoubtedly only made possible because all of the team members were determined to prove the value of the rotary concept. Perhaps this was a fitting conclusion to what I regard as the first chapter in the RE's history.

As we enter the 21st century, the rotary has a long road ahead of it. Regulations become tighter and tighter, and the needs of the end-user are constantly changing. However, I have no doubt that Mazda's engineers will continue to take up the challenge. In fact, the next chapter in the history of the RE has already begun, with the introduction of the RX-8 at the Detroit Show in January 2001. Only by facing adversity will the gods smile down on you.

It was a great pleasure to be asked to write the Foreword for this worthy publication, as it follows each step in the laborious process of refining the rotary engine (a power unit that was ultimately unique to Mazda) and the development of the sports cars that mean so much to us. I am sure the words on these pages will enable readers to get a good idea of the hardship we suffered along the way, whilst, at the same time, allow them to share in our numerous moments of joy. Banzai to Brian Long's book. I look forward to seeing a second instalment in the near future!

Takaharu 'Koby' Kobayakawa
Tokyo, Japan

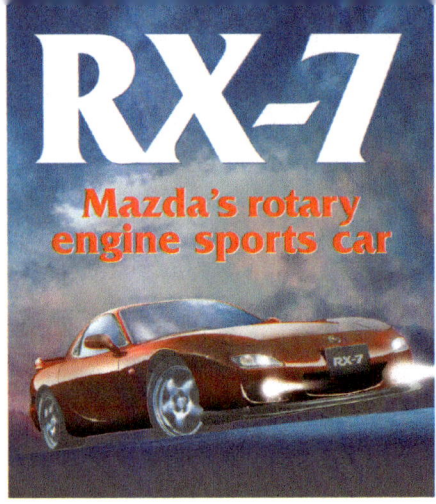

Introduction & Acknowledgements

The RX-7 followed in the footsteps of the Datsun 240Z as a pretty, reasonably-priced sporting coupé. However, at the time the RX-7 was launched, the Z-car moved into a different sector of the market, leaving the field virtually clear for the new Mazda.

In keeping with Mazda's other sporting models, the RX-7 Savanna was powered by the Wankel rotary engine, a power unit that most manufacturers predicted would take the world by storm, but one that was eventually almost exclusively used by the Hiroshima concern.

With almost half-a-million RX-7s on the road, and an excellent competition history to boot, the heavier but equally attractive second generation was launched in time for the 1986 model year. This car moved the RX-7 into the true Grand Tourer category, and spawned a whole array of models, including a convertible.

The early-1990s saw the birth of the third generation. With the MX-5 taking up the mantle of Mazda's affordable sports car, this latest incarnation of the RX-7 went even further upmarket, firmly establishing the marque in the supercar arena. Sadly, with ever-tighter emissions and noise regulations, this may be the last of the breed for export markets, although it continues to be sold in Japan – at least for now.

Fortunately, for enthusiasts of the RE and sports cars in general, the future looks bright. At the 2001 Detroit Show, Mazda unveiled the latest RX model, based on the RX-EVOLV concept vehicle. That it made its debut in America sends a clear message – rotary power is set to make a comeback in the States.

This book charts the full history of these sporting Mazdas and the people behind their development. As well as looking at the competition exploits of the RX-7, it also covers the production models in Europe, North America and the home market.

Acknowledgements

This project would not have been possible without the unfailing help of the Mazda organisation, both in Japan and America. In particular, I would like to thank Takaharu Kobayakawa for giving up a lot of his time, for reading the proof for me, and being kind enough to write the Foreword.

I just wish I could have met him earlier, like so many Japanese I have encountered during my time here. Several times I have thought about giving up writing – one seems to work endless hours for very little thanks – but the chance to meet and befriend these guys makes my job so worthwhile. Ironically, it is due to the constant encouragement of people from this great nation, like Yutaka Katayama (who I may never have got to speak to had it not been for an interview for another book), that keeps me going.

I would also like to extend my gratitude to Tamotsu Maeda and Ryota Ogawa in Mazda's Tokyo office, Brian Betz in the States, and the many members of staff who co-operated on this project. Mention should also be made of Mazda stalwart and former M2 man, Masanori Mizuochi, who came to the rescue with M2-1020 photos and information. As well as official factory material, the contents have been enhanced by the brilliant artwork of my good friend Yoshihiro Inomoto, and the photography of fellow RJC member,

Hideo Aoki. Thanks also to the staff at the Japan Motor Industry Federation Library, to Peter Hunter back in England for sharing his extensive archive with me, and Win Percy for being as helpful and friendly as ever.

Last, but certainly not least, a big thank you to my wife, Miho, not only for ploughing through piles of press releases and other Japanese material, but for always being there, and for giving me Louis – the next generation of car buffs in the family.

Notes on the Second Edition

On a personal note, so much has happened since I wrote the Introduction & Acknowledgements for the original book back in mid-2001. A 2002 RX-7 now sits in the garage (one of the last RB S-Package models ever built), taking the place of the NB2 Roadster (MX-5) I'd bought in the summer of 2000. This car will stay with me forever, and I look forward to handing the keys to my son, Louis, when I get too old to drive it, assuming our second child – Sophie-Mercedes, born earlier this year – doesn't beat him in getting them first!

Mazda memories have been plentiful. Not many RX-7 fans can say they have driven a fast lap of a test track in a Mazdaspeed-tuned car with Takao Kijima at the wheel, met and had dinner with every RX-7 Chief Engineer, and have Takaharu Kobayakawa as godfather to their daughter. For a dedicated fan of the marque, the last couple of years have been wonderful – the stuff of dreams.

As for the book, you'll notice this Second Edition has 16 more pages. These have been used to bring the RX-7 story up-to-date, and add a few words from RX-7 project leader, Takao Kijima, bringing this volume to a fitting conclusion.

The original book carried details of the early RX-8 prototypes. This car, already voted RJC 'Car of the Year' and elected to the Japan Automotive Hall of Fame (JAHFA), is now on sale around the world, and will be covered in a separate volume to be published by Veloce at a later date. The decision to do this has freed up more space for RX-7 material in this book, and we can do full justice to the effort of the Mazda engineers behind the new car.

Whether or not there will be a fourth generation RX-7 remains to be seen. Production of the turbocharged rotary rocket ended in 2002, so this may be the last time I need to update a book on the subject. It will be a shame if that is the case. Meanwhile, however, I sincerely hope you enjoy this Second Edition, which I'm dedicating to the 47 samurai, whose perseverance gave us the RE.

Notes on the Third Edition

Just over a decade has passed since the Second Edition of this book was published – enough time for a lot of fresh archive photographs to come my way, despite there being no replacement for the beautiful FD as yet.

While the world waits with bated breath for a fourth generation model, at least the RX-7 still has a strong following as a usable classic, with a recent event drawing several hundred cars from across Japan, for instance, and measures are slowly being put in place by enthusiasts to help keep vehicles on the road via new thinking on the spares situation. As it happens, the author sees a number of FC and FD models being driven on the roads of Chiba virtually every day, which is a very pleasing sight.

On a personal note, the author still enjoys a special friendship with Takaharu Kobayakawa, with all manner of projects keeping our bond as strong as ever. Believe it or not, our latest undertaking relates to horse equipment! It is the RX-7 that people will always identify Koby with, though, and I hope this book will stand as a lasting tribute to his sterling work, as well as that of the many other Mazda engineers that shared his level of passion in creating a series of magnificent rotary-engined machines.

Brian Long
Chiba City, Japan

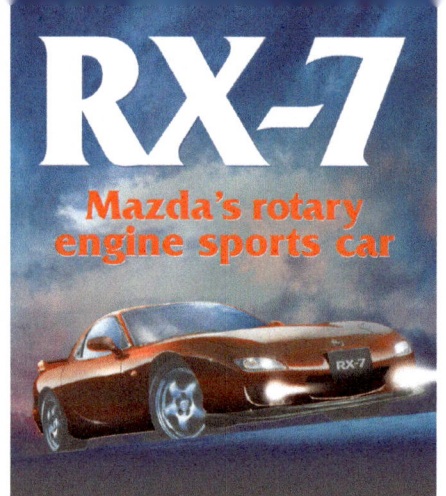

Contents

Foreword 3
Introduction 6
Acknowledgements 6
Notes on the Second and Third
  Edition 7

**Chapter 1: A brief history of
  Mazda** 9
The Mazda marque 10
Post-war growth 11
The rotary revolution 11

Chapter 2: Birth of the RX-7 14
Wankel's dream 14
Mazda and the rotary engine 15
The Cosmo Sport 110S 17
Other Mazda rotaries 18
A harsh situation 22
Project X605 23
Rotary update 29
X605 chassis details 31
The rumour mill 32
The Savanna RX-7 35
The new car in America 38

Chapter 3: The legend grows 43
A Stateside view 45
The car's impact in Britain 47

The RX-7 reaches the UK 50
Revival, and links with Ford 54
Savanna news 55
The US 1981 model year 58
The 'Mk.II' in Britain 59
The Elford Turbo 59
Japanese specials 60
American update 61
The 1982 model year 62
The 6PI rotary engine 63
1983 65
Corporate news 66
The Avatar 66
The RX-7 goes turbocharged 67
The US 1984 model year 69
European update 71
The home market 75
End of the line 76
Bowing out from Europe 76

**Chapter 4: The second
  generation** 79
Project P747 80
A new body 80
The powertrain 85
Chassis details 87
P747 reaches production 90
The new RX-7 in Japan 90
America greets the new model 92
Press reaction 94
The latest RX-7 in Europe 97
The Turbo in the States 100
1987 102
The RX-7 Convertible 104
Other 1988 model year news 105
The 1989 season 112
The 1990 model year 117
European update 119
The US market in 1991 122
Japanese specials 123
End of another era 124
Looking towards the future 124

Chapter 5: The third generation 126
A clean sheet of paper 126
Establishing a concept 126
The powertrain 127
Chassis details 128
A styling competition 132
'Operation Zero' 139

The new model in Japan 141
The American scene 143
The car's arrival in Europe 149
News from Japan 152
American update 152
Changes for 1994 155
Japanese specials 157
The US 1995 model year 157
The RX-01 160
A sad situation 161
The legend continues 163
Corporate news 163
The 1998 model year 164

**Chapter 6: The RX-7 in
  competition** 166
IMSA racing 166
Mazda at Le Mans 171
Racing in Britain 173
Other European races 174
SCCA racing 176
The RX-7's WRC record 177
Group B capers 177
Rallying in America 178
Facing reality 179
Racing in Japan & Australia 180
LSR attempts 181
IMSA update 181
SCCA news 184

Chapter 7: The twilight years 185
The 1999 model year 188
The 1999 Tokyo Show 190
Entering the new millennium 193
The end of a glorious era 201
RX-8 update 201
Afterword by Takao Kijima 204

**Appendix 1: RX-7 buyer's
  guide** 206
Engine & transmission 207
Suspension, steering & braking
  system 208
Body & interior 209
The best buy? 209

**Appendix 2: Production
  figures** 210

Index 215

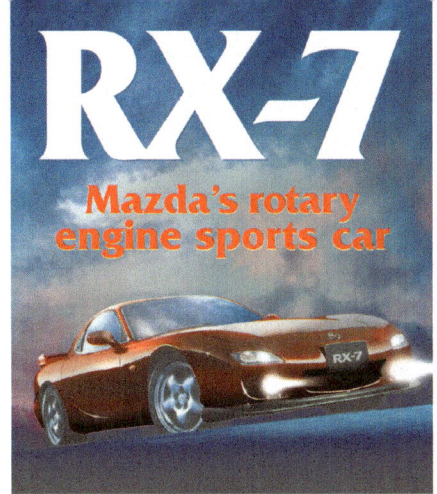

1

A brief history of Mazda

The history of the Japanese motor industry is a complex one, moulded and shaped by government decisions taken in the early-1930s and the reconstruction of Japan following the Second World War.

Mazda's origins date back to January 1920, with the founding of the Toyo Cork Kogyo Company Ltd by Jujiro Matsuda. As the name suggests, the Hiroshima-based firm initially concerned itself with cork products, but in the following year Matsuda decided to move into the manufacture of machinery.

Matsuda was born in August 1875, and, despite being brought up in the fishing trade, developed an early interest in metalworking. By the age of 19 he had his own business; sadly, destined to fail. After various other enterprises, Matsuda eventually decided to move into the supply of cork, as the First World War stopped exports from Europe and left Japan in short supply. When Europe started exporting again, Matsuda guided the company back into light industry.

The car was still not a popular means of transport for the Japanese at that time. In the early 1920s, there were still fewer than 15,000 vehicles in the country, so automobile production was not considered commercially viable. However, a few two-wheeled machines were built following the devastating Kanto Earthquake of 1923.

That year brought a flurry of imported trucks and buses from the United States in an attempt to get the country mobile again. Most of Japan's population was centred around the Tokyo Bay (Kanto) area, and the earthquake had totally destroyed thousands of buildings, and most of

Jujiro Matsuda – entrepreneur and founder of the Mazda marque. His son, Tsuneji Matsuda was recently inducted into the Japan Automotive Hall of Fame.

the communications in Tokyo and Yokohama. Matsuda's Hiroshima-based concern, on the other side of the country, was not affected, and did its best to ease transport problems by building small two-stroke motorcycles.

Although the firm still dealt in cork (this section of the business wasn't sold off until 1944), light industry became increasingly important. In line with this gradual shift in emphasis, in July 1927, the business was renamed the Toyo Kogyo Co. Ltd, which roughly translates into the Orient Industry Company.

A certain Mr Edison also found inspiration in the Ahura Mazdah myth, some years before the Japanese company.

The Mazda marque

Production of Toyo machine tools began in 1929, but, by 1930, thoughts were already turning toward motor vehicles. Design work was initiated on a three-wheeled truck (the 482cc Mazda DA), which entered production in October 1931.

As an aside, there is an interesting story behind the choice of the Mazda name. In Persian mythology, the "lord of light and wisdom" was called Ahura Mazdah. The Mazdah title sounded good in almost any language and had an ideal meaning, with the added bonus of the founder's family name being Matsuda (in Japanese it sounds very similar to Mazdah). Subsequently, the letter 'h' was dropped, and the Mazda marque was born.

The DA was a great success, and within a few months of starting production, Toyo Kogyo began exporting the three-wheeled Mazda to Manchuria – an area of China occupied by Japan. Toyo Kogyo continued to develop the three-wheeler, giving it a larger engine, and also started to manufacture gauge blocks and machine drills.

The company's capital increased no less than four times during 1934, and the factory – based in the Fuchu area of Hiroshima – was duly enlarged. However, military considerations soon led the government to pass the 1936 Motorcar Manufacturing Enterprise Law. Although only Nissan, Toyota and Isuzu complied with the new law at the time, it effectively ended the activities of the foreign car companies, with both Ford and General Motors initially cutting back production and then closing their factories in Japan during 1937.

Toyo Kogyo was forced to make munitions for the Army, although a few three-wheelers continued to leave the factory, despite the Enterprise Law. By 1940, Mazda had built a small prototype coupé, but before it could be developed further, production switched completely to armaments in the build-up to the Pacific War.

After the attack on Pearl Harbour, America declared war on Japan, but no-one could have foreseen the dreadful events that would follow. On 6 August 1945, Hiroshima became

The first vehicle to bear the Mazda name was a three-wheeled truck. Commercials of this type were built throughout the 1930s, and were revived again shortly after the WWII. This example dates from 1949.

Mazda's three-wheeler took on a more substantial appearance with the arrival of the CT series in 1950. Three-wheelers continued well into the 1960s; this T2000 of 1962 vintage has a two-ton load carrying capacity. By this time, Mazda's first car had appeared on the market.

The first Mazda car was the R360 Coupé of mid-1960, powered by a tiny air-cooled V-twin. Over 20,000 examples were sold in the first year of production.

a scene of complete devastation. A broadcast from Tokyo Radio stated: "Most of Hiroshima no longer exists. The impact of the bomb was so terrific that practically all living things, human and animal, were literally seared to death by the tremendous heat and pressure engendered by the blast."

Despite this, the Toyo Kogyo factory, partially sheltered by a hill, was just far enough away from the centre of the blast to escape heavy damage. Sadly, though, the bomb dropped by Enola Gay claimed 78,000 lives and injured countless others. The end of the Second World War came later that month, but it would take many years to restore some kind of normality to the lives of those – on all sides – who suffered as a result of the conflict.

Post-war growth

Although the factory was being used as a makeshift hospital and 'town hall', Toyo Kogyo managed to resume production of the Mazda three-wheelers at the end of 1945. Three years later, the company's capital had doubled, and up to 200 vehicles were being built each week. Larger commercials were announced in 1950, but it would be another decade before the company moved into the passenger car business. Various laws were passed to help the Japanese motor industry, and gradually it found its feet. Production rose steadily, new roads were built, and Tokyo streets began to fill with Japanese cars rather than ageing imported models. Steel and components were being produced in Japan, as by now most of the factories had been returned to their previous owners by the Occupational Forces, thus lessening the need to buy from foreign countries.

Commercials continued to sustain the Hiroshima concern, but in April 1960 the company introduced its first car – the R360 Coupé. It went on sale in May with an air-cooled V-twin engine mounted at the rear; although the 356cc unit developed only 16bhp, the R360 could be bought with either a manual or automatic transmission, and was capable of 56mph (90kph). It sold exceptionally well, with over 20,000 being built in the first year.

After the war, a number of Japanese manufacturers had taken the opportunity to enter into technical co-operation agreements with companies in the west. The Toyo Kogyo concern was quite late in taking up this offer, but eventually, in mid-1961, signed a deal with NSU of Germany.

NSU held the rights to the Wankel rotary engine, a rather advanced piece of engineering. However, corporate opinion at Mazda was that being the first vehicle builder in Japan to acquire this technology would enable it to catch up with the likes of Nissan and Toyota, thus ensuring its survival.

Over the next five years, while the rotary engine was being developed, Toyo Kogyo introduced a number of new Mazda cars – the Carol P360 and P600, the first generation of Familia models, and the Luce 1500 (the coachwork on the latter being designed by a famous Italian styling house – in fact, Giugiaro has been credited with the design during his time with Bertone).

Meanwhile, cumulative production of cars and commercials reached one million units in March 1963; two years later, the Miyoshi Proving Ground was completed. By this time, Toyo Kogyo was the third largest car producer in Japan, continually expanding operations at a staggering rate. In 1966, a new passenger car plant opened in Hiroshima, and in the following year, full-scale exports for the European market began.

The rotary revolution

Toyo Kogyo – under the leadership of Jujiro Matsuda's son, Tsuneji,

One of the prototype Cosmo Sport models – the first of over 1,800,000 Japanese road cars to be powered by the rotary engine. (Courtesy Nobuya Matsuda)

Above & inset: The rotary-engined Cosmo Sport 110S reached the market in May 1967. Around 350 of these early models were built before the Cosmo underwent a minor facelift in mid-1968. Its high price tag limited total sales to just over 1500 units over a six year production run.

since 1951 – was certainly a forward-thinking organisation, installing its first computer system at Hiroshima as early as 1958. Six years later, at the 1964 Tokyo Show (held at Harumi that year), the Mazda Cosmo Sport 110S made its debut.

Powered by the company's first Wankel engine, it was extremely advanced, and caused the Rotary Engine Development Division more than a few teething troubles in the early days. It underwent an extraordinary period of development before going on sale to the public, with a total of 60 pre-production models being road tested. Consequently, the Mazda Cosmo did not go on sale until 30 May 1967, by which time company engineers had perfected the power unit. Selling at 1,580,000 yen, it was very costly (only the Toyota 2000GT was more expensive in the sports car sector of the Japanese market), and this was reflected in a total run, from 1967 to 1972, of just 1519 units.

In October 1969, the Japan Automatic Transmission Company (JATCO) was formed, a joint venture between Toyo Kogyo, Ford and Nissan for the manufacture of automatic gearboxes. The rotary engine passed Federal tests that year, and exports

Seductive Japanese advertising for the 1968 Luce saloon. Designed by Bertone in Italy, it had been introduced two years earlier.

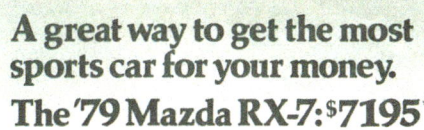

Although not the most interesting Mazda ever built, the Familia (known as the GLC in America and the 323 elsewhere), with its conventional fuel-efficient engine, helped Toyo Kogyo to survive an uncertain period in the company's history. This American advert dates from early 1979, by which time the RX-7 was already on sale in the States.

to the United States began shortly afterwards. The first cars – with both rotary and more conventional powerplants appearing in the line-up – arrived there in the spring of 1970. Within a year, Mazda dealerships were selling vehicles before they even had time to unload them from the transporters.

Following the death of Tsuneji Matsuda in November 1970 (he was 74), the reins were passed to his son, Kohei, the third generation of the Matsuda family to head the company. There was a whole string of important introductions during the early-1970s: the Mazda Capella (RX-2) was followed by the Savanna (RX-3) and, in 1972, the Luce (RX-4) made its debut. Mazda cars were now beginning to outsell trucks year after year. By the end of 1972, cumulative production had reached a staggering five million units, and the Mazda Technical Centre had been established in Irvine, California.

The oil crisis held up a number of interesting projects, such as the X020G 2+2 coupé. Rotary units, some rated up to 200bhp, were being prepared, but the timing, sadly, was all wrong, and sales of rotary-engined models as a whole began to suffer as fuel economy became an overriding consideration with new car buyers. As a result, Toyo Kogyo soon ran into financial troubles and had to turn to the Sumitomo Bank for help to keep the business afloat. The company eventually received the bank's backing, but the Matsuda family lost some of its power in the process.

1977 saw the introduction of the Familia (the original GLC/323, powered by a conventional four-stroke engine), which doubtless helped combat the downturn in Mazda sales. However, it was the car launched the following year that was significant to enthusiasts of sporting machinery.

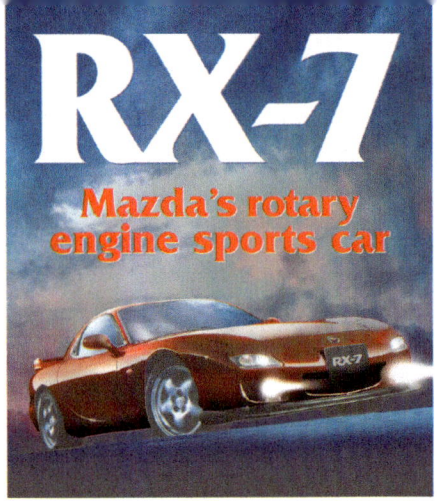

2

Birth of the RX-7

The rotary engine had already proved itself in a decade of service but, being at the heart of the RX-7, it is well worth reviewing the history of this unique powerplant, as well as explaining how it works, for however familiar one may be with four-stroke engines, the Wankel unit – although far from complicated – is so very different to anything else the average enthusiast will have encountered.

Wankel's dream

Legend has it that, as a teenager, the young Felix Wankel dreamt about driving a car he'd built that was powered by a rotary engine. This led him to investigate the commercial possibilities of the rotary and, by 1924,

1: The fuel/air charge is drawn into the uppermost chamber through the port at the top of this diagram (intake). 2: As the rotor continues to rotate, the movement of the eccentric output shaft keeps the apex seals tight to the trochoid housing, and the fuel is compressed (compression). 3: At maximum compression, the spark plugs ignite the charge and because of the chamber shape, formed by the gap between the rotor and the housing, combined with the eccentric shaft, the rotor continues to revolve (ignition/expansion), thus generating torque. 4: The final sweep of the rotor pushes the exhaust gases out through the lower port (exhaust), and the cycle is ready to start again. Meanwhile, the continuous process means that the output shaft will rotate three times for every revolution of the rotor, ie. three power pulses are delivered for each full turn of the rotor.

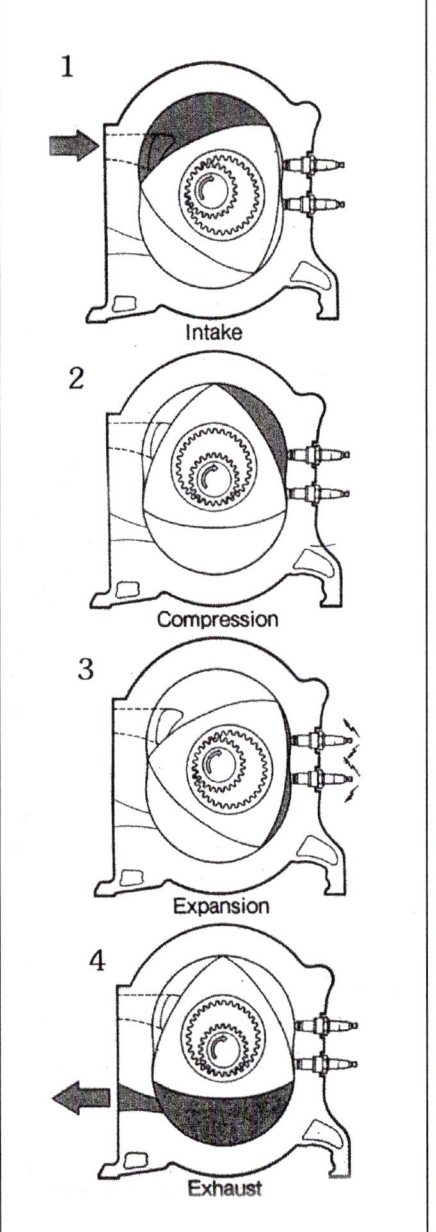

when the German was just 22 years old, he had established a small laboratory to carry out research and development appertaining to this advanced power unit.

There was nothing particularly new about the idea of a continuously rotating internal combustion engine – it has been around in principle for almost two centuries – but it took Dr Felix Wankel to turn it into a reality. It was Wankel who determined the optimum shape of the trochoid housing, and, combined with other experimental projects (such as refining rotary valves for application in the field of aviation and his work on superchargers), it was technology he developed that made it all possible.

The rotary engines found fitted to early aeroplanes were quite different, as they employed traditional four-stroke, Otto-cycle combustion, with all the pistons, con-rods, crankshaft and valvegear that this system necessitated; the only similarity here is the name.

So, how does the Wankel rotary work? With the Wankel engine, the main components are a triangular-shaped rotor enclosed in an oval-shaped outer shell known as the trochoid housing. Due to the shape of the rotor, the housing is always divided into three sections, and it is within these chambers that the four cycles of intake, compression, combustion and exhaust are carried out successively in a different area of the unit.

However, it is the mounting of the rotor on an eccentric output shaft (turning at three times the speed of the former due to the relative number of teeth on the two components) that makes it all work, as this allows the volume in the chambers to change during each rotation of the triangular rotor. Thus, the expansion force that follows combustion pushes the rotor round, which in turn moves the eccentric shaft to start the cycle over again.

The main advantage is that a rotor need only revolve once to effectively achieve what a piston in a reciprocating powerplant takes four strokes to do, by which time the rotor has delivered three power pulses. The end result is less torque fluctuation and smoother running, particularly at high rpm. It was an ingenious invention – compact, light and relatively simple – but refining the housing shape (which had to match the three apexes of the rotor at all times), and the various seals and port positions, would take a long while to perfect.

Because of its modest weight and size, compared to a more conventional engine with a similar output, in addition to its smooth power delivery at higher revs (the fact that all components turn the same way helped reduce vibration levels), naturally enough the German aircraft industry showed a great deal of interest in Wankel's project.

The good doctor was fortunate to meet and befriend a man called William Keppler, who later became economic advisor to Adolf Hitler. Keppler arranged for Wankel to carry out his research at Daimler-Benz, but he soon left Stuttgart to join BMW. However, just before war broke out, Wankel returned to Benz and worked closely with Goetze, a famous piston ring company. Due in part to his links with Keppler and the Nazi Party, during the Second World War, it was the German Aviation Ministry that financed his studies, although this was to backfire after the conflict, when Wankel was jailed by the French authorities for his part in the German war effort.

However, shortly after his release, he set up the Technical Institute of Engineering Study at his old laboratory in Lindau, and continued to develop the rotary engine and rotary compressor. Wankel approached Porsche with the idea of developing the rotary but, with limited resources, the Stuttgart company turned him away. It was at this point, through Keppler, that NSU became involved.

NSU, a German concern whose origins could be traced back to the 19th century, was better known for its motorcycle racing exploits at this time. However, NSU had been part of the automobile industry from the beginning; first as supplier and then as manufacturer.

The Great Depression had a dramatic effect on the firm, though, as the majority shareholder was actually a speculator. As a consequence, car production ceased in 1929. With NSU two-wheeler sales picking up, the NSU model designed by Dr Ferdinand Porsche – a definite forerunner of the Volkswagen – sadly, was destined to remain a prototype.

NSU-Werke AG was formed in 1937, but the factory was badly damaged during World War II, and it wasn't until 1949 that motorcycle production was resumed. However, bikes were abandoned in 1957 to enable the firm to concentrate on a return to building cars. The Prinz, a light car powered by a 600cc, air-cooled twin, arrived in autumn 1957 and was an immediate hit. It was followed by a succession of commercially-successful vehicles that eventually led to the introduction of rotary-engined production models.

NSU had first become involved with Dr Wankel when it had sealing problems with the rotary valves on racing motorcycle engines. Five years later, in 1956, Wankel's supercharger was adopted on a 50cc NSU record-breaker, enabling it to travel at a phenomenal 120.3mph (192.5kph).

Thanks to NSU and the help of Ernest Hoeppner, February 1957 saw the first rotary engine up and running. The Type DKM was followed by a more practical version with a fixed housing, and this 1958 design – the Type KKM (which stands for 'Keiskolbenmotor'), devised by NSU's Dr Walter Froede – became the basis for the modern rotary as we know it today.

NSU duly launched the Wankel Spyder in 1963, powered by a single-rotor unit rated at 64bhp. Meanwhile, though, this new form of motive power had attracted a lot of attention from other manufacturers.

Mazda and the rotary engine
In order to recoup some of the development costs incurred on the project, NSU officially announced its success at rectifying the rotary engine's inherent design difficulties in November 1959, sparking off worldwide demand from other car producers desperate to buy licences in order to acquire Wankel's new technology.

One of the many companies to show interest was the Japanese Toyo Kogyo concern, better known nowadays as Mazda. Tsuneji Matsuda, Mazda's charismatic President since 1951, who was often referred to as the Soichiro

15

Tsuneji Matsuda (to the lady's right) on his way to sign a preliminary contract with NSU in Germany in late-1960. This Japan Airlines (JAL) flight would change the history of the Mazda marque forever.

Honda of western Japan, saw the rotary engine as an ideal opportunity to bring his company up to the same level as the likes of Toyota and Nissan. Via the German Ambassador in Japan and a German friend of his, Matsuda personally began direct negotiation with NSU.

The decision to invest heavily in the rotary engine (or RE) was indeed a bold one for the time, as Japanese car production as a whole was little more than 200,000 units annually, and Mazda was accounting for only a very small proportion of this figure. Fair enough, by 1970, car production in the Land of the Rising Sun was up to 200,000 units a month (still a far cry from today's figures!), though it does give a good indication of how far behind Europe and America the Japanese were in the early 1960s.

Having gained approval from the Japanese government, a contract with NSU was formally signed in July 1961, granting Mazda the rights to the rotary engine for the princely sum of 280 million yen – equivalent to a years' wages for 8000 workers. Over 100 companies had applied (surprisingly, almost one-third of them were based in Japan), with major licence holders eventually including General Motors (via Curtiss-Wright, the giant aviation firm), Mercedes-Benz, Citroen, Ford, Alfa Romeo, Rolls-Royce, Porsche, and British Leyland.

Meanwhile, a group of technicians were sent to Germany, and NSU duly shipped a KKM400 (400 standing for 400cc) prototype engine to Japan, as well as a vast number of technical drawings. Impatient to get on with the project, by November that year, Mazda had built its own prototype based on

Kenichi Yamamoto (centre) looking over design drawings with Takashi Kuroda, the man who would eventually succeed him as head of the RE Department.

these drawings, whilst testing of the German single-rotor Wankel was taking place; this first Mazda rotary was given the Type 40A designation.

Both REs suffered from the same affliction – uneven wear patterns on the inner surface of the trochoid housing that ultimately caused the German unit to stop working completely after just 12,500 miles (20,000km) on the testbed. In reality, while this design fault persisted, there was no way the rotary engine could be sold on the open market. These so-called 'chatter marks', caused by the apex seal during vibration periods, soon became known internally as Devil's Nail Marks.

During April 1963, the Rotary Engine Development Division was formally established, headed, at the behest of Matsuda, by Kenichi Yamamoto. Born in Kumamoto on 16 September 1922,

his family moved to Hiroshima when he was a child. However, during the war, when Yamamoto trained as an engineer and designer in the aviation industry, he was based in far-away Ibaraki Prefecture. When hostilities ceased, Yamamoto returned to Hiroshima and a scene of complete devastation. One of the few places he could find work was at the Toyo Kogyo factory, but it must be said, initially he took the job grudgingly, as he had to start at the bottom, and all his studies in aircraft design would be wasted in the process. After a while, though, he began to feel proud of his small part in his home town's rebirth: fortunately, his talent was soon spotted and he was quickly moved from the production line.

With no fewer than 47 engineers working in four different sections (research, design, testing and materials), Yamamoto and his team set about curing the RE's problems. The group, consisting of mainly younger, enthusiastic members, later became known internally as 'The 47 Samurai' in reference to the 47 honourable warriors who famously avenged their master's death in 1702.

After months of toil and seemingly little progress, Yamamoto, with a stomach ulcer brought on by stress, despaired. He went to Matsuda's office to tell him he was quitting, but was surprised by the older man's response. Matsuda told Yamamoto that his brother had perished during the bombing of Hiroshima, and reminded Yamamoto of the younger sister he had lost. He said that for their sakes, and that of the city, they had to succeed with the RE. Matsuda told him to take as long as necessary, and Yamamoto duly went away full of fresh determination. This spirit, in the face of adversity, would serve them well in the future.

Eventually, after trying no fewer than 500 different compounds, a cross-hollow seal was developed to keep the chatter marks at bay. Thanks to this new design, a prototype ran for 300 hours at high speed without showing any signs of wear. However, a slightly different approach was taken for production, following extensive research into the structure and materials used in the original seals.

Inadequate sealing was the cause of another aggravating problem – oil leaking into the combustion chamber. This not only increased oil consumption, but also created a cloud of white smoke from the exhaust. Fortunately, it was later overcome when Mazda joined forces with the Nippon Piston Ring Co. and the Nippon Oil Seal Co. to produce a rubber seal and a special lubricant.

As the project progressed, it became obvious that a single-rotor RE was not viable for commercial applications. Whilst fine at higher speeds, it was liable to vibrate at low revs and was distinctly lacking in low-speed torque. As a result, to obtain smoother power delivery, the engineers concentrated their efforts on developing two-, three- and four-rotor units.

The first two-rotor engine was an original Mazda design with a 399cc x 2 capacity, known as the Type L8A. (RE displacement is generally expressed by the unit chamber volume, i.e. the difference between the minimum and maximum of a working chamber, multiplied by the number of rotors, incidentally.) This was duly fitted to a prototype Cosmo Sport, a car for enthusiasts designed specifically for rotary power.

As it happens, thanks to the sterling work of Yamamoto and his team of talented engineers, the Japanese were actually in a position to launch a rotary-powered model before NSU but, perhaps rightfully in view of the RE's origins, the German company was given the honour, introducing the Wankel Spyder at the 1963 Frankfurt Show, which opened a couple of weeks ahead of the equivalent event in Tokyo.

The Cosmo Sport 110S
Two twin-rotor Wankel engines were displayed at the 1963 Tokyo Show, but the car they were destined to power – the Cosmo Sport 110S – didn't make its debut until the following year, and did not appear in Mazda showrooms before mid-1967 (at about the same time as the infamous Ewald Praxl-designed NSU Ro80 was launched, as it happens).

As mentioned earlier, the rotary unit had given Mazda's engineers more than a few headaches. Needing to be absolutely sure they had a product that would enhance company image rather than sully it before it really got off the ground as a serious car manufacturer, proving tests took place over some 1,860,000 miles (3,000,000km).

Consequently, new apex seals were developed, produced with the aid of pyro-graphite (a strong carbon-based material) and specially-processed aluminium sintering. Even after a 62,000 mile (100,000km) test drive, wear was marginal, and there was a complete absence of the dreaded chatter marks that had plagued earlier prototype engines.

In addition to this exhaustive testing period – quite extraordinary for the time – the company decided to field a team of Type L10A Cosmos in the 1968 Marathon de la Route. The theory was that if the car could last this gruelling 84-hour event, no-one could question the reliability of the rotary engine.

Two mildly-tuned Cosmos duly turned up at the Nurburgring at the end of August, one manned by Japanese drivers and the other driven by European racers. Sadly, the Japanese team, led by Yoshimi Katayama, fell by the wayside with only a few hours to go as a result of a broken axle, but the second car managed to finish a gallant fourth overall behind the works-entered Porsche 911E of Herbert Linge and co.

The Cosmo was heralded as a new age automobile. Charles G. Burck called it "A car that may reshape the industry's future." The production model was equipped with a new 110bhp 10A (491cc x 2) RE, the first prototype of which was completed at the end of 1964. The 10A, the world's first two-rotor production rotary engine, had a side-port intake system coupled to a two-stage, four-choke carburettor; two spark plugs were employed for each rotor. With a 9.4:1 compression ratio, maximum power came at a heady 7000rpm, while peak torque, quoted at 96lbft, occurred at 3500rpm.

A July 1968 facelift saw power increase to 128bhp (torque output was also enhanced, now quoted at 103lbft) and the additional benefit of a five-speed gearbox, but sales were still slow. Although not a great success commercially – probably due to its high price as much as anything else – the Cosmo did at least establish Mazda as a builder of sports cars, and the name became inextricably linked with the Wankel unit. Over the years that followed, the Japanese company launched a series of sporting machinery exploiting the beauty of the rotary engine.

Other Mazda rotaries

The R16A was a low-slung, mid-engined sports prototype that Mazda employed to test the experimental three- and four-rotor REs. Testing took place at the recently-opened Miyoshi Proving Ground, at the time the most advanced facility in the whole of Asia. In addition to the one-off Spyder version, a clay model was made of a closed coupé, but this was as far as the latter project went.

The R15A, powered by a two-rotor RE mounted at the rear, was put forward as a possible replacement for the Cosmo. Designs dating from the tail-end of 1968 also proposed a mid-engined configuration, although neither progressed further than the drawing board.

The RX-500 was a typical dream car from the period – basically, a Japanese version of the Mercedes C-111 built to commemorate the company's 50th anniversary. However, not only did it generate a great deal of publicity when it first appeared at the 1970 Tokyo Show, on the practical side, it also provided Mazda's engineering team with masses of valuable research data, both on the rotary engine, all-round disc brakes, and the performance of plastic bodies.

A team of engineers was assigned the job of looking into the possibility of putting an RX-500 derivative into production. The RS-X, as it was called, was supposed to announce Mazda's presence in the US market, with an annual sales target of around 3500 units. Unfortunately, the proposal never got off the ground, although Akio Uchiyama, head of the project, did become a very important figure in the Hiroshima company's sports car history.

The facelifted Cosmo was duly given the L10B designation.

Production of the Cosmo Sport 110S.

A picture from the first Japan Car Test Day at Brands Hatch, England. The event, held in March 1968, featured such cars as the Cosmo Sport 110S (farthest from the camera), the Toyota Crown, Mitsubishi Colt 1100 fastback sedan, and Honda's S800. The diminutive size of the Mazda is easy to gauge in this shot.

The fabulously wacky RX-500, seen here with an early Cosmo in Hiroshima. At one point, there were thoughts of producing a road car based on this model, but the proposal was never followed through.

Right: Another view of the RX-500.

Prototypes were used to improve reliability, and power and torque output, whilst at the same time reducing fuel consumption and exhaust emissions. This research led to the development and eventual introduction of the thermal reactor system, which dramatically cut hydrocarbon levels (it was later further improved by adding a heat exchanger into the exhaust system to enhance reaction efficiency), thus allowing Mazda to pass some of the strictest anti-pollution regulations the world has ever seen: it also brought about leaner fuel/air mixtures, making the unit cleaner and substantially more frugal.

As for the production cars that benefited from these advances, the Familia Rotary Coupé came in mid-1968. Based on the RX-85 show car displayed at the 1967 Tokyo Show, this pretty two-door model – known as the R100 Coupé in export markets – was augmented by a slightly cheaper four-door saloon variant in 1969. Both were powered by a 100bhp version of the 10A twin-rotor RE.

Like the Cosmo before it, the R100 found success on the race tracks of Europe, taking fifth overall in the 1969 Marathon de la Route. In the following year, an R100 attained eighth place in the RAC Tourist Trophy, and another came fifth in the equally important Spa-Francorchamps 24-hour Race (one works car, with around 200bhp on tap, had actually been leading until problems struck halfway through the event).

In addition to the highly-successful Familia Rotary models, Mazda marketed a pillarless coupé based on the Luce. First seen as the RX-87 prototype displayed at the 1968 Tokyo Show, this gained a bigger 13A (655cc x 2) unit rated at 126bhp, which was enough to give this beautiful machine a top speed of 119mph (190kph). Launched in late-1969, it was priced at 1,750,000 yen.

Mazda continued to introduce new rotary models in quick succession, and duly received an award from the Japanese Mechanical Engineering Society for successfully commercializing the Wankel powerplant. By the end of 1970, Mazda had built in excess of 100,000 rotary engines.

The X020A/Z was an interesting design proposal from this period –

A Japanese advert dating from mid-1970 for the Mazda Familia Rotary Coupé, known in Britain as the R100 Coupé; it was also sold in the United States, but acquired round headlights for that market. Its elegant lines were bettered only by the contemporary Luce Rotary Coupé – a pillarless, two-door model based on the Luce saloon.

basically, a Mazda equivalent of the Datsun 240Z, but powered by a two-rotor RE. The idea was stillborn, sadly, but on careful examination, one can see a number of similarities to the car proposed in Project X605 – the subject of this book. Later on, there was the X110 design study (which bore a remarkable likeness to the RX-7), and also a much larger GT aimed at taking on the Jaguar E-type and Porsche 911 markets. This was known as the X020G, with power coming from 15A (737cc x 2) or 21A (1046cc x 2) REs, but, with the 1973 oil crisis, the timing was all wrong for such a vehicle.

Meanwhile, the Capella Rotary (or RX-2) went on sale in May 1970, with automatic transmission becoming an option in the following year. A high-performance, five-speed manual version known as the GSII came in 1972, when the RX-2 was given the 'Import Car of the Year' award by the American *Road Test* magazine. With the Capella Rotary came another new two-rotor engine – the 12A – with 120bhp being extracted from a capacity of 1146cc.

The 10A-powered Savanna was introduced in September 1971, the GT version of which (equipped with the larger 12A unit and a five-speed gearbox) had an enviable reputation, both on road and track, where it successfully faced up to the all-conquering Nissan Skyline GT-R. The standard 105bhp Savanna came with saloon, coupé and estate body options, incidentally. It was known abroad as the RX-3, where it used the same 12A engine as the RX-2 and Savanna GT.

Although less than 1000 of the first Luces were sold, its elegant styling made it a brilliant advertisement for the company. In October 1972, the second generation was announced, which came initially with the 573cc x 2 12A rotary. The first production car to be equipped with a full emissions control package as standard, again, saloon, coupé and estate models were made available, with the buyer able to choose between manual and automatic transmission.

In export markets, where it employed a 110bhp 13B RE (a two-rotor unit with a 654cc x 2 capacity), the second Luce was called the RX-4. It was very well-received in America, as this *Car & Driver* report demonstrates: "Mazda has mated its new fifth generation rotary engine to a fresh hardtop coupé. The end result is a Japanese two-door edition of the Jaguar XJ – impeccably mannered where comfort is involved and fleet of foot to set the pace in rapid transit. The RX-4 is going to be one formidable contender in the $4000 division." However, times were changing fast outside Japan.

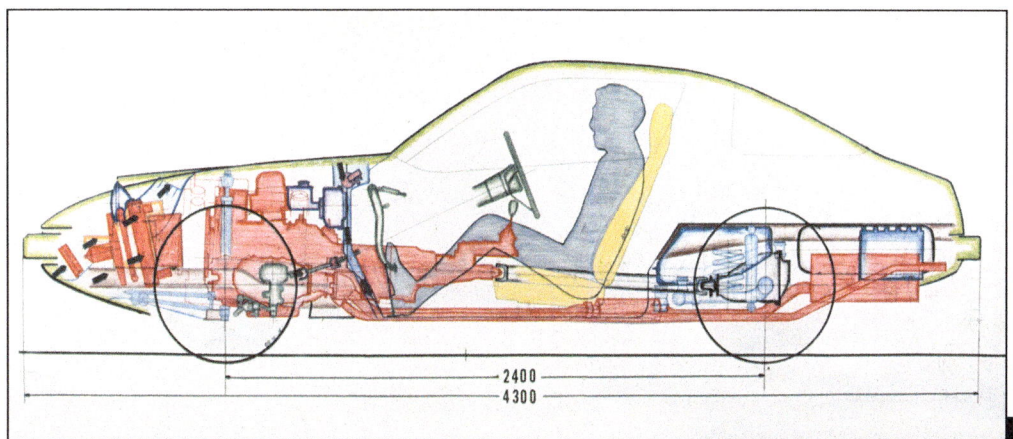

Drawing showing the layout of the X020A, which had an independent rear suspension; the X020Z proposal featured a live rear axle. The project was started in the summer of 1970.

A design sketch submitted by Hiroshi Zaima as part of the X110 study. A model with a targa roof was also put forward.

Above & right: A couple of sketches from the X020G proposal. Note the likeness to the Porsche 924 in profile, especially around the rear quarters.

21

One can see from this picture why the Japanese gained a reputation for being over-fussy in their detailing. Nonetheless, the basic shape of this 1973 model year Savanna GT is very attractive.

A harsh situation

By this time, the American market was becoming increasingly important. In 1970, the first year of official sales in the States (the rotary engine had only recently passed the Federal emissions test), just 2100 cars were sold. However, by the following year, sales had increased almost ten-fold. Mazda Motors of America continued to boom: by 1973, US sales had topped the 100,000 mark, with rotary models accounting for over 90% of this total.

In the background, however, a potential problem was looming. The floating exchange rate system was introduced in 1971. Almost immediately the yen began to strengthen against the dollar, so that, by 1972, 300 yen would buy a dollar instead of the 357 needed at the start of the previous

An official photograph of the 1974 RX-4 saloon from the UK concessionaire. The era known as the 'Sporting Forties' (1965-74 in Japanese Emperor years) spawned a number of exciting vehicles from the Land of the Rising Sun.

The Savanna GT was labelled the RX-3 abroad. Like the RX-2 (which was also rotary-engined), it came as an attractive coupé (as seen here in 1977 guise) or with four-door saloon bodywork. An estate version augmented the RX-3 range.

year. With the oil crisis of 1973, the yen was quoted at 253 per dollar before the American currency recovered dramatically.

Whichever way one looks at it, this was not a good situation for Japanese manufacturers as it pushed up prices in export markets. When the Wankel's reputation went sour (NSU was known to be replacing powerplants at 15,000 miles, or 24,000km), combined with the after-effects of the Arab-Israeli War, sales in the States – where almost all of Mazda's range was rotary-engined – dropped to disastrous levels, especially after the well-publicised EPA fuel consumption figures showed the RE in a bad light. As noted in the previous chapter, it took a massive injection of cash from the Sumitomo Bank to keep the company afloat.

Meanwhile, other automobile companies who'd bought licences to develop the Wankel had turned their backs on it. General Motors had invested a fortune in the new unit, which had been expected to power the entire GM range by 1974. Ultimately, though, despite having poured $150 million into the RE, GM had to give up on this idea: however hard the company tried, it struggled to curb the rotary's high output of unburnt hydrocarbons. Regarding emission control, GM's then-President, Pete Estes, admitted in the *Detroit News*: "We have made no progress in four years."

Even NSU was struggling with the twin-rotor unit in the Ro80. A lack of low-end torque and poor economy (at least when compared to a piston engine with similar displacement) meant the rotary unit was not really suitable for a heavy luxury saloon. Warranty claims had hit NSU's finances hard in the early days of the Ro80 and, as the effects of the fuel crisis were felt, sales fell to unacceptable levels. By this time, Volkswagen had long since taken over control of NSU, but there was no finance available for developing the RE. In the spring of 1977, after just over 37,000 Ro80s had been built, production ceased, thus signifying the end of the NSU marque.

Fortunately for Mazda, which was planning something to compete with the Datsun Z in a lightweight sporting machine, a reliable version of the rotary engine was a completely different proposition. Indeed, the inherent character of the Wankel powerplant was ideally suited to a sports car. Not that Mazda had an easy time introducing the rotary. The company employed a rich mixture to guard against detonation and to fuel the thermal reactor, so the unit quickly acquired a reputation for being something of a gas guzzler. In addition, there were problems with overheating on 1970-73 engines (caused by O-ring failure), which cost Mazda dearly in sales and in court.

There were also severe doubts about whether the Wankel could meet forthcoming emissions levels, as the large ratio of surface to volume in the working chambers tended to leave cool, and hence unburned, mixture around the edges, which was then pushed straight out into the exhaust. Two spark plugs for each rotor helped the situation, especially at lower revs, but it was largely unavoidable given the engine's basic design.

However, through sheer determination, Mazda had pretty much conquered the problems associated with the RE. Fuel consumption had been improved by up to 40% as a result of modifications made by the Japanese company during the so-called 'Phoenix Project', and, against the odds, Mazda had successfully adapted the unit to comply not only with the home market's anti-pollution laws, but also the outrageously strict Muskie Act in the States. By adopting the thermal reactor, air injection and retarded ignition, the company cleared the American test in February 1973, almost two years ahead of time, duly giving vehicles that qualified the AP (Anti-Pollution) appellation.

By not allowing outside firms access to patented improvements, Mazda managed to keep others from trying to develop the RE further. Indeed, Toyota is said to have produced an even better version of the Wankel unit, but, limited to the use of NSU patents only, without encroaching on the Hiroshima company's registered designs, it was a lost cause.

The rotary basically belonged to Mazda, and a lightweight sports car powered by this unique unit looked

NSU was struggling with the rotary in the Ro80. Sales of the model ceased in 1977, signalling the end of the German marque.

like a marketing man's dream. After all, very few significant sporting machines had been launched during the early 1970s. However, by the end of the seventies, when the RX-7 eventually arrived on the scene, the exchange rate had dropped to below 200 yen to the dollar, and was still moving in the same direction. If the new LWS model was to be successful, specifications notwithstanding, pricing was going to be of critical importance.

Project X605

Following the demise of the X020A/Z project, Mazda's designers put forward a number of sports car proposals based on the earlier sketches. During the peak of the 1973 fuel crisis, when the company found itself in massive debt, RE specialist, Makoto Kinutani, and Jiro Maebayashi (a chassis man, whose name will crop up again later in the book), put their heads together to come up with the X408 – an outline for a lightweight two-seater coupé.

The X408 was then taken a stage further in the X516/X517 design proposals, in which 516 was a sports car sharing the same floorpan and basic suspension components as

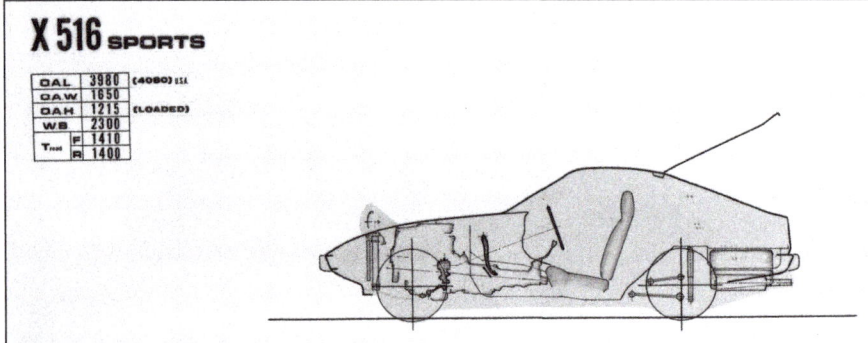

The X516 sports car proposal eventually led to Project X605.

the saloon outlined in 517. It made sound commercial sense, as it would dramatically cut production costs, and therefore made the project all the more tempting for the Mazda Board.

Sure enough, as the company's financial position improved, with the support of Shinpei Hanaoka (a Mazda Director put on the Board by the Sumitomo Bank), who had personally surveyed the American market, this project was given approval for further development. The two models were duly separated: X517 later became X606, the original rear-wheel drive 626, powered by a conventional piston engine, while X516 was transformed into the X605 – a rotary-engined car, better known as the RX-7.

Project X605 began in earnest in May 1976, headed by Kohei Matsuda, with Moriyuki Watanabe as his right-

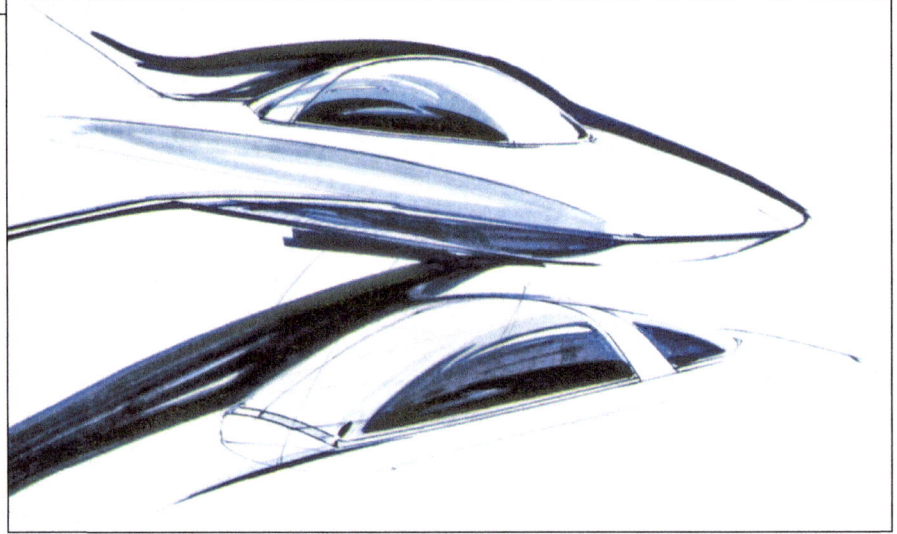

Maeda and his team of stylists initially looked towards the aeroplane for inspiration.

Sumio Mochizuki – Chief Engineer on the first generation RX-7.

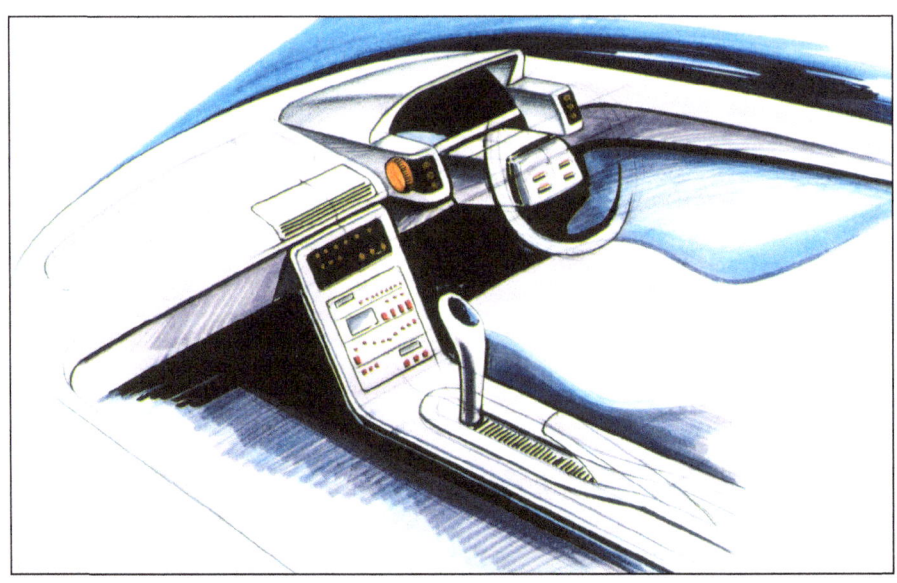

Early interior sketches were equally futuristic, but quickly toned down.

A series of early design sketches showing the evolution of Project X605.

The four one-fifth scale clays. This photograph clearly illustrates the exposed headlights favoured by the management. At that time, there was a question over the reliability of pop-up headlights, but the minimum height regulations still had to be met, thus the Frogeye Sprite arrangement.

hand man. Sumio Mochizuki was given the job of Chief Engineer, ably assisted by Akio Uchiyama, who was responsible for the vehicle's layout. It was Uchiyama who planned the chassis layout on X516, incidentally.

Hundreds of design sketches were produced by Matasaburo Maeda's team of stylists. They wanted to avoid bodywork geared too specifically at one market, citing the RX-5, with its very Trans-Atlantic lines, as a mistake. They were looking for something that would have universal appeal but, at the same time, be distinctive enough to stand out from the crowd – something a little exotic.

Of the key styling themes, Maeda asked his staff to avoid an 'aggressive'

A full-size clay model. This could so easily have been the RX-7, but fortunately, after a great deal of testing, the call for retractable headlights won through.

The rear hatch arrangement was a real sticking point, causing another battle of wits between stylists and product planners, who had to keep the costs down. Eventually, the one-piece wraparound glass, which was extremely difficult to make, had to be rejected in favour of three separate panes.

Right: A final prototype being tested in the wind tunnel. The Cd was a highly creditable 0.36, or 0.35 if a rear spoiler was fitted.

front end, whilst at the rear he requested something full of character. A light aircraft-type canopy was put forward as the inspiration for the glass area, and, despite the 2+2 seating arrangements (a feature that had already been established), it was to display the fastback lines of a pure two-seater.

Below & next page, top: Various proposals for the X605 dashboard.

after a great deal of testing, this factor won through at the last minute, despite an increase in weight and production costs, and indeed, the consequent similarity to a certain Stuttgart product.

Another sticking point was the rear hatch. Original design drawings specified a one-piece wraparound item, rather like that found on the Porsche 924 series, but cost prevailed, and eventually it became a three-piece affair, with two fixed rear quarter panes and a relatively flat lift-up centrepiece

Early proposals led to the completion of four one-fifth scale clays. Three of the four had exposed headlights, sitting proud, rather like those of the Austin-Healey Sprite, while the fourth model could just as easily have been a prototype for the second generation RX-7.

All displayed very crisp, modern lines, with the air intake situated under the front bumper, but the headlamp problem had still to be resolved. Although pop-up headlights were hardly new, they were far from common; quite strange when one considers their styling and aerodynamic benefits, especially for a sports car. Eventually,

helping to visually reduce the height of the body."

The side protection mouldings ran the full length of the vehicle, but would be reserved for higher grade models when the 7 eventually entered production, although a body crease, which was usually hidden by the rubbing strips, was equally effective from a styling point of view, if not in the car park.

The clean lines and steep windscreen angle promoted a Cd figure of 0.362 – better than that of the Datsun 280ZX of the same vintage, and about the same as that quoted for

supported by two hydraulic struts when open. It has to be said, the cunning use of black window graphics made the arrangement perfectly acceptable, hiding adhesive marks and saving the company a small fortune in the process. The laminated windscreen was also bonded in place, and all glass was tinted, incidentally.

The sunroof could be either tilted or removed completely, being based on a BMW design. Available only on export models at first, *Car & Driver* highlighted it as one of the very few areas in which the Mazda failed to shine. Indeed, the magazine even went as far as to call it a "hopeless disaster" because of its overly-complicated latch mechanism and cheap air deflector, which needed to be put in place manually after the panel was stored in its vinyl pouch.

A Targa top was investigated during the design phase, as the heavy B-post (which would serve as a roll-over bar in the event of the car flipping in a crash) lent itself ideally to such a modification. However, it was rejected at a very early stage, presumably due to the extra costs involved in tooling up for such a vehicle, the time and resources necessary to seal the roof effectively, and, of course, the loss of rigidity in the structure – an important factor in the face of Federal crash tests.

The final clay was approved in November 1976. Werner Buhrer,

Right: Design sketches for X605's interior. Tartan check was definitely the height of fashion at this time, but looks so dated nowadays.

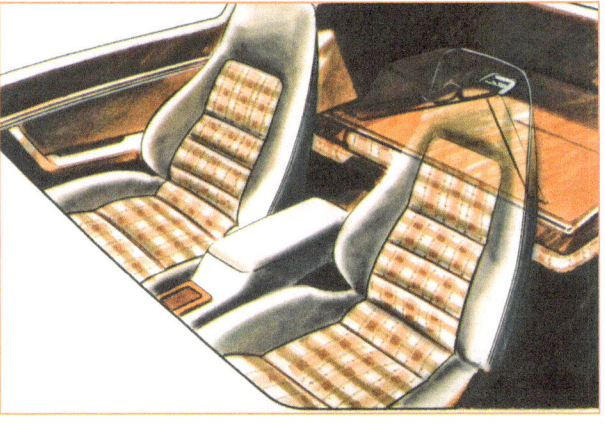

resident *Road & Track* design critic, noted: "The RX-7 follows the trend of modern sports car styling ... [It] is a remarkably clean styling sample without unnecessary 'show' elements. Therefore, it is a double pity that the responsible stylists must have been absent when the tail was created. The baroque depression for the license plate does not match at all with the rest of the car, which is very good looking!"

After highlighting the elegant alloy wheels, he continued: "Black rubber strips on the sides not only give good protection, but also visually stretch the car and therefore emphasize the low body ... The profile of the rocker panel [or sill] is also very good, not only improving the body stiffness, but also

a Porsche 924; the optional rear spoiler not only dramatically reduced lift at the back end, but further enhanced the coefficient of drag, lowering it to 0.352. Mazda's aerodynamic work certainly paid off in the end, as a number of contemporary press reports pointed out the RX-7's superb high-speed stability and distinct lack of wind noise.

Torsional rigidity was exceptional, and, to prolong the life of the vehicle, some of the more exposed panelwork was galvanized and the inside of the door skins was finished with zinc-rich paint to stop rot developing from condensation running down the panel, or a partially blocked drainage hole. A PVC coating was applied to other corrosion-prone areas.

Moving inside, stylists were seeking a classier interior than that of a pure sports car. Ultimately, this was one area which Maeda-san was less than happy with. In an interview shortly after the launch, he revealed his dislike of the colour schemes and materials used, and dryly commented that he was looking forward to the first minor change!

However, the compact RE allowed more space in the cockpit, and, it has to be said, ergonomics were excellent for the time, with clear, easy to read instrumentation and comfortable front seats. Pedals and other controls were all well positioned.

I have read in a number of places before that Japanese law prohibited the sale of two-seaters on the home market, and this is why the RX-7 was designed as a 2+2. This simply isn't true, as Nissan happily sold two generations of its two-seater Fairlady Z throughout the 1970s (the period in which the new Mazda was being developed), and continued to do so, without a break, into the new millennium. And what about the Toyota MR2? Certainly, the Ministry of Transport frowned upon two-seaters, but they were definitely not illegal.

The decision to go with 2+2 seating configuration was made purely and simply because Mazda's extensive market research showed that the sporting coupé sector was still growing, whilst that for pure two-seaters was steadily shrinking. Like most 2+2s from the period, though, the rear seats were something of a joke. In reality, the designers would have perhaps been better keeping it as a strict two-seater, and using the extra space as additional load-carrying capacity. Ultimately, the Americans would only receive a two-seater version, but this was down to nothing more sinister than a packaging problem – a lack of suitable space after making the car meet the increasingly strict Federal rear impact regulations.

Under the skin, the RX-7 came with rotary power. Indeed, the new car was designed around the RE; in this case, a new version of the 12A unit.

Rotary update

By now, Mazda had accumulated a wealth of experience concerning the Wankel powerplant, but following the fuel crisis (when petrol was three times its normal price in the States) and the unit's rejection by other companies, the RE was far from popular – even within factions of the company. In 1974, Toyo Kogyo was a staggering 17,300 million yen in the red, and many blamed the high cost of developing the rotary for this dire situation.

As already mentioned, the RX-7 was actually designed around the rotary engine, so its success was absolutely crucial for a number of reasons. It was something of a gamble, as the marketing people wanted to price the vehicle to compete with cars like the Triumph TR7 in the US (the new model's primary market). However, they also wanted to provide a greater degree of driving pleasure and refinement, so, with an unfavourable exchange rate, production levels had to be reasonably high to keep costs in check. Brisk sales were a must.

It was never going to be easy, but it was hoped that the RX-7 would also revive the fortunes of the RE for other models. Only time would tell, of course, but, having invested a fortune in refining the Wankel unit, one could only hope that for Mazda's sake – and the future of the rotary engine – this turned out to be the case.

The low-emission AP version of the rotary had long since been superseded by the even more efficient REAPS type; the models displaying the REAPS (Rotary Engine Anti-Pollution System) designation qualified for the tight set of regulations outlined for 1976.

Recent RE models included the export version of the Luce Rotary, the RX-4, which was equipped with the 13B

The lightweight and compact nature of the Wankel engine is a real bonus for automotive applications. Weight reduction is a factor, of course, but it also allows the designer to position it to enhance a vehicle's aerodynamics (via a lower bonnet-line, for instance), cabin space and weight distribution. Combined with a fairly flat torque curve, low levels of noise and vibration, and the promise of good reliability (there are substantially less moving parts to go wrong), it is not really surprising that virtually every car-producing company took an interest in this new form of motive power when it was first announced. This is the Mazda 12A unit, as employed in the X605 project.

unit (654cc x 2). Introduced in spring 1975, the luxurious Roadpacer was also powered by the 13B engine. This was a joint project with Holden in Australia, who supplied a number of body panels and mechanical components, but the timing of the launch of such a large vehicle could have been better. As a result, only 799 were sold during the car's three year run.

Much more successful, at least in Japan, was the new Cosmo, which made its debut at the 1975 Tokyo Show. Offered with 135bhp 13B or 125bhp 12A power (both with full emissions equipment), it quickly established a good reputation, becoming known as the RX-5 in export markets. In the USA, where it wasn't as successful (ironically, perhaps as much to do with the very American styling as any other factor), the model was given the 13B, rated at a modest 110bhp and with 120lbft of torque on tap.

The Luce Legato (or 929L) came in late-1977. Offered with two four-door bodies, like the Cosmo, it was powered by either the 13B or 12A RE. As we can see, Mazda certainly had a great deal of experience with the Wankel engine and, by the end of 1978, had already built more than a million rotary-engined cars.

During its bid to improve long-term reliability and fuel consumption, Mazda improved the chrome plating of the trochoidal surface and the housing interior (the latter via the Sheet-metal Insert Process, or SIP), enhanced the durability of the side housings by gas nitriding, refined the shape of the combustion recesses, and opted for more durable iron alloy apex seals – actually, it was now a similar material to that used for piston rings in a traditional engine. The 12A unit employed in the RX-7 naturally featured these latest innovations, and there were further improvements in the pipeline. Indeed, Kenichi Yamamoto had recently addressed the Society of Automotive Engineers, stating that fuel consumption would be cut by a further 15 to 20% in the near future. Mazda was known to be looking at catalytic converters and Bosch L-Jetronic fuel-injection with a view to production.

Ironically, it was contemporary accessories that were holding Mazda back from developing the RE to its full potential. A rotary unit could easily run beyond 10,000rpm (as proved in NSU racers), thus releasing more power, but low-cost, mass-produced coils and distributors with the capacity to handle at least 30,000 sparks per minute were just not available at that time. The red-line was therefore kept at around 7000rpm, which meant a larger cubic capacity (and, as such, a larger unit per se) had to be adopted to compensate.

The RX-7 engine design called for two side intake ports and a peripheral exhaust port in each of the two chambers. The adoption of side ports was found to curtail misfires when the throttle was suddenly closed, a situation caused by excessive overlap with peripheral ports (ie. ports in the same plane as the rotor).

A hot start system was devised in which the throttle valve in the downdraught Nikki two-stage, four-choke carburettor automatically opened if the water temperature was above 60 degrees C (140 degrees F). Although Mercedes had employed fuel-injection on its experimental Wankel engines, it would be some time before Mazda adopted it on one of its production cars. Incidentally, the choke automatically returned to standby position thanks to an electro-magnet, and the floats in the carburettor were modified to prevent fuel cut-off during hard cornering.

Spark plugs with three electrodes instead of the usual one were employed to help stop fouling, which in turn reduced emission levels, as the air/fuel mixture was burnt more efficiently. Other measures to stop pollution included EGR, with an air pump directing exhaust gases through a heat exchanger before being fried in the thermal reactor. By the way, the RX-7 had two coils (one for the leading, and one for the trailing plugs), but only one distributor.

The rotary engine featured a total-loss lubrication system, circulating oil to the eccentric shaft and injecting a small amount into the combustion chambers, rather like a two-stroke, to keep the apex seals in good condition; a sensor and warning light were fitted to inform the driver if the oil level dropped to a certain level.

For the X605, an oil cooler was specified, and cooling was further improved by refining the water passages in the housings and end covers. Oil capacity was listed at 5.2 litres (1.15 Imperial gallons), whilst cooling capacity was 9.5 litres (2.09 gallons).

The physical size of the RE made the decision to go for an FR layout (front engine, rear-wheel drive) an obvious one for a practical sports car. Because the power unit was so compact, it could be fitted quite a long way back in the engine bay. Indeed, on the earlier RX-3, the RE was positioned 240mm (9.4in) further back than the reciprocating engine in the same model. This so-called 'front midship' mounting of the engine was quite an important factor in the model's design, as it helped keep the bonnet-line as low as possible, enabled engineers to position emissions equipment more efficiently, and also enhanced handling characteristics by optimizing weight distribution, quoted at a near-perfect 51/49%. The 12A unit tipped the scales at just 142kg (312lb) dry, incidentally.

The gearing was selected to make up for the poor low-end torque, so the first two ratios were quite short. The basic four-speed manual transmission had ratios of 3.674:1 on first, 2.217 on second, 1.432 on third, and a direct fourth. Most cars would come with a five-speed gearbox, the overdrive fifth (0.825:1) being up and to the right, outside the traditional 'H' selector pattern. With both manual transmissions, a 3.909:1 final-drive ratio was specified, and a limited-slip differential was under development.

A single dry plate clutch was employed, with a 215mm (8.5in) outside diameter. By the way, a warning buzzer sounded as the engine approached its red-line, as the unit's smooth running at higher rpm could be very deceptive.

As for the optional automatic, first gear had a 2.458:1 ratio, second was listed at 1.458:1, and top (third) gear was 1.000:1; this 'box also came with a 3.91:1 final-drive. The selector was a simple T-bar arrangement that failed to impress Jack Yamaguchi when he tested the car in 1978. It should be noted that he was also disappointed with the kickdown facility on the JATCO-built gearbox.

On the other hand, the five-speed manual gearbox received virtually universal praise. "The gearbox," said *Road & Track*, "like every other facet of the car, gives you the feeling that it's working with you to promote the highest possible degree of driving pleasure with the car."

X605 chassis details

The suspension was developed by Uchiyama and Ishida-san of the Test Department, with ultimate responsibility for testing resting with Mazda racer, Yoshimi Katayama. There was a MacPherson strut set-up at the front, but the low nose dictated a very short version. An extra tension rod was added to avoid wheel shimmy at high speed and, because of the steering geometry, the lower part of the coil spring was tapered to stop it fouling when the suspension was at its limit of compression; a 23mm (0.90in) diameter anti-roll bar was specified as standard on all models.

At the back, there had been thoughts of an independent rear suspension (irs), and even a four-link system with a Panhard rod. Ultimately, however, it was decided to employ a live axle located by a four-link system with lower trailing and upper angled links, and a Watt's linkage – an arrangement successfully used by Katayama on his racing cars, and similar to that found on the Rover 3500. This gave good ride quality, and was an efficient package in terms of space usage. Unlike the SD1, though, the gas-filled dampers were positioned aft of the coil springs, and certain models came with an 18mm (0.71in) diameter anti-roll bar.

Steel 5J x 13 wheels were standard, coming with either 185/70 SR13 or 165 SR13 radials, or 6.45-13 crossply tyres, depending on the grade. Alternatively, there was also a cast aluminium alloy wheel (slightly wider at 5.5J x 13) for top models or available as an option on cheaper cars, and this rim came shod with low-profile 185/70 rubber.

Interestingly, because of the good results obtained with 13-inch wheels and tyres, there was no question of using 14-inch rims. Mochizuki declared himself happy with the cornering power achieved with the smaller-diameter items, so rather than looking at them

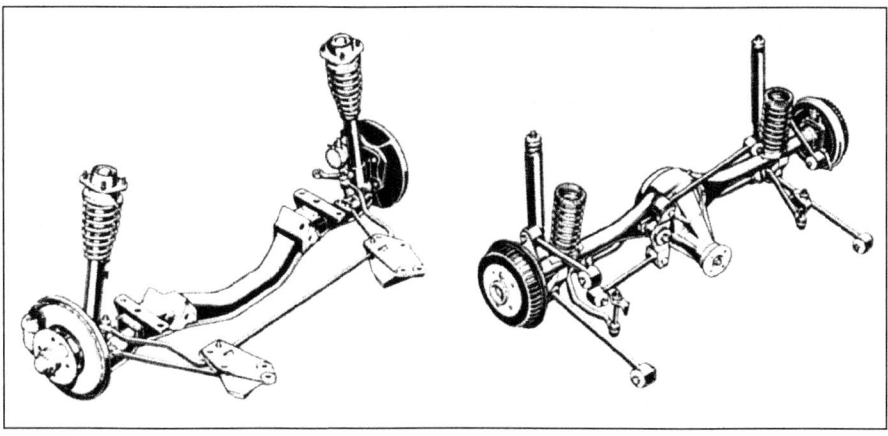

The front suspension for X605, later christened RX-7 (left), and to the right, the rear suspension and live rear axle. Note the drum brakes, complete with cooling fins to dissipate heat build-up.

as a disadvantage, he considered them a distinct advantage: they kept the unsprung weight down (one engineer calculated a saving of almost 5kg – or 11lb – per corner) and reduced production costs at the same time.

However, it was no easy task developing a competitive brake package around 13-inch wheels and tyres. The designers, naturally, wanted discs all-round but, in order to keep production costs down, were told this was simply not possible. Discs were duly specified at the front only (227mm – 8.9in diameter, and internally ventilated), while 200mm, or 7.9in, diameter drums with cooling fins were employed at the rear. In reality, though, on such a light car with modest power, discs were hardly necessary on all four corners, and it should be noted that the Porsche 924 was also specified with a disc/drum set-up. Generally speaking, this arrangement afforded a much more efficient handbrake as well.

New calipers were adopted just before production started, as the original items were not of high enough quality, and were found to distort after prolonged hard usage; the Bendix servo was also modified at an early stage to improve brake feel through the pedal. Incidentally, there was a rear brake pressure limiting valve, and, rather than a more commonly used diagonal split on the braking circuit, Mazda opted for a front/rear split.

Strange as it may seem today, the steering on earlier Mazdas had often been criticised for being rather vague. While improving the accuracy and feel of the steering was a priority, the rack-and-pinion system was rejected at an early stage, as the engineers found it difficult to isolate kickback. Instead, they refined the traditional recirculating ball set-up, beefing up the shaft from 25.5 (1in) to 33mm (1.3in) diameter to stop flexing, and changing the bearings it ran in for more accurate location and smoother operation of the mechanism. Thanks to a variable ratio (17-20:1), it was fairly light at parking speeds, but not too busy on the move; there were 3.7 turns lock-to-lock. For the sake of safety, the column itself was collapsible in the event of an accident.

Perhaps the biggest compliment regarding the chassis came from *Car & Driver*'s Don Sherman: "With 25 rubber bushings of every shape and form between the tyres and the body in back, there was plenty of opportunity to mush up road feel in the RX-7. We have yet to drive it on real highways, but our proving ground experiences suggest that Mazda's road rocket will have little trouble holding its own in ride and handling. The ride is an impressive combination of isolation over rough pavement and firm motion control when you need it ... expansion joints that felt like two-by-fours through a Porsche 924's suspension felt more like garden hoses beneath the RX-7's tyres. The only magic involved is astute tuning of

Japanese advertising from 1978, with a cutaway drawing showing the location of all the RX-7's major components.

The rumour mill

In mid-1977, an official in Mazda's American arm let it slip that Mazda was currently testing a two-seater sports coupé (the first of 50 prototypes had been completed in January at the Hiroshima Plant Complex in the Ujina area of the city). It was stated that production should begin by the end of the year, with US sales starting somewhere around April 1978.

It was perhaps a little premature, but an extensive development programme had been instigated at Miyoshi, and the third prototype to be built had already successfully passed its crash test. Promised features included a two-rotor RE, a five-speed manual transmission, four-wheel disc brakes, and styling "like nothing you've seen out of Japan before. It will be much more European in look." Competitive pricing was guaranteed.

Things were certainly starting to happen in Japan as far as the sports car world was concerned. Nissan had been building the highly-successful Fairlady Z since late-1969, but production of the first generation models was about to come to an end, with its successor expected to take a distinct move upmarket during the summer of 1978. The timing was perfect for a cheap but competent coupé to take up the market position of the old Z.

Shortly after, Kohei Matsuda (Tsuneji's son, and Mazda's President following the death of his father in November 1970), went on record stating: "A two-seater sports car may well represent the ultimate design compliment for the rotary engine." Naturally, the rumour mill went into overdrive.

To fuel the fire, staff at Mazda in America released a 'spy' picture of the forthcoming model, and, although based on the X020G, in reality it looked more like a Maserati than the actual Hiroshima product. Before long, though, journalists were starting to piece together specifications, and had even managed to obtain the name of the new car – the RX-7. "Debuts of entirely new sports cars are rare and cause for celebration," declared *Road & Track* in the March 1978 issue, "so we are excited about the coming Mazda

shock valving, spring rates and rubber bushings. Mazda engineers have done a terrific job, and the ride is second only to the rotary engine in its ability to leave a favourable impression."

Over at *Road & Track*, John Dinkel echoed Sherman's view: "Driving the RX-7 and the [Porsche] 924 across various rough roads proved quite educational as well as entertaining. Where the 924 thumps, vibrates and rattles, the RX-7 is tight, compliant and composed. There's little kickback through the Mazda's steering and the live rear axle is well behaved. Overall, the RX-7 probably has the best combination of shock absorber control of any Japanese car I've driven."

RX-7, scheduled for unveiling this spring. Mazda officials have been very [tight-lipped] about what they describe as a high-performance two-seater, but they are finally beginning to dribble information out in limited doses.

"The RX-7 will use the twin-rotor RX-4 version of Mazda's rotary engine which displaces 1308cc and develops 110bhp (SAE nett) at 6000rpm. Mazda's Director of Rotary Research & Development, Kenichi Yamamoto, comments that 'We have designed and built this sports car for all-out road and track performance. The rotary engine's attributes of light weight and high acceleration make a unique and exciting combination for a sports car powerplant.'

"Yamamoto went on to say 'Drivers of the Mazda RX-7 will not – as you say in the United States – get lost in the dust.' Mazda tests of the new sports car indicate a top speed of 120mph.

"In positioning the RX-7 in the automotive marketplace today, Kohei Matsuda, President of Toyo Kogyo (Mazda's parent company in Japan), claims that there is a gap between 'value-performance and price. Our market research has shown this. The Mazda RX-7 was designed specifically to fill this gap ... Fortunately, the rotary engine is crucial to the solution. In fact, I don't think any other manufacturer using conventional automotive powerplants could have accomplished this new level of value-performance at reasonable cost. A sports car seems to just naturally maximize the overall performance potential of rotary power – good handling, quiet and smooth ride, quick acceleration. Frankly, at this moment in technological time, we believe a two-seater sports car may well represent the ultimate design compliment for rotary engines.'

"Matsuda also says American consumers will be pleasantly surprised when they see the RX-7. Mazda has kept the car carefully under wraps thus far but our sources say it looks somewhat like a cross between the Porsche 928/924 and the new Toyota Celica Liftback. It's a fixed-top coupé with no provision, at least at this time, for a Targa-style opening or convertible top.

"Mated to the RX-7's twin-rotor

The home market launch came on 30 March 1978. The press, however, had the opportunity to try the car somewhat earlier – this is Hideo Aoki at the wheel of the new RX-7 at Miyoshi. That day, he recorded a top speed of 125mph (200kph), which dropped down to 122mph (196kph) with the headlamps in the raised position. (Courtesy Hideo Aoki)

Another picture from the time of the press launch. It is interesting to note that the stylists didn't want the Mazda badge on the nose, preferring nothing at all, or at least a matt black decal to blend in more readily with the rest of the design. It was at the insistence of the management that this rather bulky item was fitted.

engine will be either a five-speed manual or three-speed automatic gearbox, and four-wheel disc brakes (as found on the RX-4) are an integral part of the package. We are eagerly awaiting the RX-7's introduction."

By the time this article appeared in the newsagents, 50 pilot build cars had been completed, with production vehicles starting to roll off the line in March. Schedules originally proposed 3000 units a month for the domestic market, with an additional 2000 for the USA starting in April (although the first month's production for America was actually set at 3000 cars to meet the forecast initial demand). At this stage, European dealers were told they would have to wait, with 1979 being pencilled in as a possible launch date for EEC countries.

As mentioned earlier, the all-round disc brakes were dropped as part of a

Yoshiki Yamasaki was the first person outside the Matsuda family to become the head of the Toyo Kogyo company since 1922. He is seen here, in the centre, receiving one of many awards for the RX-7, from Road & Track on this occasion.

cost-cutting exercise to bring the new model to the US market at well under $7000. The transmission options would change as well, at least in the States, but otherwise it was a fairly accurate description. In March, the all-new RX-7 was launched on the home market.

The first press pictures of the all-new RX-7. The home market called for wing-mounted mirrors to comply with Japanese regulations, but for America (and ultimately other export destinations), they were moved to the doors, giving the car a far neater appearance.

Rear view of the same car, a top-of-the-range Limited model. The wraparound design of the rear combination lamp made a separate side marker unnecessary for the rear flank on US spec models.

Japanese advertising for the Savanna RX-7.

The Savanna RX-7

In Japan, the Savanna name was inextricably linked with high-performance sporting machinery, so it was retained for the latest sports car (although at that time, in view of the impending oil crisis, Mazda preferred to class it as a "high-class four-seater speciality car"), augmenting the RX-7 appellation. No-one knows what happened to the RX-6 designation, but perhaps it was a deliberate ploy to try and put a little extra distance between

The interior of the home market GT model. Note the lengthy gearlever, and also the handbrake location, which was always on the nearside (ie. passenger side for rhd, driver's side for lhd).

Fascia of the Limited grade, clearly showing the four-spoke steering wheel, the quartz clock (in the left-hand combination gauge in the instrument binnacle), and decent stereo system.

Interior of the Limited, with its full cloth trim on the seat facings and separate headrests.

the new coupé and the less than popular RX-5.

Somewhat ironically, by the time the RX-7 was officially put on sale in March 1978, Yoshiki Yamasaki had become the first person who was not a member of the Matsuda family to head the company since 1922. Yamasaki (a production engineer with a long career at Toyo Kogyo – one which stretched back to 1938, in fact) was an amiable character, not as fiery as Matsuda. He thought Mazda's biggest asset lay in advanced technology, but rightfully acknowledged that a little more effort needed to be directed towards sales. Consequently, he initiated the SE (Sales Expansion) programme, in which employees were sent to dealerships in a bid to strengthen home market penetration, thereby reducing stockpiles and cutting production without laying off workers.

In Japan, the Savanna RX-7 employed the 573cc x 2 12A powerplant. With a 9.4:1 compression ratio, the two-rotor unit delivered 130bhp at 7000rpm and 119lbft of torque at 4000rpm. All cars came with a five-speed manual transmission, with the option of a three-speed automatic (known as the RE-matic, and priced at 40,000 yen extra) on the Limited and Super Custom grades. The Custom was the cheapest model in the range, listed at 1,230,000 yen, with the Super Custom some 140,000 yen more. The GT was 1,440,000 yen, while the top of the line – the Limited – commanded 1,690,000 yen.

The price differences were reflected in the level of trim and standard features. All cars came with laminated glass, a heated rear window, an AM radio, three-point seatbelts and driver's footrest. Moving up to the Super Custom grade meant radial tyres instead of crossply items, and vinyl/cloth trim in place of the basic all-vinyl surfaces found on the Custom; the Super Custom also came with intermittent wipers, an electronic rear hatch release, and an electric clock. The GT added more features, such as halogen headlights (still quite unusual for the time), a finishing ring to brighten up the steel wheels, low-profile tyres, a rear anti-roll bar, a four-spoke steering wheel instead of the two-spoke item found on the cheaper models, a map light, a day/night rearview mirror, and luggage straps. The top-of-the-range Limited specification built on that of the GT by adding alloy wheels, full cloth trim with luxury carpets, electrical adjustment for the wing mirrors, a four-speaker stereo system with an AM/FM radio and auto-reverse cassette deck, door pockets and quartz clock.

As for dimensions, the overall length of the vehicle was 4285mm (168.7in), the width 1675mm (65.9in), and the height 1260mm (49.6in); the wheelbase was quoted at 2420mm (95.3in), while the track was 1420mm (55.9in) at the front and 1400 (55.1in) at the rear. In its lightest form, the Savanna RX-7 tipped the scales at just 1005kg (2211lb). Fuel tank capacity, by the way, was a rather minuscule 55 litres (12.1 gallons).

Without a doubt, the RX-7 was very competitive. Even in Limited form, it was still 140,000 yen cheaper than the Triumph TR7, and a massive 1,170,000 yen less than the Porsche 924. To add insult to injury, the Mazda was quicker than both (although the Stuttgart machine could boast a higher top speed) and far better equipped. The Lancia Beta Montecarlo was almost twice the price of the Hiroshima car in Japan, and the Matra Bagheera could easily be outpaced, even in larger-engined S guise.

Yamamoto was certainly confident about the package which, during an interview, he revealed was designed to satisfy three main objectives – high performance, good quality and a reasonable price for the end user. "The RX-7," he said, "is more than just a new type of car, it signifies the renaissance of the rotary engine ... For someone that has dedicated 15 years of their life to the RE, it represents the fulfilment of a dream."

It would be fair to say that *Car Graphic* was also impressed with the new Mazda. Following a test of the RX-7 Limited, it said: "The silent sports car 'designed by rotary'. Performance with 573cc x 2 rotor 130bhp engine and five-speed gearbox is favourably comparable with the 924 (Japanese version) and is accompanied by no noise or fuss. For the domestic market, the RX-7 is regulated by a device in the carburettor to do no more than 180kph [112mph] on the speedometer (the actual test speed on our car was 174.08kph). With the device removed, however, we managed to hit 186.05kph in fourth (184.14kph in fifth). Handling, with light, responsive steering, is beautifully agile, yet straight line stability is excellent. A virtually neutral steerer, it is easy to provoke power slides on slow corners. Some of our staff felt that this tendency [to slide] was rather excessive, due to, presumably, too much roll stiffness at the rear. [It provides a] firm yet smooth ride at any speed to which very comfortable seats contribute a lot. Back seats are very 'occasional' but provide useful extra luggage space when folded flat. On the debit side, the engine still shows slight unevenness around 1500-2000rpm. Although fuel consumption at cruising speeds has now improved to match that of a piston-engined car of similar performance, it is still rather

Cover of the June 1978 issue of Car Graphic.

Part of a range brochure produced in August 1978. The RX-7 is shown at top left on the cover, with its headlamps up. The headlights could be raised quickly, thanks to twin electric motors, but there was no facility for 'flashing' oncoming drivers unless in this position.

thirsty in city traffic. At 1,690,000 yen, though, the RX-7 is a most desirable proposition for a sporting twosome."

Fellow RJC member, Hiroshi Hoshijima, tested the new model for *Motor Fan* in 1978, and declared the engine quiet, if a little unrefined at low revs (the emissions equipment was thought to be at the root of the problem). He went on to state that the RX-7 was one of the best handling cars to ever come out of Japan. A different journalist writing for the same magazine thought the steering could do with being a little more direct, although he considered the new Mazda to be a "brilliant" package for the money. Not surprisingly, the RX-7 received the Japanese 'Car of the Year' award, and straight away a massive waiting list developed.

The Mazda marque had already acquired a reputation among motorsport enthusiasts for sporting machines. At the official launch of the RX-7, it should be noted that Toyo Kogyo put two 'competition versions' of the new car on display, known at the time as the RX-7R. Actually, these were early prototypes of Mazda's latest weapon in the fight for SCCA and IMSA GTU honours in America, powered by the 12A RE equipped with the so-called Sports Kit. In addition to an uprated engine (pushing out the best part of 250bhp) and drivetrain, the suspension and braking systems were suitably modified, with the package being completed by 9J x 14 wheels at the front and 11Js at the rear.

The new car in America

Introduced to the press in February 1978, the RX-7 went on the market as an early 1979 model a little while later, on 24 April. Although it was announced that Mazda hoped to sell the base model for under $6000, after taking exchange rates into account, the official retail price was set at $6395.

Nonetheless, this prompted a flood of orders. Suddenly, all of the problems reported in the press relating to the Wankel engine were forgotten. Like the 240Z before it, the RX-7 created such a stir in the States that people were willing to pay up to $3000 over the retail price in a bid to jump a few places on the ever-growing waiting list. Some were seen advertised privately for as much as $11,300!

Despite 3000 units a month being allocated for America (which was soon upped to 4000), it simply wasn't enough to keep up with initial demand. Greedy dealers, anxious to reap a profit after a number of lean years, were in an ideal position to charge extra, a situation exacerbated by the lengthy shipping times involved in crossing the Pacific. Ultimately, though, by the end of 1978, 19,359 RX-7s had been sold in the States, which equated to 26% of US Mazda sales for the year – not bad at all when one considers that the model wasn't available until the end of April.

However, the practice of asking for a hefty premium was of great concern to Mazda. R.E. Hayden, VP for Sales & Marketing, wrote a letter addressed to the dealers stating: "Sales can be lost. If a consumer is ready to buy a

The Beautiful Rotary サバンナ RX-7

ルムが心を捉える、リトラクタブル・ヘッドライトが光る。
的な評価を得て爆発的人気を呼んでいる――羨望のRX-7。

「世界に通用するスペシャリティ・カーだ!!」と絶賛。
★北米ジャーナリスト18名と山口京一氏がRX-7に試乗――そのレポート

先ごろ、北米のジャーナリスト18名と山口京一氏ら自動車評論家が東洋工業の三次テストコースでRX-7に試乗。各氏とも素晴らしさを絶賛し、予想以上の評価をいただきました。

高速性能がすばらしい!
山口京一氏（自動車評論家）
出来栄えが立派だ。低速回転からの引張りが特に良く、5速で1500rpmからきれいに立上る。高速性能がすばらしい。ギアボックスも良く、オートマチックも非常に優れており、スムーズである。ブレーキについても、ヨーロッパ車以上に安定している。ステアリングの安定さも印象的。一般のハイパフォーマンスの車にありがちな神経質なところがなく、女性にも容易になじめる味つけがしてあると思う。また、低中速のネバりも実にすばらしい。

すべてがNICEだ!
Mr. D. Sherman（アメリカ大自動車雑誌『Car & Driver』誌の記者）
加速力が非常に強い。ブレーキも良く、シフトも大変良い。ハンドルの位置もとても気にいった。室内すべてのレイアウトも申し分ない。車に乗った瞬間の異和感がまったくなく、とてもなじみやすい車だ。120マイル～130マイルで走行したが、とにかくすべてがナイスだ。

世界に通用するクルマだ!
Mr. Karl Ludvigsen（『PLAY BOY』誌に執筆のフリーランサー）
どんな新車でも何か更に改善する部分が残されて、発売後も開発が必要なものだが、RX-7は、実にほとんどのものが備えられ、このままでも世界に通用する。

安定したロードホールディング!
Mr. J. Lamm（アメリカ三大自動車誌『Road & Track』誌の記者）
パワーがあり、加速力は特に印象的。しかもとても静か…この点は、アメリカのスポーツカーユーザーに非常に高評価するだろう。とにかく、加速力、静かさ、安定したロードホールディングなどのコンビネーションが抜群。素晴らしいクルマで問題点は何もない。

レシプロでは真似のできない素晴らしさ!
Mr. C. Norpel（アメリカ三大自動車誌『モータートレンド』のエディター）
期待をはるかに上廻るクルマだ。ハンドリングは大変安定している上、シャープだし、高回転でのトルクも強く、バンクでも安心して乗れる。非常に静かなクルマであり、低速でも高速でも実にスムーズ。ハンドリング、パフォーマンスも文句ない。スタイリングもすばらしく、特にリアが気に入った。すべてにバランスのとれたクルマであり、これはレシプロでは決して真似はできない。

CARS for a changed world 1978

圧倒的好評「10ベストカー」の1台に選ばれる。

ある自動車専門誌"TRACK"誌の、恒例の10台のベスト車にサバンナRX-7などの表彰以来、アメリカでも話題を呼び、同誌でもその良さを絶賛、いまは最も注目されています。

…ドシップ
…ランスの良いシャ

T $25,000以上	ポルシェ928
T $12,000～$25,000	ポルシェ911SC
T $7,000～$12,000	アルファロメオ・スプリントベローチェ
T $7,000以下	マツダRX-7
ports Sedan $19,000以上	BMW733i
ports Sedan $11,000～$19,000	BMW530i
ports Sedan $7,500～$11,000	Audi5000
	etc.

シー、最も理想的なフロントミッドシップ、快適な室内、スマートなクーペタイプボディが組合わされ、"実質上比類のないコンビネーションになっている。"（記事抜粋）

素晴らしいロータリーエンジン
「ロータリーエンジンに期待される全ての特徴（スムーズさ、静かな回転、すばらしい性能、そしてフレキシビリティー）は、いずれもRX-7において明白である。」（記事抜粋）

文句なしのベストカー
「10台のベストカーの中で、本誌スタッフが満場一致で選出したのが7000ドル以下のスポーツカー＝RX-7だけ、他はかなり票がわれ、微少差で選ばれた車も少なくない。」（記事抜粋）

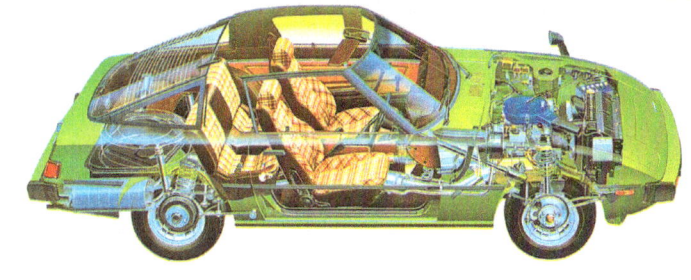

Mazda RX-7 and is confronted with an excessive price, he will likely purchase another sports car – and be lost as a Mazda owner for several years, perhaps forever. Meanwhile, he'll spread the word to his friends and associates, and they too will likely not buy a Mazda RX-7 – or any Mazda products.

"Our market position can be destroyed. As you know, the Mazda RX-7 was designed and built to be an 'affordable' sports car, one that would compete with the [Datsun] 280Z and [Porsche] 924 in performance and styling but would be available at a much lower price. If it is priced excessively then it is no longer the same car in terms of value and marketing rationale, and the image of the car in the eyes of the consumer becomes distorted.

"Mazda, in general, and the Mazda RX-7 in particular, become vulnerable to press criticism. The high demand for the car is attributable in large part to favourable press reports based on the suggested retail price, and we hope to earn the continued support of the press based on the merits of the car. But if the press believes that salesmen at Mazda dealers are exploiting this demand by abusing consumers on pricing, they are likely to be extremely critical. I hardly have to tell you how difficult it is to conduct a positive marketing campaign in the face of negative press reports."

In America, there was the base S model, and the better-equipped GS. Both were pure two-seaters (for reasons cited earlier), powered by the 12A rotary engine, which, in US trim, with a 9.4:1 compression ratio, developed 100bhp at 6000rpm, and 105lbft of torque at 4000rpm – both subtle improvements over the contemporary RX-3 unit.

Even the cheapest variant came with an AM/FM stereo radio with electric aerial, tinted glass with a heated rear window, reclining seats,

Superb American advertising from the time of the launch. Takaharu Kobayakawa, the gentleman who wrote the Foreword to this book, was one of the team involved in the original market research. He revealed that US dealers were not entirely confident of selling a rotary sports car in large volume – perhaps around 1500 units a month – but it was enough to make the project viable. Ultimately, of course, this figure proved very conservative.

carpets, a quartz clock and front anti-roll bar. The $6995 GS had a five-speed manual gearbox (instead of the four-speed unit fitted to the S), wider 185/70 HR13 Bridgestone rubber in place of the standard 165 HR13 radial tyres, a rear anti-roll bar, a four-spoke leather trimmed steering wheel (instead of the two-spoke item found on the S), intermittent wipers, a remote hatch release and side protection mouldings. Air conditioning was a $525 option on both models, although the three-speed automatic transmission (priced at $325) was only available on the GS. Other options included the attractive 5.5J aluminium alloy wheels at $250, a sunroof, also $250, two types of accent stripes (priced at $92 and $105, respectively) and the California emissions package at $75.

Compared to the competition, the 122mph (195kph) RX-7 offered better performance than most of its contemporaries in the same market sector – often by quite some margin. The GS, even with air conditioning, could cover the 0-60 yardstick in a shade over nine seconds, with the standing quarter being covered in 17 seconds dead at a speed of 83mph (133kph). Only the Fiat X1/9 came close in cornering capability, braking efficiency was almost identical to that of a Porsche 924, and the Mazda was exceptionally quiet. If anything, economy was a little disappointing in some tests, although others showed up better than average fuel consumption. Consequently, almost immediately, the RX-7 was showered with accolades and praise in the press.

Road & Track voted it the 'Best Sports Car Under $7000' in its list of the "Ten *Best Cars* for a Changing World." A couple of months later, in the August 1978 issue, the same magazine stated: "'New standards in performance and elegance for medium-priced two-seat GT cars' is the way we described the 240Z in our initial road test (April 1970), and those same words can now be applied to the Mazda without equivocation. In its evolution from the 240 through the 260 to the 280Z, the

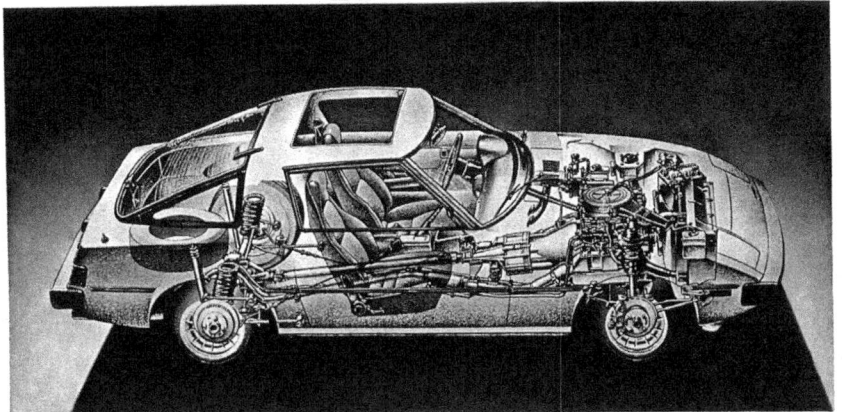

Another early advert from the States, outlining the problems Mazda's designers faced, and the various solutions found to overcome them.

Datsun has given up some of its agility and sporting attributes in favour of more refinement and comfort. The RX-7 is a blend of the best of both worlds; a true sporting GT.

"Every person on our staff returned from driving the Mazda with glowing praise for its performance, handling and comfort features – enthusiastic unanimity of that sort is exceedingly rare ... The Mazda RX-7, at less than $7000, is an enthusiast's dream come true."

Car & Driver was equally impressed: "At its Japanese introduction, Mazda's prodigy was like the star of spring training: radiant with promise, but totally unproven against established pros. Now that we've driven it here, we feel as though the Mazda RX-7 has just pitched its first game and scored a no-hitter. The car is even better than our first brief encounter suggested it might be.

"The heart of the matter is the Mazda's personality, which makes its acceleration far more useful in the real world than its arch rival [the Datsun 280Z, which according to C&D tests, was slightly quicker on paper]. From the first eager hum of the RX-7's rotary engine, you know you've got a tear-around tiger. It begs to be red-lined through the gears, likes to be tossed into turns, and loves you when you twitch its steering wheel affectionately through traffic. There's plenty of incentive to move quickly in the Mazda because the engine does its job without the usual thrashing of a piston engine. There's a whoosh from the exhaust and a whir from under the hood, but none of the cacophony you have to contend with in a 280Z squeezed for acceleration ... This is your front-row seat for Mazda's stereophonic symphony of scintillating engine sounds ...

"Mazda's rotor motor feels like a speed vending machine. The longer you hold the right pedal down, the more you get. Heavy flywheel action damps the thrill of acceleration somewhat, but the engine keeps on winding higher and higher up a horsepower curve that seems straight-edge linear. The rush feels as though it will last forever, until the over-rev alarm goes off at 6500rpm to remind you to pull the shift lever at the 7000rpm red-line.

"It's reasonable to expect great handling in a sports car, and the RX-7 delivers full satisfaction in this regard ... With the RX-7 GS's combination of front and rear anti-sway bars acting through 5.5-inch aluminium wheels, this car will deliver whatever posture you prefer in the turns. Take your choice of any attitude between neat-and-tidy understeer and ferocious oversteer; it's all controlled by the power pedal. If you'd prefer a nice, smooth ride home from work, go lightly on the gas across the apexes and the RX-7 will hang in its tracks like a caterpillar. But if you feel a little more adventuresome, just turn up the wick and the RX-7 will slide around a bit at both ends as it annihilates the best ET you ever posted in your old commuter." In the same magazine, Patrick Bedard mused: "Every once in a while a car

Kenichi Yamamoto toasting the 1,000,000th rotary-engined car.

comes along that seems too good to be true. The original 240Z was one. The Honda Accord was another. And now we have the Mazda RX-7. This car cannot lose. It has power, smoothness, comfort, reasonable looks, and a generally sophisticated demeanour, all for about $7000. A value like that will make people gouge eyes and pull hair to get on a dealer's waiting list.

"I can't blame them. Even if the RX-7, the 280Z, and the Porsche 924 all sold for exactly the same price, I would opt for the Mazda simply because of its Wankel engine. None of the others will rush for the red-line singing such a happy song. And none of them comes with a three-year/50,000 mile warranty either.

"Still, there is more to the RX-7 than its engine. The car feels delightfully light and nimble, just the opposite of the Z. You don't have to muscle the RX-7 around. It responds to your suggestion instead of your command, like any fine piece of equipment. But such virtue usually costs more. The fact that you can buy the Mazda for less than its obvious competitors is what makes it too good to be true."

Regarding the cockpit, in the May 1978 edition of *Road & Track*, John Dinkel wrote the following appraisal: "The interior can best be described as 'enthusiast friendly', imparting a feeling of instinctively knowing where all the major controls are located the first time you slide into the driver's seat. Directly in front of the driver is a single pod containing the central tachometer, a speedometer [marked up to 130mph] to the right, and fuel-level and coolant temperature gauges and a clock to the left. A clever feature of the tachometer is an insert voltmeter. When the ignition is turned on, but before the engine is started, the tach needle swings up to read battery voltage. Neat.

"The seats have fairly decent contouring and better than average thigh support, but tall drivers may be faced with a mild case of the Porsche 924's well-known thigh/steering wheel interference. The pedals are well-positioned for heel-and-toe downshifting and the footrest (standard only on the GS version) is an appreciated item.

"Few sports cars, regardless of price, have as effective a heating and vent system ... There's only one area where the RX-7 draws criticism: The level of some of the materials, for example the upholstery, door panels and the boots around the handbrake and shifter, isn't up to Mazda's usual high standards."

Motor Trend compared the RX-7, Porsche 924 and Datsun 280Z, citing them as perfect examples of a modern breed of sports car that had to balance practicality with the more usual aspects one expects from sporting machinery. The test highlighted the 280Z's marginal advantage in speed, but the lightweight Hiroshima vehicle – the kerb weight of the US spec base model was listed at 1068kg, or 2350lb – took the honours in the braking category. Amazingly, the big Datsun was the most frugal of the bunch, with the Mazda not far behind. The Porsche, a car the author rates very highly, was actually quite disappointing in this company.

In conclusion, it was stated that each had its merits and flaws. In summing up, Peter Frey observed: "Which one of the three you might choose will be a function of what shape you like to have your fun in ... They are a wave of the future, and the future looks bright indeed."

From reading a large number of contemporary press reports, it became obvious to the author that perhaps only one sports car has made a similar impact on the motoring world in more recent years – the MX-5 – which says an awful lot for the enthusiastic engineers at Mazda. The last words go to Don Sherman who, writing for *Car & Driver*, declared that "this two-place rotary rocket has more sex appeal than Charlie's Angels."

The American market had a choice of six coachwork colours initially, including three metallic shades. Cars came with a 12-month warranty, with the engines covered for three years, or 50,000 miles (80,000km) – a sign of Mazda's faith in the unit. Unlike home market production, which started with the number SA22C-100000, US chassis numbers began at SA22C-500000.

3

The legend grows

On 10 January 1979, Kenichi Yamamoto stepped up to receive the *Motor Fan* 1978 Car of the Year award. Then, two months later, exactly a year after the vehicle made its debut, the home market received two more variations on the RX-7 theme – the SE-GT and the SE Limited.

The main feature brought in with the SE series was a sunroof, previously only available on export models. This steel panel could be tilted or removed completely, though the air deflector was listed as an option – it looked awful, but it did at least work.

With the SE-GT 130,000 yen more than the standard GT, one would expect a little more than just a sunroof, and it came with moquette seating surfaces, better quality carpet, a silver finish on the centre console insert, and an AM/FM stereo. The SE Limited added air conditioning, electric windows, digital clock, leather-wrapped steering wheel and gearknob, and moquette/knitted trim.

The manual only SE-GT was announced at 1,570,000 yen, whilst the five-speed SE Limited was 1,990,000, or 2,030,000 yen in automatic trim. To

Inset: Interior of the SE Limited, complete with air conditioning and a digital clock.

A press photograph dated 2 March 1979, showing the new SE Limited grade for the home market. Although the steel sunroof was the main feature of the SE series, a number of other items were included to raise the standard specification.

An overhead shot of the SE-GT, clearly showing the sunroof, which could either be tilted or removed completely, as it has been here.

Tasteful Japanese advertising for the new SE series.

The entry level Custom grade for the 1980 model year. From the outside, the Super Custom didn't look much different.

Interior of the Custom, Japan's base model. Incidentally, vents were integrated into the A-posts to direct air onto the side windows to prevent them misting up.

The interior certainly inherited a high-quality atmosphere for 1980. This is the home market GT.

By the time the RX-7 appeared at the 1979 Tokyo Show (held at Harumi from 1 November), a number of minor changes had been carried out in accordance with the details outlined in a Mazda document, code number P642 (the 'P' standing for production).

A breakerless, transistorized ignition system was adopted on all cars (a useful modification which could easily be retro-fitted to earlier 7s), and new colours and fabrics were introduced for the 1980 season, including a leather

put these prices into perspective, the contemporary Custom (the cheapest in the RX-7 line) was still 1,230,000 yen, with the Limited – what was the top-of-the-range model – also unchanged at 1,690,000 yen. The introduction of more expensive variants was doubtless a move to counter the new threat posed by the latest version of the Datsun Z, introduced on the home market during August 1978. Like so many sporting machines from the era, this latest model was a much more upmarket version of its predecessor, the emphasis changing from pure sports to refined GT as the years passed.

The SE-GT from October 1979 ...

trim option on the SE Limited. A rear wash/wipe system came on certain models, along with an internal louvre for the top edge of the rear hatch.

A Stateside view

By the start of 1979, the RX-7 'S' was priced at $7195, while the 'GS' was $800 more. To put this into perspective, the GLC range started at $3695, and even the most expensive 626 was $1400 less than a basic RX. Options – which included air conditioning ($555), stripe kits ($92 or $105), alloy wheels

... and the Limited from the same time.

A superb shot of the 1980 SE Limited, seen here with optional leather trim. Note the air deflector at the leading edge of the sunroof aperture, which was also an option.

Below: An arty shot showing the rear wash/wipe and window louvre mentioned in the text. It also shows the car's tail in detail.

Below, inset: An SE Limited photographed at Manganji in Tochigi. (Courtesy Hideo Aoki)

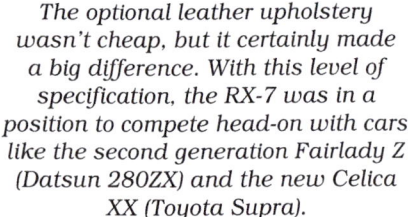

The optional leather upholstery wasn't cheap, but it certainly made a big difference. With this level of specification, the RX-7 was in a position to compete head-on with cars like the second generation Fairlady Z (Datsun 280ZX) and the new Celica XX (Toyota Supra).

($275, or $550 if batched together with a sunroof) and automatic transmission ($355) – took the sticker price even higher.

These prices were held until the end of the year and, in fact, the cost of California emissions equipment was reduced from $80 to $50. To make up for this loss in dealer margins, the automatic gearbox was priced at

Advertising for a US limited edition model, dating from mid-1979.

(the 924 was by far the best in this department), and there were other areas in which the legendary 'Vette was disappointing.

Overall, the most points went to the Datsun (1054), with the Mazda second (1033); the Porsche scored 957, 102 more than the Chevrolet. In conclusion, it was stated: "It would be difficult not to choose the RX-7 or the 280ZX when buying one of these sports/GT cars. Both made a fine showing and serve to remind us that the Japanese are serious about their products."

By the end of 1979, production was already up to 7000 units per month. The factory was still having trouble keeping up with demand but, nonetheless, the time had come to make the car available in Europe, which could only further burden the over-stretched workforce in Hiroshima.

Incidentally, a questionnaire revealed that most owners in the States were attracted to the RX-7 because of its handling, fun-to-drive factor, performance and styling, and, to a lesser extent, its price and engineering features. Interestingly, apart from fuel economy, one of the biggest complaints to surface during the survey concerned the heating and ventilation system, which had received a great deal of praise in most road tests, although some were less complementary when air conditioning was fitted – more than two-thirds of American buyers had specified this option, which perhaps provides the answer. Other problems cited included a lack of interior space, and running expenses combined with poor dealer service. Thankfully, the latter is now a thing of the past!

The car's impact in Britain

Complete with a picture of the home market model (with a blacked-out number plate, to hide the Savanna appellation), *Thoroughbred & Classic Cars* magazine – known nowadays simply as *Classic Cars* – introduced the RX-7 to the British public in its August 1978 issue. It said: "The new, glamorous rotary-engined sports car from Mazda has hit the USA but it will remain tantalisingly distant, so far as the UK is concerned, for some time to come. Rotary-engined cars have a somewhat tarnished reputation in this

$30 more if it was specified on the 'S' model. However, there was no shortage of buyers, with the RX-7 accounting for 54,853 of the 156,000 Mazdas sold in the States during 1979.

Tests of automatic sports cars are rare in enthusiast publications, so I will take this opportunity to quote *Road & Track*, which compared top-spec automatic versions of the RX-7 GS, the 924, 280ZX and the Chevrolet Corvette.

The Mazda was the cheapest in the group, with the Porsche by far the most expensive, priced at $17,790 as tested. Surprisingly, despite the massive gap in engine capacity and horsepower ratings between the contenders, top speed was similar, but in performance tests, the American car showed its advantage, embarrassing the others into submission. However, one paid for the power in poor fuel consumption

The 1980 Mazda RX-7 GS

Just one look is all it takes to appreciate the exceptional value of the Mazda RX-7 versus Datsun 280ZX or Porsche 924.

As remarkable as the Mazda RX-7 is on its own merits, it looks all the better when compared with the competition. Because the sleek, aerodynamic RX-7 is virtually everything you could want in a refined sports car—at an almost unbelievable price.

It can reach 0-50 in 6.3 seconds. Its inherently compact rotary engine is placed <u>behind</u> the front axle, for ideal weight distribution and superb handling.

In auto racing, a specially-prepared RX-7 won its class at the Daytona 24-hour race. Another RX-7 set a world speed record at Bonneville.

The smoothness of the rotary engine makes the RX-7 a quiet sports car. All this performance from a car that can attain excellent gas mileage on the open road.

17 EST. mpg **28** EST.** hwy mpg

But the front mid-engine RX-7 offers infinitely more than performance. It also provides extraordinary comfort.

So if you know what you want in a sports car, and you don't want to pay a king's ransom to get it, take a look at the RX-7 GS or S Model. The beautifully-styled, high-mileage, high-performance sports cars from Mazda.

You're also going to like the looks of RX-7 GS standard features.
• AM/FM stereo radio with power antenna • Side-window demisters • Cut-pile carpeting • Tinted glass • 5-speed • Tachometer
• Styled steel wheels • Steel-belted radial tires • Front and rear stabilizer bars • Ventilated front disc and finned rear drum brakes with power assist • Electric remote hatch release. 3-speed automatic transmission, air conditioning, aluminum wheels and sun roof available as options.

$8295*

*Manufacturer's suggested retail price for GS Model shown. S Model $7495. Slightly higher in California. Actual prices established by dealers. Taxes, license, freight, optional equipment and any other dealer charges are extra. (Wide alloy wheels shown $275-$295.) All prices subject to change without notice.
**EPA estimates for comparison purposes for GS Model with 5 spd. trans. The mileage you get may vary depending on how fast you drive, the weather, and trip length. The actual highway mileage will probably be less. California, 16 estimated mpg, 27 estimated highway mpg.

Mazda's rotary engine licensed by NSU-WANKEL.

MAZDA
The more you look, the more you like.

American advertising for the 1980 model year. At first, US specification cars came with a driver's-side mirror only, but for 1980, they came equipped with a pair fitted as standard. In addition, tiny overriders were added on the rear bumper (in line with the number plate light housings), although they soon disappeared when the model received a facelift the following year.

speed of 120mph. The styling will appeal much more to European taste – embellishment being kept to the absolute minimum. It is low and lean, and has the engine set well back which augers well for balanced handling. There are retractable headlamps, and a hatchback luggage entrance with heated glass panel.

"Mazda hope to make substantial inroads into the American sports car market – the big worry for British manufacturers will be the degree of penetration."

As one will gather from the opening statement, the RX-7 was not yet available in the UK, but the final paragraph did raise an interesting point. Japanese sporting machinery had already made a massive impact on the US market by this time – more than 380,000 Datsun Z-cars and well over 500,000 Toyota Celicas had found their way to American shores since 1970, but the British industry had little with which it could mount a counter-offensive.

The days of the open car seemed numbered, and the new breed of GTs from the UK – vehicles like the Triumph Stag and TR7 – were simply unable to compete. As I said in my history of the Datsun Z, also published by Veloce: "The Japanese have often been blamed for the demise of the British car industry. My view has always been that it destroyed itself by arrogantly sitting on its laurels for far too long – unwilling to build cars aimed at specific markets, and failing to keep up with the changing times."

Japanese pricing policy was another factor. Most people seem to think that Japanese prices were so competitive because wages were lower. This simply isn't true – summer and winter bonuses often equate to the average wage in the UK. No, it was productivity that was the key. While the British industry was being crippled by strikes, usually for no good reason, Japanese factories had excellent labour relations. Furthermore, the designers made the cars easier (and therefore quicker) to build. Maurice Ford, an old friend with many years' experience in the industry, once said: "The Japanese could throw a door from ten yards and it would fit. You could be messing around for ages

country due to poor petrol economy and rapid wear of the rotor seals. However, Mazda have carried out a rigorous development programme and we are assured that these problems have been sorted out. The main plus points of this engine are its compactness and turbine-like smoothness of operation. Mazda rotaries meet all the current emission regulations, too.

"The engine is rated at 2.3 litres, producing 130bhp DIN at 7000rpm. The car will accelerate to 60mph in 8.7 seconds and has a maximum

The advance information sheet prepared for the 1978 Motor Show, held for the first time at the NEC near Birmingham.

An early Mazda UK press photograph, still using a Japanese specification model, but with the wing mirrors removed. The rubber bungs used to fill the resulting holes look far from professional.

trying to get an early Jaguar door right, and then you'd have to adjust it again once all the electrics went in."

In other words, the Japanese spent their time and energy on tooling and refining production techniques first, rather than letting the men on the track make the best of a bad job. This also explains why cars from this part of the world have an unrivalled reputation for build quality. If you think that last statement is biased, take a close look at a Lexus LS400!

But the RX-7 was not such a threat to sales on British soil. Due to outrageous taxes (and a certain

A rear three-quarter view of the same car. A 'Rotary Engine' badge was fitted on the tail of the pre-1981 models, at least as far as home and American markets were concerned. In fact, in Europe, the longer registration plates made it necessary to relocate the number plate light housings, thus leaving no space for the aforementioned item. This vehicle, which is actually Japanese specification, despite appearing in photos presented to the UK press, carries the badge.

amount of greed, it has to be said), the new Mazda was hardly a bargain.

The RX-7 reaches the UK

As noted in the *Classic Cars* article, the RX-7 was considered to be a 2292cc car in Europe due to a different way of measuring the Wankel unit's capacity – fortunately, the Japanese classed it as a 1146cc powerplant (as did the Americans), otherwise it would have attracted a heavy tax in its home country for having an engine of over two-litres.

A different system of horsepower measurement soon brought the 130bhp figure quoted down to 105bhp at 6000rpm, although this was slightly more than the Americans got, and the 106lbft of torque (developed at 4000rpm) was almost the same maximum figure as that listed in US catalogues.

Testing with leaded fuel – which was basically the only type of petrol available in EEC countries – highlighted an interesting and totally unexpected problem. The SIP process, whereby steel sheet is bonded to the trochoid housing and then chrome plated, called for tiny pores in the surface to aid oil retention (obtained via acid treatment). However, the leaded fuel reduced longevity of the trochoid surface unless the pores were of a uniform pattern, so only a small number of housings were selected for use in Europe.

The apex seals were also modified to make them more suitable for European conditions, where an engine could be expected to do far more high-speed running than in Japan or the US. This had a slightly adverse effect on emissions, but contemporary EEC regulations were nowhere near as strict as those for the home market or California, so for the sake of reliability, this was considered an acceptable trade-off.

In line with Japanese and Stateside models, the UK spec 12A rotary had a 9.4:1 compression ratio, a four-choke Nikki carburettor and, like other 1980 MY cars, the newly-introduced transistorized ignition system. The unit would run on either two-star or higher octane four-star fuel.

Without the need to meet Federal rear impact regulations, like that for the home market, the European RX-7 could be sold as a 2+2. The European model had different side repeater lights to its counterparts in America and Japan, the front indicators incorporated side lights with clear lenses to comply with EEC law, and the rear combination lights were of a slightly different design, as side markers were unnecessary.

Another change for Europe was the adoption of Pirelli CN36 tyres instead of Bridgestone rubber, though size and rating were the same as the low-profile radials used elsewhere. However, it should be stressed that although the author has found a number of detail differences, given the period when US spec cars were traditionally quite different to those supplied to other markets, the RX-7 was remarkably similar in all parts of the globe; even the overall dimensions were the same, thanks to standardized bumpers for all countries.

An advance information sheet (complete with colour photography featuring the Savanna RX-7 minus its distinctive wing mirrors) was prepared for the 1978 Motor Show, held for the first time at the NEC. (Thereafter, of course, the venue would alternate between Earls Court and the Birmingham Exhibition Centre.) A beautifully-prepared example was shipped over for the event and given prime position on the Mazda stand, though it would still be some time before full importation began. The sheet read as follows: "The sleek look that draws admiring glances combined with the smooth, surging power of a new generation Mazda rotary engine.

"The power-unit, equivalent to 2.3 litres, is allied to a five-speed gearbox, which ensures a sparkling performance. The rotary engine is placed well back in the chassis giving an excellent fore to aft weight ratio.

"It's a 2+2 and there's an amazing amount of interior space within that smooth, aerodynamic body silhouette. Front seats are bucket style with integrated headrests and are orthopaedically designed to take any stress out of long-distance driving.

"The cockpit design has received special attention and all instruments are easily visible either through, or to the side of, the steering wheel. Add that to a well-planned centre console with the gearlever falling easily to hand and you have the recipe for comfortable, effortless driving.

"There's a flat rear deck too, for luggage, and a lifting rear window for easy access.

"Front suspension is by struts with coil springs plus an anti-roll bar and tension rods. At the rear there are four trailing arms and a Watt linkage together with separate anti-roll bar, coil springs and telescopic dampers to ensure that roadholding matches the performance.

"Sleek modern styling and superb rotary engine efficiency are combined in the Mazda RX-7 to produce the shape of things to come. It is anticipated that the Mazda RX-7 Rotary will be available in the UK during the summer of 1979."

The RX-7 eventually reached British shores in 1979, officially going on sale on 1 September. There was only one version sold in the UK (there were no trim variations, and the automatic transmission was not available). It was listed at £8549, but to go some way towards justifying the high price, it came with an equally high degree of equipment.

Standard features included a five-speed gearbox, alloy wheels shod with 185/70 low-profile radial tyres, front and rear anti-roll bars, halogen headlights, integrated front spoiler, tinted glass with a laminated windscreen and heated rear window, a leather-covered four-spoke steering wheel, full instrumentation with a panel light dimmer switch, reclining front seats and a fold-down rear seat (both finished in vinyl with cloth inserts), an AM/FM stereo radio with four speakers, an electric aerial and a separate cassette deck, intermittent wipers, cut-pile carpeting (the luggage compartment was also trimmed), an adjustable driver's footrest, door pockets, an electric hatch release, quartz clock, cigarette lighter, luggage straps, a day/night rearview mirror, driver's door mirror, full-length rubbing strips, and a locking fuel cap.

Despite the undoubted high level of specification (similar to that of the Limited model in Japan), £8549 was a lot of money in 1979 (metallic paint was classed as optional, adding another

At last, a proper UK specification model, as illustrated in the first British catalogue. Note the different badges on the front wings, and new location of the side repeater light.

£86), and the RX-7 found itself pitched against some tough and established competitors.

The Porsche 924 and the new Datsun Z – the 280ZX – were a little more expensive, but both had a loyal following, especially the Stuttgart thoroughbred. From Italy, there was the beautiful Alfetta GTV, from Germany, the BMW 323i, and there were British bulldogs like the Reliant Scimitar GTE and the TVR Taimar. High on the

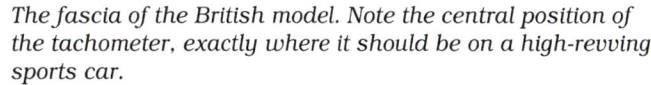

The fascia of the British model. Note the central position of the tachometer, exactly where it should be on a high-revving sports car.

value-for-money rating were cars like the Capri, the X1/9 and the TR7 – the Ford, even in three-litre Ghia trim, being just £6620, while the Fiat and Triumph were a measly £5320. The cheap and cheerful MGB provided yet another alternative at this end of the market.

Three years had passed since the RE was withdrawn from the UK market amid a storm of controversy. However, billed as 'The Orient Express' in British advertising, there is no doubt the RX-7 and the rotary had its supporters.

Regarding the Wankel unit, *Motor* magazine stated: "It is a more satisfying engine to drive hard than those of many rivals, with good driveability apart from a slight rough patch in the carburation just before the carburettor second stage comes in, which it does with some abruptness.

"When it's idling you'd hardly know the engine is running, and apart from a momentary vibration just above idle

Another view of the interior. Although sales figures were never going to match those of America and Japan, the RX-7 was nonetheless an instant hit in Britain.

speed, it remains astonishingly smooth throughout the rev range, whether you are pottering about at modest revs using just the carburettor's primary stage, or bringing in the full force of all four barrels to surge through the gears to the 7000rpm red-line."

In the same month, Clive Richardson of *MotorSport* observed: "First impressions of all who drove our test RX-7 were of the ease and pleasantness of control, a complementary combination of light and smooth steering, a delightful five-speed gearbox, light, progressive clutch, well-placed controls and above all a feeling of tautness, smoothness and tractability right through the driveline."

UK advertising from September 1979.

Summing up, Richardson noted: "At £8549, this attractive Mazda is aimed at an expensive and demanding market sector where charisma can count almost as much as engineering excellence. Unusually for a Japanese car, the RX-7 has the looks which ought to gain it that charisma in the right circles. More than that, it is especially easy and pleasant to drive, comfortable and uncannily smooth and vibration free. It is a league away from the old hairy-chested sports car theme, a delightfully civilised and practical sports car which should hold no qualms for the inexperienced and give plenty of pleasure for the experienced. Mazda seem to have conquered all the bugs which gave the Wankel engine a bad name in its early days and made the benefits of turbine smoothness well worth having. Cleverly engineered and well finished, the RX-7 is very easy to live with; I enjoyed it immensely."

The magazine gave the 2340lb (1064kg) RX-7 a 121mph (194kph) top speed and 18.6mpg average – not that bad for a hard-driven test car that also had to contend with heavy London traffic. Oil consumption, which also has to be considered with the rotary, was found to be around 800 miles (1280km) per litre, incidentally. The 0-60mph time was quoted at 9.2 seconds, and the standing-quarter was clocked at 17 seconds flat.

Interestingly, comparing figures in *Motor* and *Autocar* (both of these magazines used the same press car, which was a different one to that tested by *MotorSport*) revealed remarkably similar results with one journal, but not the other. Only *Motor*'s 0-60 time was a little on the slow side, quoted at 9.9 seconds, otherwise, even the fuel consumption was almost spot on. However, *Autocar* recorded slower times all round, and an average of 18.2mpg.

It would be fair to say *Autocar* wasn't as impressed with the car, either, concluding: "The Mazda appeals strongly to many people with its looks; it holds the road well, but could do with better steering. The question mark over its engine is today a faint one – reports suggest that there is nothing amiss with it in ordinary service – but one wishes that its mechanical refinement was matched by better sound reduction."

On the other hand, *Motor*'s summary, whilst containing some valid criticisms, was far more complementary, virtually echoing the views of *MotorSport*: "To a man our testers liked the RX-7, differing among themselves only in the degree of their enthusiasm – tempered in some cases by disappointment with the outright acceleration figures (though nobody felt it lacked performance on the road), and in other cases by a degree of intake/exhaust noise that is not so much excessive, as simply unnecessary. The RX-7 isn't very well packaged either: as a two-seater, legroom is unnecessarily restricted, while it is very cramped as a four-seater and luggage space is poor. In addition, the fuel consumption can be heavy if you drive it very hard.

"It is, however, a very satisfying driver's car, with thoroughly entertaining handling, tireless brakes, a good control layout, pleasant gearbox, and of course the outstanding smoothness of that rotary engine. Without sacrificing any comfort compared to its rivals, it is arguably a more enjoyable car to drive hard than any of them, and for that reason alone it deserves to sell well."

Oddly, European cars only came with a standard 12-month unlimited mileage warranty, with no additional cover for the engine. Servicing was scheduled for every 12,000 miles (19,200km) in the UK, with a free service after the first 600 (960km), although oil changes were recommended every 6000 miles to keep the RE in tip-top condition.

However, a distinct advantage for the Mazda over competitors was its proven record in the British Saloon Car Championship (later the BTCC), as Tom Walkinshaw had successfully been

A rear three-quarter shot of a proper UK car. Compare this with the tail of the vehicle in the earlier press photograph.

The engine that powered the European RX-7.

The RX-7 page from a Mazda UK range brochure dated January 1980.

racing one from the start of the season, months in advance of it going on sale in the UK. Indeed, at the time of the car's launch, Walkinshaw was leading the series. Before long, in conjunction with Mazda UK, Walkinshaw was offering a TWR (Tom Walkinshaw Racing) version, which had front and rear spoilers, wheelarch dress pieces, 6J x 13 spoked alloys shod with wider tyres, a TWR steering wheel and attractive decals.

In the USA especially, there was no shortage of firms lining up to offer uprated components and other modifications. Of the better-known specialists, perhaps Quickor Engineering of Beaverton, Oregon, deserves at least a brief mention for its RX-7 handling package, which employed shorter, stiffer springs to lower the car by 45mm (1.8in), Bilstein shocks, and a 28mm (1.1in) diameter front and 16mm (0.63in) rear anti-roll bar, as opposed to the standard 23 (0.91in) and 18mm (0.71in) combination. In addition, an adjustable 19mm (0.75in) rear bar was available, along with harder polyurethane bushes for the trailing link bushings to improve the chassis' response. With a limited-slip differential and wider wheels and tyres, the Quickor conversion stopped the inside rear wheel spinning in sharper turns (a common occurrence noted in many contemporary tests) and provided the RX-7 with far superior handling and roadholding.

As an example, one magazine recorded an average speed of 52.9mph (84.6kph) through a slalom course with the standard model, but with the beautifully-balanced Quickor vehicle, the same journalist was able to clock 57.8mph (92.5kph) – a vast improvement that readily translated into quicker cross-country times on the road for the enthusiastic driver.

Revival, and links with Ford

Madza's sales started to pick up again thanks to the introduction of the conventionally-powered Familia family car and the popularity of the RX-7. Cumulative production reached ten million vehicles in 1979, but in November that year Ford acquired a 24.5% equity stake in the Hiroshima company. Within three years, Mazda was marketing Ford-brand vehicles through its Autorama sales channel in Japan. This arrangement actually worked both ways, as a number of Mazdas (such as the B-series pick-up) had been badged as Fords in the States, and vehicles were later developed jointly on both sides of the Pacific.

Tom Walkinshaw easily won his class in the BTCC in 1979, and Win Percy took the championship outright with the RX-7 in 1980 and '81. Walkinshaw had prepared Percy's racer, and these are TWR-modified road cars from 1981. From left to right: the front-wheel drive 323, the 626 Coupé, and the RX-7 Turbo.

In the meantime, 1980 brought with it the introduction of the front-wheel drive Mazda Familia (also known as the GLC or 323, depending on the market). The Familia was presented with the coveted 1980-81 'Japanese Car of the Year' award; over one-million had been produced by 1982.

During 1980, to celebrate its tenth anniversary in the States, Mazda introduced a limited number of GLC, 626 and RX-7 models finished in Renaissance Red, and featuring special interior fabrics and commemorative badging. The RX-7 version was based on the GS, but came with alloy wheels, a sunroof, an uprated stereo, so-called 'competition seats' and power door mirrors.

The 'Leather Sport' was another special for the American market, introduced at the end of May. As the name implies, leather was used to trim the interior (the seats were the same design as those found in the anniversary model), including the steering wheel and gearknob. The LS also came with a sunroof, a high quality stereo system, power mirrors, and unique badging. The alloy wheels were painted gold, which nicely set off the Brilliant Black, Aurora White or Solar Gold paintwork.

By the summer of 1980, whilst the GLC cost much the same (only $100 more than it was 18 months earlier), RX-7 prices in the USA had risen by quite some margin. The 'S' was now $7645, with the higher spec 'GS' listed at $8395. Options and their prices, however, were unchanged.

The 60th anniversary special edition for the Japanese market.

As a matter of interest, Japanese manufacturers built seven million vehicles between them during 1980, helping Japan to become the world's number one car-producing country.

Savanna news

On 25 February 1980, when prices for the home market ranged from 1,250,000 to 2,130,000 yen (or 2,170,000 yen, if automatic transmission specified), a limited edition variant based on the GT became available in Japan. Introduced to commemorate the 60th anniversary of the company, this attractive model featured alloy wheels, Cibie foglights, and black paintwork with a heavy silver and red coachline; the same striking colour scheme was used in the interior.

However, just in time for the 1981 season, in accordance with the details set out in project P815, the RX-7 range was simplified and received an extensive facelift. At the front, it was given a new colour-coded, polyurethane-covered bumper with a smooth, integrated spoiler, helping to lower the Cd to a creditable 0.34 and reduce lift. Behind the new panel, the bumper was mounted on tiny shock absorbers, rather like those found on the Jaguar XJ-S, in order for the design to meet with the Federal 5mph (8kph) impact regulations.

A matching rear bumper with a cutaway for the number plate cleaned up the tail, while revised 'full-width' combination lights with smoked lenses gave the car a more modern appearance. These revisions added 55mm (2.2in) to the length of the vehicle, and 20mm (0.8in) to the width. In addition, broader rubbing strips were introduced, lower positioning allowing the front side marker on Japanese and American spec models to be mounted on the leading section, and the badging was predominantly black, just as the stylists had requested back in 1978.

Inside, as part of the restyling exercise, the 7 was provided with new, more supportive seats featuring independent headrests; the handbrake design was changed, and the shorter

The American 'Leather Sport' (or LS) model from 1980.

Interior of the limited edition car, introduced in February 1980. Note the way the upholstery matches the vehicle's coachwork finish.

55

The 1981 model year facelift brought with it the introduction of the GT-J grade for the home market – basically replacing both the Custom and Super Custom models. Note the new front bumper and latest wheel design, also part of the facelift.

Interior of the GT-J, displaying the new dashboard arrangement. The door panels were also revised at this time, along with the headlining, thus providing a recess for the sunvisors.

Interior of the GT grade.

Below: Japan's 1981 model year GT in ideal sports car country.

The tail-end treatment was totally revised for 1981. This, as can be seen from the badge on the left-hand side, is the SE-GT model.

gearlever was relocated slightly nearer to the driver, finished with a new gearknob.

The door panels, headlining and dashboard design were also modified, with all meters featuring orange on black markings instead of the previous white on black. The voltmeter function was separated from the tachometer, placed low down in the central gauge (which just so happened to house the tachometer!), while the left-hand combination dial now featured an oil pressure gauge. As a result, the clock was moved to the revised centre console.

1981 saw the end of thermal reactors and the use of catalytic converters, at least in countries where unleaded fuel was available. Although the 'cat' had been around for some time, Mazda was having trouble getting it to work properly with the Wankel unit. The RE's high levels

The SE Limited continued as the top-of-the-range model, easily identified by its rather novel alloy wheels, designed to resemble the rotor in the RE engine.

At first glance there wasn't much difference between the SE-GT and SE Limited inside, but careful inspection revealed a digital clock and leather-trimmed steering wheel on the top model. In addition, the SE Limited was still available with optional leather trim.

of hydrocarbon emissions had to be reduced without the aid of the thermal reactor, and early experiments revealed a severe misfire when the engine was not under load. These problems were resolved in a typically inventive way, through the introduction of a two-stage catalyst, split secondary air control and further improved sealing in the chambers, combined with a reactive exhaust manifold, a special valve in the intake system to prevent misfires, and a revised, high-energy ignition system feeding new spark plugs, each with four electrodes instead of three.

The Cosmo had received this novel catalytic converter set-up almost a year earlier than the RX-7 and the Luce, by the way. With a relatively lean mixture, it was said to reduce fuel consumption by up to 20%, whilst improving low-speed torque characteristics and engine response in general. Of course, only road test results would give the true story, but the new emissions package certainly looked promising.

Other changes included adoption of a thinner 16mm (0.63in) anti-roll bar at the back (when fitted) instead of the former 18mm (0.71in) item, and a new steel wheel design. Top models received a rather novel 5.5J x 13 alloy wheel, its inner shape aping that of the triangular rotor in the rotary engine.

As mentioned earlier, the home market range was simplified somewhat, with the new 1,395,000 yen GT-J grade taking the place of the Custom and Super Custom. The GT continued, listed at 1,540,000 yen, although the Limited fell by the wayside, leaving the SE-GT and SE Limited at the top end of the line, catalogued at 1,770,000 and 2,200,000 yen respectively. The entry-level GT-J came with manual gearbox only; the others could be specified with automatic transmissions for an extra 40,000 yen.

The US 1981 model year

The updated RX-7, often referred to as the 'Mk.II', was introduced to the USA in November 1980. It displayed the modified nose and tail styling, the revised interior, and of course, a catalytic converter, but there were new alloy wheels and a new grade added for the American market at the same time.

When the 1981 models were announced, the RX-7 price tag started at $8595, but, by the middle of the year, prices were quickly adjusted. The basic S was listed at $9395 (although it now featured a rear anti-roll bar and intermittent wipers, items previously reserved for the more expensive GS, and a remote fuel door release button), whilst the GS (with halogen headlights and a 'lights on' reminder chime, power adjustment for the door mirrors, a built-in map reading light and illuminated ignition key barrel) came in at $9895. The newly-introduced GSL was priced at $11,395 – $900 more than when it first appeared on the scene.

For 1981, the four-speed gearbox was deleted, so all models fell into line with other markets and came with five-speed transmissions (the three-speed automatic continued as an option, and all gearing remained the same as earlier cars), while the speedometer was marked to 85mph to comply with the latest, albeit short-lived, Federal regulations. Americans – who were still offered a two-seater version of the RX-7 rather than a 2+2 – also got a larger 63 litre fuel tank (equivalent to 13.9 Imperial gallons) and storage bins behind the revised seats.

The luxury GSL grade added disc brakes all-round (236mm or 9.3in diameter discs were fitted at the rear, although their worth was open to question during early independent tests), four-spoke 5.5J x 13 cast alloy wheels with 185/70 low-profile tyres, and a limited-slip differential. Additional features included power windows, cruise control, a removable sunroof, a stereo radio/cassette player, quartz digital clock and a rear wash/wipe facility; leather trim was listed as an option on the GSL, priced at $695.

With maximum power and torque output unchanged from last year (100bhp and 105lbft, respectively), the RX-7 GSL was remarkably similar to the Datsun 280ZX and Porsche 924 in overall performance, and cost substantially less than the Stuttgart machine, even in basic trim. Testing the luxury model for *Road & Track*, Joe Rusz noted: "The rotary runs on leaner fuel mixtures than previously and averages 24mpg in the EPA's city-highway cycle, compared to 20mpg last year.

"Although, according to Mazda's figures, the 1981 RX-7's performance is only slightly improved (0-60mph times have been reduced from 8.7 to 8.6 seconds), driveability and smoothness are better than before, because the factory has devised a system that diverts air/fuel mixture from the rear to the front rotor during deceleration. This reduces misfiring and the resultant increase in emissions.

"The RX-7, with its standard-equipment five-speed transmission, is extremely quiet on the highway. The air/fuel bypass contributes to this, eliminating most if not all of the popping and occasional banging that we formerly found during deceleration. The GSL's four-spoke steering wheel

America's luxurious 1981 model year GSL. As well as being fitted with many extras as standard to pamper the owner, the GSL also received a number of mechanical upgrades.

gives the car a proper sports car feel, which is further enhanced by the generously bolstered leather seats. On the track, the limited-slip differential and the optional four-wheel disc brakes make an already topnotch showroom stock racer (just check the SCCA records) even better. The RX-7 has tended toward power oversteer, and Mazda knows this. So all the 1981s get thinner rear anti-roll bars. Yes, the 7 is still a bit rear biased but it's more neutral than before."

In the USA, options included air conditioning at $595, a sunroof ($325), automatic transmission ($355 on all grades), and aluminium alloy wheels. The latter option was priced at $325 individually, or $595 if bought as a package with the sunroof; for the base model, low-profile 185/70 HR13 tyres added a further $65. A rear spoiler was also listed.

Regarding the automatic 'box, having recorded a 0-60 time only one second shy of a manual model, *Car & Driver* noted: "Formal track-burning aside, whenever the GSL automatic was available for staff use, a line formed from the key board all the way back to the art department. Generally, the nature of most hardcore sports cars is not suited to automation in the gearbox. Mazda's rotary engine, however, is perfectly in tune with its three-speed automatic. Even during wide-open-throttle upshifts, which occur at an ambitious 5500rpm, the rhythm of the rotary's quiet refrain is barely disrupted by the smooth, fluid shifts of the transmission. But although we were impressed by the automatic, particularly by how little it loses to the five-speed in acceleration, we'd rather twitch the tiger's tail through the stick than just hang around for the ride."

The 'Mk.II' in Britain

Due to the distinct lack of unleaded fuel in Britain at the time (ironically, it has now become difficult to source leaded fuel in the country!), a catalytic converter had to be ruled out, as the lead content in the petrol would have destroyed it. Therefore, the thermal reactor continued for European markets, a set-up that easily conformed with EEC emissions regulations of the period.

The 'Mk.II', at £8750, was only £200 more than the original model when it finally arrived on the scene in spring 1981 (although sales didn't officially begin until 3 June). The highly-specified UK cars came with a moulded rear spoiler (which dropped the Cd down even further, to a quoted 0.32), a different rear bumper (the number plate was fitted between the rear lights), a rear foglight, and old-style repeater lamps on the front wings – features which readily identified European models; the alloy wheels were of the new, four-spoke design recently introduced for the American market. In addition to items found on earlier vehicles, a sunroof was now standard, along with headlight washers, electric windows, driver's mirror power adjustment (there was still no mirror on the nearside as yet), a map light, remote fuel door release and rear wash/wipe facility. A luggage cover, rather like that found on the 924, plus warning chimes for an open door and if the driver forgot to turn off the headlamps, were also provided. As a result, there were no major options.

Mechanically, European cars gained 10bhp, taking the maximum output to 115bhp at 6000rpm, while peak torque increased slightly to 112lbft at 4000rpm. At the same time, they inherited the American GSL's rear disc brakes, combined with a larger brake servo and Dunlop tyres. The kerb weight of the UK model, by the way, was catalogued at 1050kg, or 2310lb.

MotorSport said: "The RX-7 must represent exceptional value for money, being better equipped than, and having equal characteristics to, some cars with fancy names costing nearly twice as much ... It is an ideal car for covering long distances fast and comfortably."

It is interesting to note that over an extended 12,000 mile (19,200km) test, the magazine returned an average fuel consumption figure of 23.4mpg – more than reasonable for a car of this type. The top speed was said to be in excess of 120mph (192kph).

The Elford Turbo

With the rotary engine, because the rotor turns three times slower than the output shaft, the more relaxed timing constraints of the intake and exhaust processes readily support the addition of equipment intended to extract more performance from the unit.

After several complementary road tests of Elford's prototype RX-7 Turbo towards the end of 1980, Mazda UK decided to give the conversion its blessing. All Mazda mechanics were trained to deal with the servicing and maintenance of this turbocharged variant.

Elford Engineering was based near Bournemouth in England, and was actually a Mazda dealer. Malcolm Cole designed the installation, employing a Garrett AiResearch T04B turbocharger in conjunction with an SU carburettor; surprisingly, the relatively high 9.4:1 compression ratio was retained.

Naturally, a new exhaust system was required. Consequently, all of the emission control equipment was lost, but the unit still complied with European exhaust regulations, which, at that time, were nowhere near as strict as those for America and the home market. This not only released more power, it also relieved the vehicle of some weight, so that even after the addition of the blower and its ancillaries, the turbocharged model was actually no heavier than the standard car, and the chassis' balance was undisturbed.

With maximum boost restricted to 5psi via a wastegate, the Elford model developed 160bhp at 6000rpm and 150lbft of torque at 4000. This endowed the car with a seven second 0-60 time – 0-100mph coming up in just 18 seconds. There was also a notable improvement in mid-range performance, allowing the driver to carry out safer, effortless passing manoeuvres. Fuel consumption suffered by about 15%, which can be considered a fairly small price to pay given the increased horsepower and torque, but it did tend to limit the vehicle's range.

While nothing dramatic was deemed necessary to cope with the extra horses, the front brakes were modified to include larger air scoops to improve cooling, and given harder pads. Other, more obvious changes, included a glassfibre front airdam with built-in driving lights, a rear spoiler (also grp and colour-keyed to the body), unique Wolfrace wheels (these 6J x 13 items, shod with broad Pirelli rubber,

FORMULA ONE WORLD CHAMPION GETS INTO A LEADING POSITION.

Alan Jones, a man accustomed to being out front, has recently joined the board of Richard Knight Cars Ltd.

We are the leading Mazda dealer in London, England's largest RX7 specialist and sole distributor of the 'RX7 Elford Turbo'.

And everyone at Richard Knight Cars would like to wish Alan as much success on our board as he is having on the racetrack.

Richard Knight Cars Ltd
35a-37 Fairfax Road, Swiss Cottage, London NW6 Telephone: 01-328 7714/7727/7738

MOTOR SPORT, JULY 1981

British advertising for the Elford Turbo featuring the Australian ex-F1 Champion, Alan Jones. A later Elford advert carried the line: "Mazda make them fast, Elfords make them faster."

gave the car a slightly wider track), and Elford badging. The interior was left untouched, except for the addition of a boost gauge tacked on under the dash. As a Mazda agent, Elford was in an excellent position to sell complete cars from new, which it did for £10,900 (instead of £8750 for the standard model), although a number of clients had their own vehicle converted afterwards. Although the conversion was of extremely high quality, sadly, early cars were not as reliable as had been hoped, so a new company, Elford Turbo Ltd, was established to tackle the problems. New manifolds were cast (the exhaust one in iron, with the inlet one in alloy), and the lubrication system received a great deal of attention. Owners were given the chance to forsake the headlamp washing system in favour of better windscreen washers, and larger wheel and tyre combinations were made available.

With electronic fuel-injection, the official power output was being quoted as 165bhp at 6500rpm, while maximum torque had increased to 166lbft; at the same time, the price had risen to almost £12,000. Around 500 of the 135mph (216kph) Elford Turbos were built in the end. Not surprisingly, the company went on to offer turbocharger kits for other Mazdas, too.

A lesser-known but nonetheless worthy turbo conversion was offered by Mazda dealers Bob and Mike Redrup, trading as Bruce Garages in London. Their 'Motospeed' RX-7 featured a Janspeed-designed installation comprising a RotoMaster turbocharger, an intercooler, twin-choke Weber carburettor, a free-flow exhaust and a Micro-Dynamics black box. Giving 7psi of boost, there wasn't much improvement in torque output at low revs, but maximum power was in the region of 200bhp – enough to endow the Motospeed car with a 6.2 seconds 0-60 time, and a top speed of 145mph (232kph). For speed freaks, this was enough to justify the price, which was £3000 more than an Elford Turbo. But there were other modifications, including a full glassfibre body kit (the bulging panels could be ordered separately, without the performance conversion, if required), a 15-inch wheel and tyre package, and a boost gauge for the interior.

Japanese specials

In a bid to reverse falling sales in Japan, 7 March 1981 was the date a GT-based variant known as the 'Spring Shot' was launched on the home market. Limited to 200 examples, it featured a limited-slip differential, front foglights (sourced from Cibie), four-spoke alloy wheels (usually reserved for export) shod with Michelin 185/70 HR13 tyres, and a unique fabric for the seats. Finished in Sparkling Black Metallic with a red coachline, it sold very quickly.

The 'Spring Shot' special was followed exactly three months later by the so-called 'Summer Shot' edition. Limited to 100 models, like its predecessor, it was based on the GT and featured an lsd, along with four-spoke alloys with Michelin tyres. This time, though, it was pitched at a slightly different clientele, having two-tone blue paintwork (a combination of the

UK advertising from September 1981.

American update

In August 1981, *Road & Track* voted the RX-7 'Best Closed Sports Car' in its list of the "Ten *Best Car*s for the 1980s." The same journal had an RX as part of its long-term test fleet, and at 12,000 miles (19,200km), it reported: "When we first tested the Mazda RX-7 in August 1978, we described it as an enthusiast's dream come true and, after living with the car for 12,000 miles, our judgement is confirmed." Once the same distance had been covered again, the magazine had this to say: "The automobile limelight moves fast these days, shifting from European motor shows and Japanese introductions to an alphabet soup of models spilling from Detroit in response. Such is the ebb and flow of consumer curiosity, but true benchmarks linger to become legends – and our long-term RX-7 is quietly and surely treating us to this transition."

Even at 36,000 miles (57,600km), there was still nothing major to report, only fading trim due to the strong sunlight and a broken steering lock, and at double that distance, *Road & Track* concluded: "It turned out to be a peach of a car." Interestingly, in spite of the RE's reputation for being a gas guzzler, at the end of the test period, overall running costs were surprisingly low.

Mazda (North America) Inc. – better-known as MANA – was established during 1981. As the years passed, this developed into a key organisation within the company fold, putting forward design proposals and carrying out useful market research to make

The RX-7 had a glamorous image in Europe, as this reproduced ad shows.

A US specification GS model for the 1982 season.

Tender Blue and Canal Blue shades), seats trimmed in black moquette, and headlight washers. However, home market sales continued to fall off, with only 2349 units being sold in 1981, compared with 4301 the previous year.

61

Interior of the UK car for 1982.

Cover from a Dutch catalogue, dated September 1981. This particular car, the SDX model, featured the 'Wankel'-type alloys and a rear spoiler. A cheaper DX version was also available, although most European countries had only one grade.

British specification RX-7s from early 1982. Note the different rear number plate arrangement compared to Japanese and American models.

cars more suitable for the market they were destined for.

Despite unfavourable exchange rates, around 166,000 Mazdas were sold in the States that year – the GLC being the best-seller in the economy sector, while the facelifted RX-7 appealed to enthusiasts. By the end of 1981, a total of 43,418 RX-7s had found new homes in the US, a figure which represented roughly a quarter of American Mazda sales for the accounting period.

The 1982 model year

There were no major changes for export markets in 1982. In America, Bridgestone RD207 tyres replaced the former RD106 type, as they were supposed to provide improved steering feel and enhance the car's handling characteristics. In addition, better quality cut-pile carpets were adopted across the range.

The basic S model was priced at $9695, $600 less than the GS. The top-of-the-range GSL came in at $11,895, and could be trimmed in leather for an extra $695. Other options included air conditioning ($625), cruise control ($200), sunroof ($325), automatic transmission (for the GS or GSL only and priced at $360), and alloy wheels ($325 on the GS, or $350 for the S, complete with wider 185/70 rubber).

While Mazda sales in general dropped slightly on the previous year, the RX-7 did quite well. During 1982, a total of 48,889 were sold in the States – an improvement of around 5500 units on 1981.

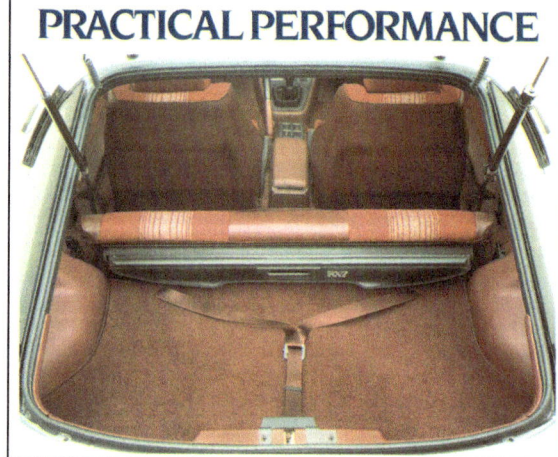

For a sports coupé, the RX-7 was surprisingly practical, with a shallow but decent-sized boot (complete with cover, a la Porsche 924) and its 2+2 seating for Europe. The rear seat could be folded, of course, to provide additional luggage space.

The 6PI RE.

The new GT-X model featured on the cover of the Japanese catalogue that introduced the 6PI engine for use in the RX-7.

Interior of the new GT-X grade.

The higher quality carpeting was naturally carried over to the European models, but there was little else to report. In Britain, the 1982 model year RX-7 was priced at £9199 (there was still only one variant listed for the UK and most other EEC countries), bringing it into direct competition with the likes of the Datsun 280ZX, Lancia Beta Montecarlo, Porsche 924, and Alfa GTV. However, in a bid to increase sales, this price was held over for the following season.

On the home market, the GT-J provided the entry level model, listed at 1,426,000 yen (manual only). The GT commanded 1,574,000 yen in five-speed guise, while the SE-GT and SE Limited were priced at 1,809,000 and 2,248,000 yen, respectively; the GT and the SE series could be specified with a three-speed automatic transmission, adding a further 40,000 yen. However, significant changes were afoot in Japan.

The 6PI rotary engine

In 1981, Mazda adopted six-port induction for its Type 12A rotary unit (573cc x 2). This new form of intake system employed three ports for each rotor, and by controlling these three openings in three progressive stages, economy could be improved without sacrificing low-speed torque or performance at higher revs.

First employed on the new Cosmo and Luce models (introduced at the 1981 Tokyo Show), oddly, the 6PI system was not used abroad until the 13B unit was reintroduced to America. However, as part of the P130 project, home market RX-7s received this latest piece of RE technology in March 1982. Whilst reducing fuel consumption was, of course, important, the idea behind this 'minor change' was to give Japanese drivers an altogether sportier machine. A new manual gearbox was introduced, with 3.622:1 on first, 2.186 on second, 1.419 on third, a direct fourth, and 0.858:1 on top; the final-drive remained at 3.91:1.

To go with the new engine (though still listed as having 130bhp, with 119lbft of torque) and gearbox (for the time being, employed on the home market only), a new grade was added – the GT-X – which replaced the SE-GT in the line-up.

The GT-J continued as the entry level model, with 5J x 13 steel wheels (the same four-spoke design introduced for 1981) shod with 165 SR13 radials, an AM radio with a single speaker, cheaper seats (although trimmed in cloth, nonetheless), and a vinyl-covered, four-spoke steering wheel.

The GT grade added 185/70 SR13 tyres, rear brake discs to go with the standard front discs, a rear anti-roll bar, halogen headlights, side protection mouldings, an A-shaped steering wheel, a remote hatch release switch, and an extended centre console, including an armrest.

Moving up to the GT-X brought with it 185/70 HR13 radials, a limited-slip differential, four-speaker AM/FM radio,

63

The 6PI-powered SE Limited with its unique two-tone paint scheme, pictured at the entrance to a park in the shadow of Mount Fuji. (Courtesy Hideo Aoki)

power adjustment for the mirrors, electric windows, a rear wash/wipe facility, better quality carpets, and moquette trim.

As the top-of-the-range model, the SE Limited came with the GT-X's tyres on the 5.5J alloys styled to look like an RE rotor. It also had leather trim (including on the steering wheel, although it remained an A-shaped design), a six-speaker radio/cassette, cruise control, a sunroof (optional on the GT-X), and a graduated tint on the windscreen.

Air conditioning was listed as a dealer option, as were the four-spoke alloys found on export models. Standard coachwork colours included Formula White, Renaissance Red, Sparkling Black, Sunbeam Silver, Misty Blue and, for the SE Limited, a Havana Brown/Maya Gold two-tone scheme.

Towards the end of 1982, prices stood at 1,442,000 yen for the manual only GT-J, 1,590,000 yen for the five-speed GT, 1,849,000 for the GT-X, and 2,219,000 for the SE Limited. From the GT grade upwards, automatic transmission was available for an extra

Rear view of the same car, clearly showing the number plate location and the sunroof in its tilt position. (Courtesy Hideo Aoki)

America's GS Limited Edition of 1983 vintage.

The GS Limited Edition interior was trimmed in red to give a good contrast with the silver paintwork. With so many features coming as standard, this package – restricted to 5000 units – was excellent value.

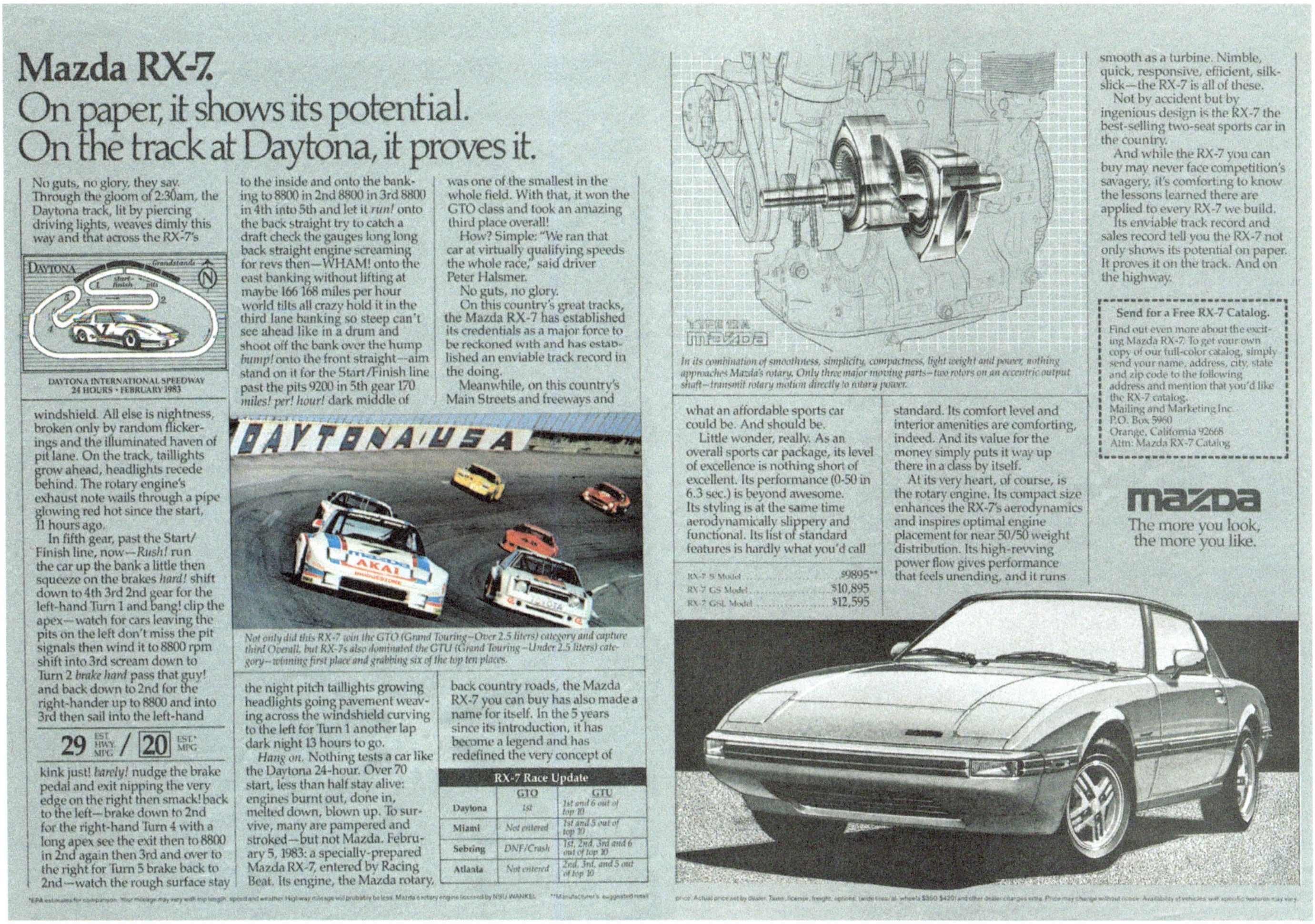

Mazda RX-7.

On paper, it shows its potential. On the track at Daytona, it proves it.

No guts, no glory, they say. Through the gloom of 2:30am, the Daytona track, lit by piercing driving lights, weaves dimly this way and that across the RX-7's windshield. All else is nightness, broken only by random flickerings and the illuminated haven of pit lane. On the track, taillights grow ahead, headlights recede behind. The rotary engine's exhaust note wails through a pipe glowing red hot since the start, 11 hours ago.

In fifth gear, past the Start/Finish line, now—*Rush!* run the car up the bank a little then squeeze on the brakes *hard!* shift down to 4th 3rd 2nd gear for the left-hand Turn 1 and bang! clip the apex—watch for cars leaving the pits on the left don't miss the pit signals then wind it to 8800 rpm shift into 3rd scream down to Turn 2 *brake hard* pass that guy! and back down to 2nd for the right-hander up to 8800 and into 3rd then sail into the left-hand kink just! *barely!* nudge the brake pedal and exit nipping the very edge on the right then smack! back to the left—brake down to 2nd for the right-hand Turn 4 with a long apex see the exit then to 8800 in 2nd again then 3rd and over to the right for Turn 5 brake back to 2nd—watch the rough surface stay to the inside and onto the banking to 8800 in 2nd 8800 in 3rd 8800 in 4th into 5th and let it *run!* onto the back straight try to catch a draft check the gauges long long back straight engine screaming for revs then—WHAM! onto the east banking without lifting at maybe 166 168 miles per hour world tilts all crazy hold it in the third lane banking so steep can't see ahead like in a drum and shoot off the bank over the hump *bump!* onto the front straight—aim stand on it for the Start/Finish line past the pits 9200 in 5th gear 170 *miles! per! hour!* dark middle of the night pitch taillights growing headlights going pavement weaving across the windshield curving to the left for Turn 1 another lap dark night 13 hours to go.

Hang on. Nothing tests a car like the Daytona 24-hour. Over 70 start, less than half stay alive: engines burnt out, done in, melted down, blown up. To survive, many are pampered and stroked—but not Mazda. February 5, 1983: a specially-prepared Mazda RX-7, entered by Racing Beat. Its engine, the Mazda rotary, was one of the smallest in the whole field. With that, it won the GTO class and took an amazing third place overall!

How? Simple: "We ran that car at virtually qualifying speeds the whole race," said driver Peter Halsmer.

No guts, no glory.

On this country's great tracks, the Mazda RX-7 has established its credentials as a major force to be reckoned with and has established an enviable track record in the doing.

Meanwhile, on this country's Main Streets and freeways and back country roads, the Mazda RX-7 you can buy has also made a name for itself. In the 5 years since its introduction, it has become a legend and has redefined the very concept of what an affordable sports car could be. And should be.

Little wonder, really. As an overall sports car package, its level of excellence is nothing short of excellent. Its performance (0-50 in 6.3 sec.) is beyond awesome. Its styling is at the same time aerodynamically slippery and functional. Its list of standard features is hardly what you'd call standard. Its comfort level and interior amenities are comforting, indeed. And its value for the money simply puts it way up there in a class by itself.

At its very heart, of course, is the rotary engine. Its compact size enhances the RX-7's aerodynamics and inspires optimal engine placement for near 50/50 weight distribution. Its high-revving power flow gives performance that feels unending, and it runs smooth as a turbine. Nimble, quick, responsive, efficient, silk-slick—the RX-7 is all of these.

Not by accident but by ingenious design is the RX-7 the best-selling two-seat sports car in the country.

And while the RX-7 you can buy may never face competition's savagery, it's comforting to know the lessons learned there are applied to every RX-7 we build.

Its enviable track record and sales record tell you the RX-7 not only shows its potential on paper. It proves it on the track. And on the highway.

DAYTONA INTERNATIONAL SPEEDWAY
24 HOURS • FEBRUARY 1983

29 EST. HWY. MPG / 20 EST.* MPG

Not only did this RX-7 win the GTO (Grand Touring—Over 2.5 liters) category and capture third Overall, but RX-7s also dominated the GTU (Grand Touring—Under 2.5 liters) category—winning first place and grabbing six of the top ten places.

RX-7 Race Update

	GTO	GTU
Daytona	1st	1st and 6 out of top 10
Miami	Not entered	1st and 5 out of top 10
Sebring	DNF/Crash	1st, 2nd, 3rd and 6 out of top 10
Atlanta	Not entered	2nd, 3rd, and 5 out of top 10

In its combination of smoothness, simplicity, compactness, light weight and power, nothing approaches Mazda's rotary. Only three major moving parts—two rotors on an eccentric output shaft—transmit rotary motion directly to rotary power.

RX-7 S Model	$9895**
RX-7 GS Model	$10,895
RX-7 GSL Model	$12,595

Send for a Free RX-7 Catalog.

Find out even more about the exciting Mazda RX-7. To get your own copy of our full-color catalog, simply send your name, address, city, state and zip code to the following address and mention that you'd like the RX-7 catalog.
Mailing and Marketing Inc.
P.O. Box 5960
Orange, California 92668
Attn: Mazda RX-7 Catalog

mazda
The more you look, the more you like.

American advertising from 1983, making the most of Mazda's success on the race tracks.

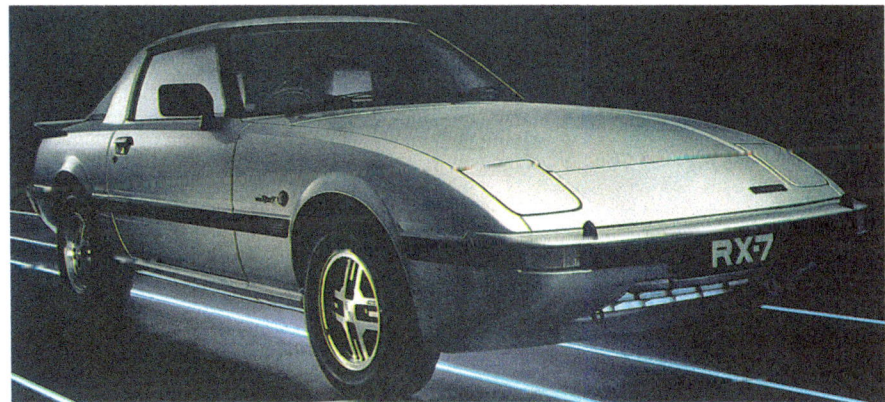

A page from the Mazda UK catalogue from spring 1983.

40,000 yen. By this time, of course, the 1983 model year had been announced in export markets.

1983

America's P130 changes included adoption of a further improved, lean-burn rotary engine, although there was no extra power or torque, and the unit did not have the 6PI system. A maintenance-free battery was added, along with warning buzzers for low oil and coolant levels.

Improved seating was also a feature; the front pair offering much better support – even the basic S grade (priced at $9895) had three-position, driver's seat adjustment, and could be trimmed in vinyl or velour. All cars now came with wide body protection side mouldings and door-mounted map pockets.

The GS was $1000 more, but the new six-speaker radio/cassette accounted for a lot of that. In addition to the usual GS goodies, there were a number of other, more minor, convenience items, such as luggage holding straps, a centre armrest with storage compartment, a graduated tint on the windscreen, and lighting for the glovebox and cargo area.

The GSL, at $12,595, was pretty much unchanged, although it now had striped tweed upholstery, or leather trim for an extra $695. Other major options for 1983 included air conditioning ($625), cruise control ($200), a sunroof ($325), automatic transmission ($360), alloy wheels ($325, or $350 for the 'S' if the customer required the low-profile tyres), and various stereo upgrades.

There was also a GS Limited Edition, priced at $12,720, and restricted to 5000 units. Based on the GS, it came with a sunroof and was finished in Chateau Silver Metallic paint with unique red pinstripes. Inside, red cloth was used to trim the seats, while air conditioning, cruise control, and a top stereo radio/cassette with equalizer and balancer were added to give the car an air of luxury. Unique multi-spoke 5.5J forged aluminium alloy wheels, finished in silver and shod with 195/60 HR14 Bridgestone tyres, completed the package.

An interesting comparison test appeared in the June 1983 issue of *Motor Trend*. "We might as well admit it," it said, "Japanese manufacturers have done more than just take control of what we call the affordable GT class of automobiles. They have elevated it, defined it, and claimed it as their own. By making fun, good-performing cars attractive to a broad range of buyers, building them in large quantities, and selling them for reasonable prices, the Orient's major auto makers have virtually created a market segment."

This was to be a fascinating clash, bringing together the RX-7 GSL ($13,075 as tested), the recently-introduced Mitsubishi Starion ($13,940), Toyota Supra ($15,991) and Datsun 280ZX Turbo ($18,659). The Mazda was not only the cheapest of the bunch, but with just 100bhp on tap, it was also the least powerful (the others had between 145 and 180bhp). However, its high-revving engine, distinct weight advantage and clean shape could be expected to make up for this shortfall in horsepower.

In the matter of top speed, the two turbocharged models showed their mettle (although, it has to be said, the Starion wasn't that much quicker), while at 117.5mph, the RX-7 just pipped the Supra for third place. In the 0-60 sprint, the Mazda fell a long way behind, but caught up with all bar the Datsun by the quarter-mile marker – at 17 seconds, it was only half a second slower than the Mitsubishi, with the Toyota splitting the two. In the braking category, the lightweight Mazda took first prize. "The RX-7 and Supra were both prone to rear lock-up," it was observed, "but their good pedal made modulation easy."

The 7 also gave a remarkably good showing during the slalom and skidpan tests. It was noted: "On the skidpan, the Turbo ZX lurched and howled around, trying resolutely to either push off the circle nose first or spin off it backwards. Yet it exactly matched the times for the RX-7, whose skinny tyres offset its near-neutral balance and best-of-the-group predictability. Top honours for sheer cornering stick went to the Supra with the Starion close behind."

Overall fuel consumption figures showed the Datsun to be the thirstiest at 18.1mpg, although the Hiroshima machine was uncomfortably close at just 18.2; the other cars gave figures of nearly 21mpg.

Regarding the interior, *Motor Trend* said: "The RX-7 shows simple, clean design in its seating, door panels, dashboard, and instrument cluster. It's unpretentious but doesn't look plain (or dated, despite its years being on the market) ... In all ways, the Mazda's interior is competent – not flashy, not busy, not even luxurious. Just completely competent. It's not likely that anyone in the market for a modern sporting GT car will find any major fault in the RX-7's cockpit."

Summing up, it was stated: "[Forget the price], and Mazda's durable rotary RX-7 comes off quite well. Consider price and it's a marvel. Despite the lowest horsepower of the bunch, the smallest tyres, and the only solid rear axle, the RX-7 needs no apologies. And it's a joy to drive ... With the smooth five-speed 'box, this is among the most fun-to-use powertrains you can buy today.

"It demands a little muscle at the wheel, but the RX-7 drives with almost the same kind of smoothness and refinement as the Supra, feeling smaller and lighter to boot. Its good balance translates into easy handling on the street, and very little appears to upset it."

The final decision went to the Supra (*Motor Trend*'s 1982 'Import Car of the Year'), but it was a close call and the "rotary rocket" remained as popular as ever. At the end of 1983, records show that more than 52,000 RX-7's were sold in America which, despite a vast improvement in sales performance across the range, represented around 30% of the total Mazda sales figure for the States that year.

Corporate news
1982 had seen the introduction of the fwd Mazda Capella (or 626). It was immediately voted the 1982-83 'Japanese Car of the Year' in its native country, was named *Motor Trend* magazine's 1983 'Import Car of the Year', and also received a large number of other prestigious accolades overseas. Sales in America continued to climb as restrictions on fuel eased and the appeal of the Mazda range widened.

Toyo Kogyo entered into an 8% capital tie-up with Kia Motors in 1983, and cumulative production reached 15 million units. From a very small beginning, Mazda had grown at great speed and developed a range of vehicles which could compete in all markets, challenging established car manufacturers throughout the world.

The next series of changes outlined for the RX-7 (under the P132 banner) would ultimately reinforce the marque's appeal. But first, a brief look at a worthy project undertaken by American Al Dooley.

The Avatar
The Avatar was the dream of Al Dooley, an engineer and sports car enthusiast, who wanted to build himself what he classed as the ultimate convertible. From the moment the RX-7 was launched, he looked into ways of creating a drophead coupé from it, without sacrificing the model's excellent structural integrity.

Steel strengthening beams were welded in the sill area, with another pair following the line of the transmission tunnel. Steel bars were then welded to the new outer frame, which extended into the windscreen frame to stop scuttle shake – the curse of convertibles. Another beam was added where the boot hinged, and a second skin grafted onto the existing boot floor.

For the coachwork modifications, fibreglass was rejected from day one, Dooley preferring to use aircraft-standard alloy panels in order to obtain a high class image; a special chip-resistant paint was employed, along with additional underseal to preserve the body. The frame for the convertible top was constructed from brass and aluminium, and made to drop out of sight when the hood was lowered.

The interior was trimmed in leather. Wood accents complemented the beautiful Nardi steering wheel, and high quality carpet added that extra touch of class; the stereo was uprated to include eight speakers.

Mechanically, changes were few. Different brake pads were specified, along with thicker front and rear anti-roll bars, new springs and shocks, and 15-inch alloys shod with Pirelli P7 tyres. In all, this elegant conversion added just 45kg (100lb) to the weight of the vehicle.

The author is not a big fan of modified vehicles, but the Avatar looked absolutely superb – a Japanese-American hybrid that resembled the Ferrari Daytona Spider. For those not happy with the standard engine (which could be linked to either the standard five-speed manual gearbox, or optional automatic), there was also a 307bhp turbocharged RE on offer, based on the 13B unit. This level of horsepower enabled the Avatar to perform like a Daytona, too!

At the same time as the Avatar took a bow, California Custom Coach was offering an RX-7 Targa conversion. Mazda was considering a Targa during this car's design process, but the idea was dismissed whilst still on the drawing board.

Meanwhile, Dooley continued to build the Avatar until 1988, by which time more than 120 had been constructed. Prototypes were produced based on the second generation model, but this project was duly abandoned after news broke of Mazda's own intention to introduce a convertible.

The 12A Turbo powerplant; sadly, only available in Japan.

The RX-7 goes turbocharged

The turbocharged 12A, with an 8.5:1 compression ratio (it is standard practice to lower the c/r on a turbo engine), produced a useful 165bhp at 6500rpm in Japanese trim. Naturally, maximum torque output was also enhanced, quoted at 166lbft at 4000rpm.

These impressive figures were achieved via an oil-cooled Hitachi turbocharger (a small turbocharger was chosen to reduce lag, then made to run faster to make up for lack of size), and the use of Nippondenso electronic fuel-injection. Although the 12A Turbo reverted back to two intake ports per chamber, there were other refinements, such as an improved finish on the trochoid, better lubrication, and adoption of an anti-knock sensor. The beauty of this particular turbo installation was that, despite the massive boost in power output, there was very little gain in weight.

The Cosmo was the first model to receive the turbocharged engine, and, in a bid to try and revive the fortunes of the RX-7 in Japan (home sales were now consistently hovering around the 1500 units per annum mark), as part of the changes outlined in project P132, the 165bhp unit duly found its way into the rotary sports car.

Launched in September 1983, the Turbo series was introduced to counter the threat of higher-powered machines from Toyota and Nissan. It ran alongside the normally-aspirated 6PI range, although the line-up was given new body colours and realigned to include three variations of each – the GT, GT-X and SE Limited grades. The turbocharged cars came with 14-inch wheels and tyres, the SE Limited having attractive 5.5J x 14 alloys shod with 205/60 Pirelli rubber (one of the few external clues to what was lurking under the bonnet), a limited-slip differential, larger diameter brakes (vented discs all round), eight-position, manually-adjustable shock absorbers, and the option of variable-assist power steering with a quicker ratio. A rear spoiler was also listed as an option.

Gear ratios for the Turbo were much the same as those found on earlier 6PI models, although the fifth gear was more overdriven at 0.791:1. Whilst the final-drive ratio was the traditional 3.91:1, the clutch and drivetrain were suitably modified to handle the extra horsepower. The automatic transmission option was not available

The GT Turbo of September 1983. Note the attractive wheels (the alloys were an option on the GT and GT-X grades), cooling slits in the front airdam, and the 'Rotary Turbo' badge on the bumper; one with similar script was mounted next to the grade badge on the tail. (Courtesy Hideo Aoki)

Interior of the GT Turbo, with the old-style fascia, but new three-spoke wheel for the turbocharged car, and the all-important boost gauge in the centre dial.

on the Turbo series, but the normally-aspirated cars had a new JATCO four-speed version with torque converter lock-up on top gear. This necessitated a new final-drive ratio, listed at 3.93:1. The manual gearbox for non-turbos was unchanged from earlier 6PI models, with fifth listed at 0.858:1.

All cars came with the larger 63 litre (13.9 gallon) fuel tank, first seen in the States on the 1981 range, cooling slits in the front airdam, and a Spacesaver spare. An independent rear suspension was considered as part of the P132 upgrade, but instead a thinner 13mm (0.51in) rear anti-roll bar was adopted, a number of bushes were revised, and the rear control arms were mounted 20mm (0.79in) lower on the body.

The Turbos came with a three-spoke steering wheel and slightly different trim. However, it should be noted that Japanese models retained the previous

Tail of the GT Turbo. By now, the RX-7 was a very purposeful-looking machine. (Courtesy Hideo Aoki)

Advertising for the Turbo, including news of a 300-off limited edition based on the GT version of the new model. Available from 8 October 1983, this was to commemorate Mazda's success in the C Junior category at Le Mans, and featured Custom Silver Metallic paintwork, Pirelli P6 tyres on 14-inch alloy wheels, a limited-slip differential, power door mirrors, and a special keyring and plaque.

year's dashboard and instruments, although on the Turbos, a boost gauge replaced the voltmeter on the centre dial. In fact, most countries continued with the old fascia, but under the P132 directives, America was to receive an updated version.

As for prices, the normally-aspirated GT was 1,623,000 yen in five-speed manual guise, the GT-X was 1,878,000, and the SE Limited, 2,274,000. The turbocharged GT was listed at 1,847,000 yen, while the GT-X and SE Limited were priced at 2,152,000 and 2,568,000 yen, respectively. With the non-turbo cars, the four-speed automatic added 82,000 yen.

Mazda's engineers obviously succeeded in their aims, as *Car Graphic* described the Turbo as "a proper sports car." Oddly, the turbocharged RX-7 was only ever available in Japan, though the American market was also destined to receive a unique version of the model for 1984.

The US 1984 model year

For some time, rumour had it that America was getting a larger engine. The 13B unit had been in service in the home market's Cosmo and Luce for several years, and had recently been updated with 6PI, dynamic-effect induction (DEI) and Bosch L-Jetronic fuel-injection. There was no doubt that a proven powerplant was available and, in October 1983, in accordance with the far-reaching details outlined in project code P132, the 13B-powered RX-7 duly made its debut.

With a 9.4:1 compression ratio, this particular RE delivered 135bhp

Colour-coding everything is a little overpowering, but perhaps this is one of the ultimate Grand Tourers from the period – a turbocharged SE Limited with leather trim.

American advertising for the new 13B-powered GSL-SE.

Rear three-quarter view of the GSL-SE. Note the badge on the left-hand side of the tail, and the beautiful 14-inch alloy wheels.

at 6000rpm, and a useful 133lbft of torque at 2750rpm. As the catalogue pointed out: "With a mere 14% increase in displacement over the 12A rotary, the 13B achieves its phenomenal potency through a myriad of refinements in design. First, its six-port, three-stage variable fuel induction system permits peak performance throughout its rpm range. Then, an ingenious dynamic-effect induction passage design creates a supercharged effect that is unique to the rotary. And finally, its computerized electronic gas injection constantly adjusts to the precise needs of the engine at that millisecond."

This was the first time that the 6PI system had been seen outside Japan, and the newly-introduced DEI system was equally noteworthy, using pressure waves from the combustion process to "supercharge" the air/fuel mixture without the need for heavy and expensive mechanical forced induction equipment. Like the Japanese Turbo engine, this RE received an improved finish on the trochoid, and better lubrication. However, after all the development work, only one model was given the fuel-injected 13B – the American market GSL-SE.

The GSL-SE borrowed many of its chassis elements from the home market turbocharged cars, including a limited-slip differential, 205/60 VR14 tyres on the new 5.5J cast alloy wheels, a tuned suspension, uprated disc brakes (250mm at the front, 257 at the rear, or 9.8 and 10.1in, respectively), ventilated at all four corners, and the option of speed-sensing, power-assisted steering (just $300 extra).

The gearing was the same as the Japanese 6PI model, except for a 0.760:1 ratio on fifth, and a new 4.08:1 final-drive. The SE also received an uprated clutch and drivetrain, although an automatic transmission was not available.

At $15,095, standard features included air conditioning, a sunroof, cruise control, power windows and mirrors, and cloth upholstery with velour side bolsters and matching door panels (leather trim was listed as a $700 option). This luxury specification naturally added to the car's weight, although at 1170kg (2575lb) it was hardly heavy compared to its contemporaries.

As part of the P132 master plan, all cars, including the SE, came with the rear suspension modifications carried out on Japan's models, and slits on the front spoiler to help keep the brakes cool.

American models also featured a revised instrument panel with four main meters in front of the driver (from left to right: an oil pressure gauge combined with a voltmeter, a tachometer, a 140mph speedometer, and water temperature next to a fuel gauge), new switchgear, a redesigned centre console including an armrest, quartz digital clock and totally different heating and ventilation controls, three-way driver's seat adjustment, a new three spoke steering wheel, and lighting and locks on the storage bins behind the seats.

The 12A engine gained a little power thanks to a new monolith catalytic converter, taking the maximum output to 101bhp at 6000rpm, and 107lbft of torque at 4000rpm. It was linked to the latest five speed gearbox which employed the same internal ratios as that on the GSL-SE, except for fifth (0.807), and the old 3.91 final-drive was retained. The optional four-speed automatic ratios were 2.458:1 on first, 1.458:1 on second, 1.000:1 on third, and 0.720 on fourth (although different to the Japanese specification, the 3.91 final-drive was kept again for America).

Differences between the grades remained much as before, with the basic S starting at $10,195 for 1984. The GS was $1100 more, but the GSL, which now came with driver's seat height adjustment, and a top stereo radio/cassette with nine-band equalizer, was priced at $13,095. Leather trim and power steering were available as options on the latter. Other major options included air conditioning, a sunroof, and alloy wheels (the familiar four-spoke design continued unchanged on the 13-inch rims).

However, it was the RX-7 GSL-SE that captured the headlines. According to independent tests, the 13B-engined model was capable of covering the standing-quarter in 16.4 seconds before going on to a top speed of 126mph (202kph). *Car & Driver* noted: "It sings an irresistible song, begging to be revved to its red-line and thrown into corners, and it communicates the joys of the sports car experience."

Road & Track was equally impressed and voted the RX-7 GSL-SE the 'Best Sports/GT' in the $14-18,000 price range in its "12 Best Enthusiast Cars of 1984." The same magazine compared the model with five other two-seaters in March that year; namely the Morgan 4/4 2000, the Alfa Romeo Spider Veloce, Pontiac Fiero SE, Honda Civic CRX 1.5, and the latest Z-car – the Nissan 300ZX. Looking for the ultimate sports car, the team at *Road & Track* thought the following of the larger-engined RX-7: "The exterior has been little changed, except for the handsome wheels, while the interior is one of the most attractive and functional we can imagine, with superb seats (one dissenter) and luxury equipment that somehow does not intrude on the car's sporting character. [However], the instrument lighting is not good and the figures are hard to read at night. The fake stitching on some (but not all) parts of the vinyl was criticized.

"The rear suspension of all RX-7s now has the lower control arms mounted 20mm lower on the body; while not eliminating the occasional rear twitchiness completely, this change and the speed-sensing variable-assist power steering make for confidence-inspiring handling. The RX-7 devours road with more appetite than any other car in the group.

"On mountain roads and at Willow Springs the RX-7 was every bit as quick as the very stable, 160bhp 300ZX, and the less experienced racers among us found the RX-7 the easiest car to drive really fast, its directness more reassuring than the softer vagueness of the ZX."

The ZX was the Mazda's nearest competitor in the marketplace, of course, and it's interesting to note that, although the Nissan had more horses under the bonnet, the power-to-weight ratio was not dissimilar, making performance and fuel consumption figures almost identical. The ZX was a little better in the braking department, and quieter at cruising speeds, although the Hiroshima machine had a slight overall advantage when it came to handling and roadholding.

As with other recent tests, it was close, but the Mazda beat the big Nissan on this occasion; rather surprisingly, though, top honours went to the nippy Honda. At the end of 1984, it was noted that 54,310 RX-7s were sold in the States during the year.

European update

The P132 changes were less dramatic for Europe, though nonetheless significant. The 1984 model year RX-7, often referred to as the 'Mk.III' and priced at £9999 in Britain, gained the Turbo's suspension revisions, its bigger 14-inch alloys shod with Dunlop 205/60 rubber and, of course, ventilated discs all round.

Reaction to the Dunlop tyres was somewhat mixed, the majority of testers tending to think they lost traction too quickly in poor conditions, making the 7 "decidedly tail happy." As *Autocar* said, though: "The brakes are well up on the car's performance potential, proving firm and progressive and remarkably fade-free."

Other modifications included adoption of a 63 litre fuel tank, the latest front airdam styling, dual mirrors (at last!), and an intercooler instead of the former oil cooler. Power outputs were unchanged in EEC countries, but, like its counterparts in Japan and the US, the European RX-7 got

Main picture: A 1984 RX-7 for mainland Europe. Unlike British cars (and those for the home market), these left-hand drive models had the new dashboard fitted to the American RX-7s.

Inset, above: Interior of a left-hand drive car for Europe.

Tail of the lhd 1984 Model Year RX-7 for Europe. Again, two grades were listed – the DX and SDX, this being the more expensive SDX, easily identified by the spoiler at the rear and headlight washers up front.

When Toyota launched the MR2, it described the car as the 'playmate of the year'. Mazda went one better with its advertising, joining forces with Playboy in Japan to produce a whole series of adverts like this one, featuring the rotary-powered Cosmo.

The last American catalogue to feature the first generation models. The car is a GSL-SE.

The S was the entry level model in the States.

The next grade up from the basic S was this one, the GS, with such items as wider tyres, halogen headlamps, power adjustment for the door mirrors, and a graduated screen.

Left: Interior of the 1985 GS, seen here with automatic transmission, an option not available on the base model. Note the later fascia, introduced to the US market in the previous season.

The GSL for the American 1985 model year.

a new gearbox (ratios were as per the Japanese 6PI models, combined with the 3.93:1 final-drive found on home market automatic models).

Having recorded a 16.1 second standing-quarter and a top speed of 123mph (197kph), *Autocar* summed up the RX-7 as "a thoroughly enjoyable car to drive, in terms of its performance, its handling and its good equipment levels. While the low-profile tyres have resulted in a slightly harsher, noisier ride, overall levels of refinement are still well above average. It is zippy enough for chasing around country lanes, smooth enough for comfortable long-distance cruising. At more than £1000 cheaper than a Porsche 924 it looks like good value."

Indeed, the £1000 figure quoted doesn't really give a true picture, as the Hiroshima machine was fully-equipped at that price (one of the few options was metallic paint at £85), while the Stuttgart thoroughbred would have cost about £13,500 if it was to match Mazda's level of standard features.

At the start of its April 1984 road test, *MotorSport* stated: "Why there are not more RX-7s on Britain's roads is a mystery." The author is very fond of the 924, but with this price difference in mind, and all the other points in the Mazda's favour, the magazine certainly raised an interesting point.

The home market

The Toyo Kogyo business was renamed the Mazda Motor Corporation on 1 May 1984, with Kenichi Yamamoto elected President shortly after his 62nd birthday. Born in 1922, Yamamoto, former MD, had served with Toyo Kogyo for many years and had been the company's Chief Engineer since January 1978. He had seen a vast number of changes along the way, both in terms of technology (he had been responsible for designing a V-twin engine for the three-wheeled Mazda trucks shortly after the war, and was heavily involved with the R360 and its descendants; he was also one of the key people behind the development of the Mazda rotary engine), and in company growth to a leading car manufacturer. Behind all of Yamamoto's achievements in the field of engineering was a dedicated enthusiasm for his work – an important factor that would have a bearing on the future.

In September 1984, a 'Limited Version' RX-7 based on the

Dashboard of the GSL. Both the GSL and GSL-SE were available with leather trim.

The 13B-powered GSL-SE, with Roger Mandeville's IMSA GTO racer.

turbocharged GT was announced. Finished in silver, it came with Pirelli P6 tyres on alloy wheels, a rear spoiler, and a spectacular six-speaker audio system. Sales were restricted to just 200 units.

Meanwhile, the standard 1985 model year range was much the same as before, with prices only 1% up on the previous season. This situation was hardly surprising, as rumours surrounding a new generation were starting to filter through into the press, and Mazda needed to clear its old stock. The Japanese are the most dedicated followers of fashion (generally speaking, one can always spot heavy initial demand, then a dramatic tailing off of sales in virtually every model on the home market), so there was little chance of selling the first generation car after its replacement became available.

End of the line
The SE received a new ratio on fifth gear (0.711:1 instead of 0.760), but otherwise there was little to report. The S was priced at $10,945, the GS at $11,845, the GSL was $13,645, while the GSL-SE commanded a hefty $15,645. Options remained much the same, with air conditioning up $20, and automatic transmission up $190 to a still more than reasonable $500; alloy wheels, on the other hand, went down to $350, representing a saving of about $150 on last year.

Coachwork colours for America included Dover White, Ocean Blue Metallic, Sunrise Red, Sunbeam Silver Metallic, Custom Silver Metallic, Sparkling Black Metallic, Tender Blue Metallic, Desert Brown Metallic, and Light Beige.

In the summer of 1985, *Road & Track* compared a fresh batch of affordable two-seaters, including the RX-7 GSL, Toyota's MR2, the Honda Civic CRX Si, Pontiac Fiero GT, Bertone X1/9 (formally badged as a Fiat), and the evergreen Alfa Spider. By now the Hiroshima coupé was starting to show its age when pitched against more dynamic machinery, and only the X1/9 was rated lower. However, Mazda already had an answer for the critics.

The second generation model was duly launched in September 1985, although the public already had a good idea of what to expect. Kenichi Yamamoto had given an interview not long after he took up the President's office, and revealed that Mazda was moving the latest RX-7 upmarket, intending it to compete directly with the Porsche 944 – a quicker and more refined development of the 924. He told people to expect a traditional FR layout, an independent rear suspension, and more power. Ultimately, like most of its contemporaries, the RX-7 was destined to become bigger, heavier, and more luxurious as the design evolved. By the time production of the first generation RX-7 came to an end, no fewer than 377,878 had been sold in America; 471,018 had been built in all. Remember, only a two-seater version was ever sold in the States.

Bowing out from Europe
While the fate of the first generation RX-7 was sealed, it soldiered on in Europe a few months after the new car was launched in Japan and America. Priced at £10,500 for the 1985 season in the UK, *Fast Lane* brought together the 7 and its old Stuttgart rival – the 924 – for a comparison test. The British magazine concluded: "Despite the steady flow of improvements, time has

Interior of one of the very last UK models. Note the old-style fascia was retained for right-hand drive cars.

gradually taken its toll on this pair. Neither can really match the standards of performance or handling that newer, cheaper hot hatches achieve with embarrassing ease.

"Yet does it matter? Many customers will probably be as interested in looks and aesthetic appeal as in outperforming the buzzing hordes of GTis. Frankly, it is very hard to split this pair. The Mazda is perhaps prettier and certainly has the more appealing engine, both for its smoothness and for its unique technical interest.

"It loses on ride and handling to the Porsche, thanks largely to the German car's more fluid ride and better seating ... Dynamically it has the edge and economically it's a shrewd bet, too. The complete equation, then, just balances in favour of the 924."

Judging by this report, a replacement 7 was long overdue. By the time the second generation model eventually appeared in the UK, the RX-7 cost £11,499 – an increase of £1000 on the 1985 model year price. Standard body colours for Europe included Dover White, Sunrise Red, Sunbeam Silver, Sparkling Black, Tender Blue, and Opal Green. Depending on the paintwork, trim came in either black, wine red or beige.

Tailpiece. A UK specification model from early 1985.

4

The second generation

The 1980s had seen the yen moving strongly against the dollar, pushing prices in export markets to unprecedented levels, with a corresponding knock-on effect in the showrooms. Cheaper models were no longer cheap, so the obvious answer – at least with existing designs – was to move upmarket and get a better return on fewer sales. The Nissan Z-cars and Mazda's own GSL-SE were perfect examples of this theory in practice.

The Germans, too, had had to rethink their strategy. Porsche dropped the 924 completely from the American market in early 1982, as it was simply not competitive in the wake of unhelpful exchange rate fluctuations. It was replaced by the 944 as an entry level model in the States, although the 924S took that mantle in June 1986, priced at almost $20,000 in basic trim!

A friend of the author's, Yoshihiko Matsuo, Chief Designer of the original Fairlady Z (240Z) and now a design consultant, gave his definition of a modern sports car in a recent interview: "It must be a two passenger automobile with attractive body styling designed for high-speed, highly-responsive driving. The engine must have reserves of power even at high rpm. It should have a manual transmission with a good feel and a fully-functional cockpit, and support pleasant high-speed handling. To state it as a category, I would say that sports cars belong somewhere between speciality cars and racing prototypes. Also, I believe, there are two main types of sports cars, one the Lightweight Sports Car and the other the Super Sports Car."

The first generation RX-7 wasn't exactly lightweight, but it was nearer the lightweight concept than most.

Kenichi Yamamoto, RJC 'Person of the Year' 1991-92, was Mazda's President at the time the Second Generation RX-7 was launched. At least with Yamamoto at the helm, the rotary's future seemed assured.

Weighing in at around 1100kg (2420lb), it was substantially lighter than Nissan's S130 series Fairlady (280ZX), and the recently-introduced Z31 models. But the 7 was destined to follow the Fairlady in its move upmarket: the P747 would be bigger, faster, heavier and better-equipped. In other words, the second generation RX-7 was going to be a Super Sports Car. Many who followed the industry knew this to be the case, and even the public got confirmation of the 7's new role when photographs appeared in most of the leading publications in mid-1985. Someone had spotted a couple of prototypes during cold weather testing in Canada, without any disguise panels whatsoever. "Mazda goes Porsche for '86," read the headline in *Motor*, which featured a three-page spread on the new machine.

Incidentally, with the new RX-7 and its contemporaries moving upwards, this left a massive void at entry level

Akio Uchiyama – the second generation RX-7's Chief Engineer.

as far as Japanese manufacturers were concerned. The Mazda marque was flying high in the States at that time, with the RX-7 dominating the IMSA racing scene and the SCCA Pro-Rally series. Kenichi Yamamoto knew that a true LWS – an abbreviation of lightweight sports car, used within the trade in much the same way as MPV (multi-purpose vehicle), and so on – would potentially have this sector of the market to itself and further strengthen Mazda's sporting image. The LWS that eventually emerged became known as the MX-5. The rest, as they say, is history ...

Project P747

The plan for the second generation RX-7 – Project P747, as it was called internally – was set in motion towards the end of 1980, gaining full approval in June 1981. Akio Uchiyama (who had been heavily involved with the first generation RX-7 from inception, and was behind many of its improvements as the original design matured) was duly given the post of Chief Engineer, with Noriaki Yoshioka as his assistant.

Meanwhile, on Yamamoto's orders, Uchiyama and a small group of Mazda engineers and planners had spent three months in the United States. This was to allow them to get a true feel for what the people in America thought of the RX-7 and, just as importantly, what they expected from the model in the future.

By spring 1982, proposals were already being put forward at dealer clinics in the States. Three configurations were suggested: a 'Realistic Sports Car' (one priced at between $9000 and $12,000, with a 110bhp engine, live rear axle, rack-and-pinion steering, 13-inch wheels, disc/drum braking, and the option of 2+2 seating); a 'Civilized Sports Car' (starting at $11,000, but featuring an extra 20bhp, independent rear suspension, power-assisted steering, 14-inch wheels, discs all round, and a high level of luxury equipment), and a 'Technologically Advanced Sports Car' (priced somewhere between $13,000 and $15,000, with a rear transaxle, adjustable suspension, ABS braking, 15-inch wheels with wide, low-profile tyres, a rear seat as standard, and electronic instrumentation).

The results from this survey gave conclusive proof that a 'Civilized Sports Car' was what the public wanted, with a base sticker price falling between $11,000 and $13,000 (remember, at this time, prices in the USA started at $9700, while the top-of-the-range GSL, even with leather trim, was $12,600). It was a very worthwhile exercise, and one which allowed Uchiyama and his team to clearly focus on the new car's specifications.

Uchiyama acknowledged that "one can only gain pleasure from a sports car when it is truly fun to drive, allowing experienced drivers, and those not so experienced, to extract the maximum amount of enjoyment from their own level of skill. No matter how much technology progresses, making high-performance machinery easier to handle, the vehicle cannot be classed as a sports car unless the driver actually feels like he is in command."

A theme was duly established; to develop a car which "creates a new level of performance, and fully imparts the joy of driving."

A new body

In the opening weeks of 1982, a small group of five designers – three exterior stylists, and two interior men – was sent for inspiration to Mazda's recently-opened MANA facility in California. With America being the model's primary market, it was felt that the design team, led by Yasuji Oda, should

Discussing design proposals in the early stages of P747 development.

This page & overleaf, top: Early design sketches.

see and experience P747's ultimate surroundings (and its competition!) first-hand. Only then could the team start sketching proposals for its bodywork and cockpit. Nowadays, of course, all of the major Japanese manufacturers have design bases in the States and Europe, but this was something quite new for Mazda at that time.

Anyway, various drawings and full-size renderings were made (of both exterior and interior), with the body designs eventually narrowed down to ten possibilities. These were then displayed at another clinic in March 1982, allowing the group to return to Japan with a clear idea of what was expected.

When Oda and his team arrived back in Hiroshima, the ten drawings were reviewed once more, and, with the aid of the market research carried out in the States, two choices were put forward for further development – one which looked remarkably like the 1986.5 model year Toyota Supra (Design F), and one which would eventually become the new RX-7 (Design E).

The two drawings were duly taken to clay model stage, leading to the production of a resin body for each proposal. After an internal review in Hiroshima, the mock-ups were then shipped to America to take part in yet another clinic in autumn 1982, anonymously placed alongside a first generation RX-7, a Datsun 280ZX, a Toyota Supra, the Chevrolet Corvette and Porsche's new 944 for comparison. Interestingly, the Stuttgart machine found most favour, but the critics put Design E in a clear second place. Naturally, shortly after (in February 1983), the decision was made to go with Design E, with further refinements to the shape after tests in the Japan Automobile Research Institute's wind tunnel, and later at the new facility installed at Miyoshi.

There were surprisingly few changes along the way. An idea was to have a Nissan 300ZX (Z31)-type headlight arrangement was rejected at an early stage, as was a proposal to use

81

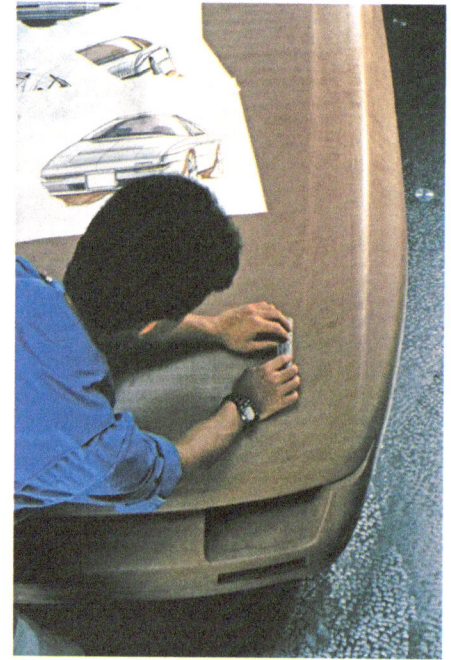

A Mazda modeller pictured in mid-1982 interpreting a designer's sketch.

P747's Chief Designer, Yasuji Oda (left), discussing the finer points of the car's styling with Matasaburo Maeda (head of the first RX-7's design, seen here in the centre), and interior man, Takashi Ono.

Right, top: A resin model of Design E – the prototype that would eventually become the RX-7.

Right, middle: The other proposal under consideration was Design F. Both resin models featured muscular lines on the nearside, and smooth wings on the other. Bulging wheelarches (seen here) and sill extensions, were duly rejected, on aerodynamic grounds and the need to keep the vehicle's width below 1700mm (66.9in) to avoid customers having to pay a heavy additional tax. Car Styling's Akira Fujimoto, a very fair critic, said he would have liked to have seen a little more curvature in the wings.

Right, bottom: Spring 1983 and almost there.

circular taillights at the rear (in honour of earlier rotary models). In reality, apart from odd details like the door handles and lighting arrangements, the design stayed very true to the original drawing – a gentle evolution of the first generation RX-7.

In an interview with *Car Styling*, Yasuji Oda stated: "After debating at the planning stage just how much to change the body styling, we decided to retain as far as possible the favourable points and features of the old body. We wanted to avoid being too conservative, and even studied a proposal which moved the greenhouse forwards to shorten the nose, as have some recent two-seater, mid-engined cars, but the general layout has hardly changed. We went for a true sports car look which stuck faithfully to the basics."

He continued: "The first generation RX-7 body had something rough-hewn about it, making one feel it was rather like a child that hadn't grown up yet, and yet it was very distinctive. We designed the body for the second generation series with a view to maturing and refining those features."

After a number of subtle tweaks, by mid-1984, the body for P747 had been finalised and given a warm reception at clinics in America and Europe. Of the main features, there was an aggressive-looking B-post which resembled that of a certain model from Germany, a one-piece glass rear hatch (rather like the one requested for the original RX-7, and with an integrated steel frame), retractable headlights that remained facing forwards to allow them to be used as passing lights or to 'flash' oncoming drivers (the beam was directed through tiny lenses in the smooth nose panel – itself a feature, produced in a unique reinforced polyurethane, and incorporating the front airdam), hidden rain channels, one-piece door pressings (ie. no separate side window frames), and smooth door handles.

Ultimately, through a series of minute refinements, the Cd was reduced to 0.31, or 0.29 with the optional aerodynamic aids (consisting of a three-piece front airdam extension kit, rear spoiler, rear wheelarch/sill trim, and an aluminium undertray), the latter being exceptional for the period. At the same time, lift was reduced, and dynamic testing (with the help of Mazda's GNC-2 computer programme) ensured shell rigidity easily surpassed

The finished design being tested in the wind tunnel. If anything, the B-pillar was perhaps a little too heavy (although it did offer a good measure of roll-over protection), and some road tests later complained about the A-posts being in the line of vision on tighter corners. Highly practical in service, the new door design allowed flush-fitting windows, and was both stronger and lighter than a traditional door. It also promoted far more efficient production methods, from time and cost points of view.

A number of early design sketches for the new car's fascia.

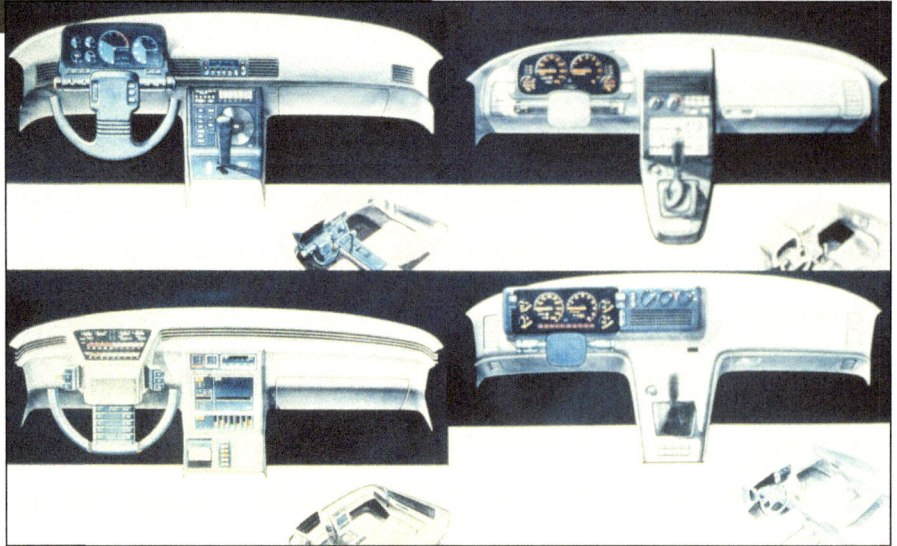

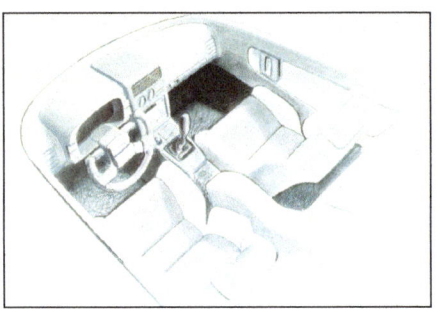

One of the many sketches put forward for the interior.

Work in progress on an early interior styling buck.

Another interesting interior styling buck for the P747 project.

that of its predecessor, in spite of there being no noticeable difference in weight.

As for the interior, design themes were drawn up in California at the same time as initial body sketches were being made, resulting in no fewer than four separate styling proposals. However, it was after the group returned to Hiroshima in spring 1982 that work on the cockpit began in earnest.

The interior styling was never going to be easy. The design team had been told quite clearly in initial market research that electronic displays were not as desirable as some manufacturers thought, but the new fascia had to be sporting, modern and functional. Cost constraints added to the designers' problem, as the management wanted to move the model upmarket, whilst clinics indicated an acceptable upper price limit that precluded the use of exotic trim materials. The interior had to look classy and expensive, but be relatively cheap to produce.

A vast number of drawings were put forward, with bucks produced to represent the more promising proposals. Ultimately, the dashboard and centre console retained a familiar Mazda look, although heating and ventilation was improved, there was more luggage and storage space, and the design of some of the minor switchgear was quite revolutionary. Two types of seat were offered initially, the cheaper version sporting integrated headrests instead of separate, adjustable items; cloth trim was standard, with leather an option on certain grades.

Work on the bodyshell ensured that the car could meet all known Federal crash regulations without having to forfeit the rear seats, something which had been necessary with the US specification first generation model. As a result, the new RX-7 would be available as a 2+2 in all markets, which would doubtless increase its appeal to those with young families. However, for true sports enthusiasts, a two-seater version was also prepared. On the latter, the fold-down rear seat (once described by *Motor* as "a vestigial bench for legless midgets") was replaced by two storage bins.

The powertrain

Work on the powertrain began in mid-

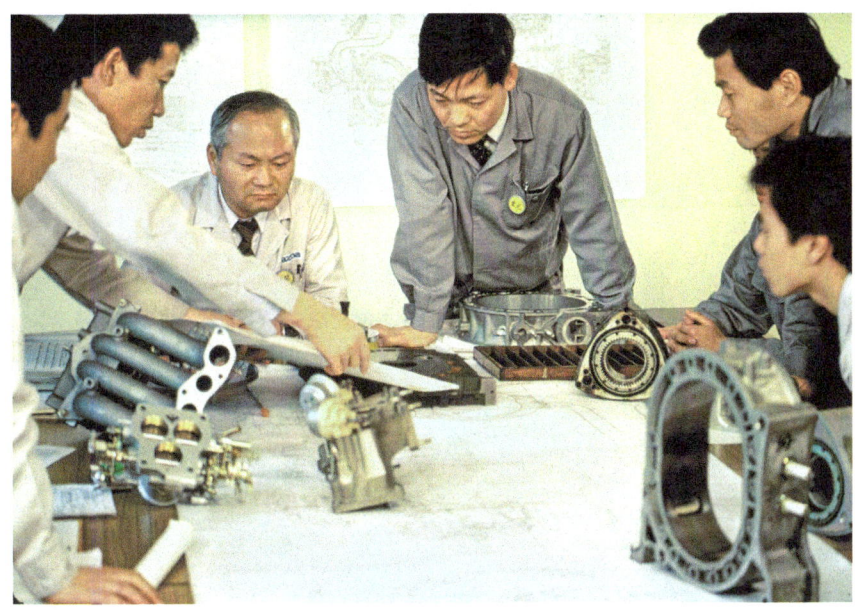

The engine development team discuss options and ways in which to further refine the unique rotary power unit. Head of the RE Department, Hiroshi Ohzeki, can be seen seated in the centre of this picture.

The 185bhp 13B Turbo. Eventually, it would become available in all the major markets.

1982. Only the rotary engine was considered, although three main options were put forward for development – the 12A 6PI unit (introduced on home market RX-7s in March 1982), the 13B DEI (scheduled and duly adopted for the USA's 1984 model year), and the 13B with forced induction, either by turbocharging or supercharging (the latter via the experimental TISC system). Having set certain limits on horsepower and acceptable fuel consumption levels relative to engine output, it was quickly realised that the 12A was not going to be suitable for the new, heavier car. Independent tests showed an average of 25.2mpg (Imperial) for the smaller RE when installed in the SE Limited, while the much more powerful fuel-injected unit could return 23.7mpg – a reasonable figure given the additional performance, but one which was uncomfortably close to attracting America's Gas Guzzler Tax.

Hiroshi Ohzeki and his team of engineers therefore concentrated on the 13B options, trying to extract more power, whilst at the same time improving fuel economy. The normally-aspirated unit – with 6PI, DEI and fuel-injection – was already in service

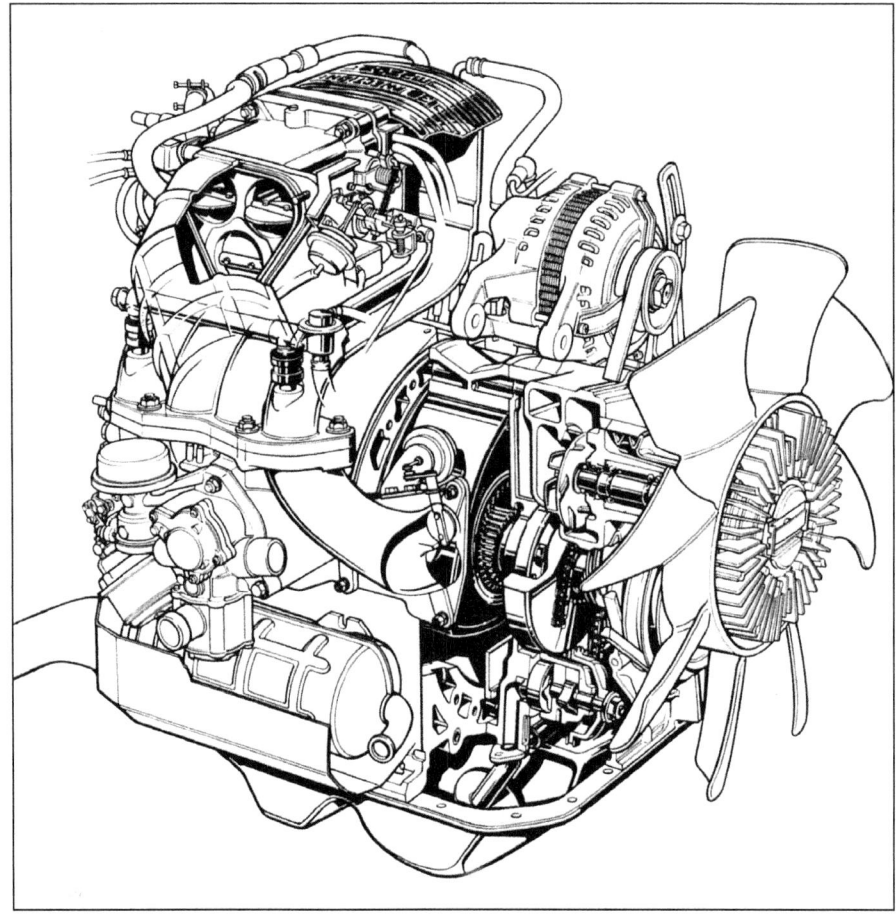

Cutaway drawing of the 13B DEI engine, produced only for export RX-7s. The new generation REs received a Teflon coating on internal chromed surfaces to enhance oil retention, and therefore prolong life.

in the States, so had a proven service record by the time the new RX-7 was launched. After a number of subtle refinements in the DEI components and the efi system, and adoption of a new ECU, relocated SSD spark plugs and lighter rotors with redesigned seals (all of which amounted to a hard-fought gain of 11bhp), not to mention improvements in engine lubrication and cooling, it was declared fit for duty in the P747 model. With a familiar 9.4:1 compression ratio, maximum power was quoted as 146bhp at 6500rpm, while peak torque was listed at 138lbft at 3500rpm.

Having decided to go along the turbocharging route for the high-powered engine, the 13B Turbo was duly developed alongside the normally-aspirated RE. The planners had originally set a target of 170bhp for this unit, but caused all sorts of headaches when they then upped it to 180 at the last minute in order to remain competitive with contemporary Toyota and Nissan outputs.

However, Ohzeki's department eventually achieved a reliable power output in excess of the later target, thanks to a specially-designed, twin-scroll Hitachi turbocharger, an air-to-air intercooler and a new version of Bosch's L-Jetronic fuel-injection. As with the 12A Turbo, though, (introduced on Japanese RX-7s for the 1984 season), the 6PI arrangement was dropped in favour of two intake ports per chamber.

With an 8.5:1 compression ratio (a piezoelectric knock sensor and an electronically-controlled ignition retard system was employed to avoid internal damage), the turbocharged RE developed 185bhp at 6500rpm, along with 181lbft of torque at 3500rpm.

Equally important, the new engine had a broad power band and, because of the water-cooled, twin-scroll charger (which basically combined the specific advantages of a large and small turbo in one compact unit), a lesser amount of lag than usually experienced in installations from this period. At 171kg (376.2lb), it was only 18kg (39.6lb) heavier than its 146bhp counterpart.

Like the normally-aspirated rotary engine, emission control was via a multi-stage catalyst, with two pre-converters (the design was slightly different on the turbocharged RE, although basically the same in principle), and a main monolith converter. Ultimately, spent gases exited from dual silencers, instead of the single rear box (with twin pipes) found on earlier RX-7s.

Whatever powerplant was specified, as with the earlier cars, the RE was placed low down behind the front axle line to reduce the height of the bonnetline and enhance the vehicle's weight distribution. For the same reason, the new lightweight radiator was mounted at an angle to keep the front as low as possible; an oil cooler was standard across the range.

Export versions of the new RX-7 came with two five-speed gearboxes, and the option of a four-speed automatic on normally-aspirated models. The standard manual transmission was an uprated version of that found in the American GSL-SE model (the Type M), while turbocharged vehicles received the new Type R 'box.

Internal ratios on the manual transmissions were very similar for export: 3.475:1 on first, 2.002 on second, 1.366 on third, a direct fourth, and an overdriven 0.711:1 on fifth for the Type M, with the corresponding ratios for turbocharged models being 3.483, 2.015, 1.391, 1.000, and 0.762. Normally-aspirated cars employed a 225mm (8.9in) diameter clutch, while the Type R was fitted with a beefier 240mm (9.4in) item.

The final-drive ratio was 4.10:1 for the lower-powered cars, with 3.91 on the turbocharged models. However, by the time full-scale production started

A cutaway of the GT Limited by master artist, Yoshihiro Inomoto. This superb drawing clearly shows the chassis components and their locations. (Courtesy Yoshihiro Inomoto)

for export, the latter was changed to 4.10 as well. An lsd came as standard on the top models, and was optional on the other grades. While on the subject of the final-drive, mention should be made of the rather novel end cover for the differential unit, which was cast in aluminium alloy and had an integrated mounting bracket. The automatic was the familiar JATCO unit carried over from the previous generation, although the first two ratios were changed for export, as its application would ultimately be quite different for the home market. First gear was now listed as 2.841:1, with 1.541 on second, 1.000 on third, and 0.720 on the overdrive fourth (selected via a push-button on the T-shift); the traditional 3.91:1 final-drive was retained for the four-speed unit.

It should be noted that gear ratios for home market models were slightly different, with the Type R gearbox having a 0.806 ratio on fifth, combined with a 4.10:1 final-drive from day one. The automatic, which could be specified on the Turbo (as it happens, only the turbocharged car was sold in Japan), had the original JATCO four-speed specifications, and also came with a 4.10:1 rear axle.

Chassis details

Uchiyama entrusted Jiro Maebayashi with the chassis layout. Maebayashi had been a strong supporter of the rotary-engined sports car, putting forward a number of proposals before ultimately working alongside Uchiyama on the X605 project.

Up front, it was decided to further refine the MacPherson strut suspension, but for the rear suspension, there was no doubt that the old-fashioned live rear axle had reached the limit of its

Testing a very heavily disguised prototype.

development, leaving no choice but to go for an irs system.

Mazda had introduced its twin-trapezoidal link (TTL) rear suspension on the 323 and 626 models, incorporating toe control to enhance handling and improve stability under braking or deceleration, but Maebayashi wanted to take the idea one step further. Takao Kijima, a brilliant chassis engineer who would later head RX-7 and MX-5 development, was pulled into the team from a different department. Together, Kijima and Maebayashi set about their task to design the ultimate rear suspension for P747.

Double-wishbone suspension was naturally an ideal choice (it was used on virtually all traditional racing and sports cars, and was later adopted for the MX-5 two-seater, of course), but it presented a packaging problem on this particular project. A semi-trailing arm irs was therefore chosen as a good compromise, and became the basic layout on which development work began.

In the background, the MX-02 concept car was progressing, and by the time it was exhibited at the 1983 Tokyo Show, it featured the perfect toe control system – four-wheel steering. But this was too expensive for a volume production model, the price of which had to fall within certain limits already outlined by the planners. Instead, an ingenious system was devised with a triaxial floating hub, an arrangement which gave almost limitless toe control variations without the need to employ expensive and heavy electronics and/or hydraulics.

Two engineering mules (based on then-current RX-7s, and designated X-0s) were completed in spring 1982 for evaluation. Both had MacPherson struts and lower A-arms of fabricated steel up front (mounted on a subframe that also carried the steering rack and, later on, the engine supports, too), but one featured the new hub with a semi-trailing arm suspension from an old Cosmo, whilst the other had Chapman struts to give the Mazda team a level of comparison. Development engineers tried both cars before three well-known Mazda racers (Yoshimi Katayama, who had helped refine the first generation model's suspension, Yojiro Terada,

Cold weather testing in Canada.

Comparison testing in the States. The blue car is a Toyota Celica Supra, by the way.

and Takashi Yorino) were enlisted for their views. By the end of the year, the general consensus was to abandon semi-trailing arms.

However, Kijima was convinced the idea could be made to work, and, in any case, the Chapman strut set-up ultimately displayed as many negative features as positive ones. Kijima went back to the computer and set about giving the new floating hub different bushing values. At the same time, each semi-trailing arm was, in effect, split in two parts to give the car better anti-squat and anti-dive characteristics, whilst also making the

Preparing a prototype for some fast laps at the Nürburgring in Germany.

Mazda quite literally went to extraordinary lengths to ensure reliability!

IRS a more compact package; camber-compensating links were added to counter another complaint. By May 1983, the first X-1 mule had been built, featuring Kijima's latest modifications, along with lighter aluminium alloy wheel hubs (saving around 7kg, or 15.4lb), and cast alloy lower A-arms at the front. This was a great improvement, and ultimately seven X-1s were produced for testing, most of which was done in Japan, although one was shipped to the Nurburgring for evaluation on the notorious German circuit. A few niggling faults still had to be ironed out, but the engineers were getting closer to the desired results.

The final prototype version, the X-2 of early-1984 vintage, employed forged aluminium alloy A-arms (saving 2kg, or 4.4lb, per car when compared to fabricated steel items), and a rear subframe was used as a mounting point for the irs and final-drive after severe NVH problems had been experienced with the X-1.

Apart from a few detail refinements, this was how the car went into production, with the novel rear suspension gaining the DTSS (Dynamic Tracking Suspension System) appellation along the way. According to Mazda, it retained the space efficiency of the semi-trailing arm set-up whilst providing a level of wheel control one would expect from double-wishbones; only time would tell, of course, but the press reports would make particularly interesting reading with regard to this element of the vehicle.

Standard anti-roll diameters were 22mm (0.87in) up front, and 12mm (0.47in) at the back. However, the top-of-the-range models could be specified with the uprated Turbo suspension – stiffer springs and shock absorber values, plus 24mm (0.94in) front and 14mm (0.55in) rear anti-roll bars – or AAS (Auto Adjusting Suspension), an electronically-controlled damper system that enabled the driver to choose between 'Normal' or 'Sport' settings.

Steering was now by rack-and-pinion instead of the former recirculating ball, and came either with or without power assistance. The advanced speed-and g-sensing power steering (standard on the turbocharged and top normally-aspirated models, optional on others) was provided with electronically-controlled variable assistance, and had a quick 15.2:1 ratio (compared with 20.3:1 for the manual rack). There was steering wheel adjustment for height (but not reach) and, for safety, the column was collapsible.

At one point, there were thoughts of adopting inboard discs at the back, rather like those found on the contemporary Alfa GTV and Jaguar XJ series, but a suitable system was devised placing the rear calipers ahead of the axle line. With the front calipers on the trailing edge of the discs, and the rear items on the leading edge, this gave the additional bonus of keeping the weight of the braking system within the wheelbase. An ABS braking system was also in the pipeline at this time.

The braking system adopted for production was naturally servo-assisted, and via discs all round (250mm diameter up front, 261mm at the rear, or 9.8in and 10.3in, respectively). Top models received vented rear discs of a larger 273mm (10.7in) o.d., and four-pot calipers up front (acting on 276mm, or 10.9in discs), which not only improved braking efficiency, but, being made in aluminium alloy instead of cast iron, saved a total of 4.2kg (9.2lb) for each pair. The vehicles with uprated brakes had five-bolt wheel fixings instead of four, incidentally.

Although the cheaper grades came with 185/70 HR14 tyres on 5.5J steel rims (with 5.5J alloys as an option), the top normally-aspirated models had 15-inch wheels and Bridgestone Potenza tyres (6J cast aluminium alloys with 205/60 VR-rated rubber), while turbocharged cars had 16-inch items -7J rims shod with 205/55 VR16 Goodyear Eagles.

P747 reaches production

A weight reduction programme was instigated in mid-1983, which even went as far as sourcing an aluminium jack to save 1.4kg (3lb). Some members of the management were less than happy about escalating production costs brought about by the use of expensive alloys and novel engineering features. At least Mazda realised the importance of the RX-7 as a flagship model, and, fortunately, the project was eventually approved in November 1983.

When the S-1 prototypes appeared, they were, essentially, the production car (although following further testing in America, Europe and Canada, a few minor changes were made). A final prototype, the S-2, was built towards the end of 1984, but this model remained in Japan. If P747 was to be launched in 1985 as planned, time had simply run out – it was now or never.

Although the second generation model was completely new, the original RX-7 had been a great success, so it was foolish not to capitalize on this popularity. Therefore, despite strong feeling in some quarters about naming it the RX-8 (RX-9 was mentioned in a number of contemporary publications, too), the latest car was also to be known by the RX-7 appellation.

Production duly started in the Hiroshima Plant Complex in Ujina (where the original RX-7 was built), with chassis numbers for the new car beginning at FC3S-100000. Initial schedules were set for around 6000 units a month, incidentally, the majority of this figure allocated for the US market.

As for dimensions, the wheelbase was 2430mm (95.7in), the overall length was 4310mm (169.7in), the width 1690mm (66.5in), and the height 1270mm (50.0in); the front track was 1450mm (57.1in), 10mm (0.4in) wider than that listed for the rear. This meant the new car was a fraction bigger in all respects, but the greatest difference was in the vehicle's wider track. The lightest model in the home market line-up was 1210kg (2662lb), while weight distribution was an ideal 51% front, 49% rear. Like the later first generation cars, the new RX-7 also employed a 63 litre fuel tank.

The new RX-7 in Japan

The Hiroshima marque displayed the MX-03 at the 1985 Tokyo Show, a four-wheel drive, four-wheel steer coupé designed by Masakatsu Kato. Another interesting facet of the design was the three-rotor engine – turbocharged in this case – which was doubtless a preview of the power unit destined for use in the forthcoming luxury saloon being prepared for Mazda's proposed new luxury division.

With no less than 315bhp on tap, it has been said that the MX-03 could top 180mph (290kph), although this was fairly academic as all manufacturers in Japan were regulated to govern production cars to run no faster than 112mph (180kph) at the time. Featuring 2+2 seating, it was sportier than the MX-02 of two years previous (which was quite staid by comparison), but sadly it, too, was destined to remain a prototype.

The 1985 event (held at Harumi

The MX-03 was an interesting exhibit on the Mazda stand at the 1985 Tokyo Show, but the event also saw the debut of the Second Generation RX-7. (Courtesy Hideo Aoki)

The home market GT-X grade, the model most suited to hard drivers, seen here at speed. (Courtesy Hideo Aoki)

One of the first GT Limited models photographed at the Nishi-Nippon race track. Perhaps unfairly, more than a few comments were made about its similarity to the water-cooled Porsches. The *Autocar* said: "Styling appears to owe a lot to the Weissach firm." (Courtesy Hideo Aoki)

Interior of the GT-X. Having the warning lights in the centre of the dashboard fascia allowed Mazda to use larger meters, but the arrangement was criticised by some, as the small bank of lights were out of the driver's direct line of vision. Most reports praised the well-shaped seats and adjustable steering and, naturally, the comfortable driving position one could achieve with them. Good pedal positioning was also mentioned on several occasions.

The turbocharged engine was certainly a snug fit ...

The tail of the GT-R model. The rear bumper was made up from similar materials to those employed in the front nose panel. (Courtesy Hideo Aoki)

Japanese advertising introducing the new Savanna RX-7. The same car featured here – a GT Limited – was used for a small four-page brochure, which had equally atmospheric photography.

from 31 October to 11 November) also saw the debut of the new RX-7, announced only a month earlier, on 20 September. At the press conference, Kenichi Yamamoto said: "The new RX-7 will extend the citizenship of the sports car in today's mature automobile market."

As mentioned earlier, only the Turbo was sold in Japan, distinguished by a power bulge in the bonnet, slightly offset towards the nearside. This was not a cosmetic appendage, as it provided an intake for the intercooler, which sat directly on top of the turbocharged engine. However, compared with the smooth panel found on non-turbo models, it was not as clean through the air and, as a consequence, the car's Cd was increased by 0.01.

With sales starting on 8 October, prices initially ranged from 1,971,000 yen for the GT model, up to 3,120,000 yen for the automatic GT Limited. There were four grades for the home market – the basic GT, the GT-R, GT-X, and the GT Limited – all in 2+2 form only.

The GT came with a five-speed gearbox, a manual steering rack, and manually adjustable shock absorbers (rather like those found on the earlier turbocharged RX-7, with an eight position selector dial). The seats had integrated headrests, and were trimmed in low-grade materials, although the uprated braking system and halogen headlights came as standard.

Moving up to the GT-R (which started at 2,278,000 yen) brought the option of automatic transmission, and power-assisted steering as part of the package. Other features included an enhanced level of trim, individual headrests on the front seats, a rear wash/wipe facility, a four-speaker AM/FM stereo, power windows, and courtesy door lights.

The GT-X, at 2,588,000 yen in manual guise, had the AAS suspension system, and came with five-spoke 6J x 15 alloy wheels instead of six-inch steel rims, although all Japanese models were shod with 205/60 HR15 rubber. The GT-X also gained a radio/cassette and power adjustment for the door mirrors.

The GT Limited was the luxury grade, with air conditioning, a sunroof, better quality, full-cloth trim (including the side bolsters), a radio/cassette with graphic equalizer, central locking, and cruise control. However, performance wasn't forgotten, as for 200,000 yen the buyer could specify a limited-slip differential and four-wheel, three-sensor ABS brakes.(Oddly, the lsd came as standard on the GT-X.)

Although a five-speed gearbox was standard on each grade, all except the GT could be bought with automatic transmission, priced at 82,000 yen. The Aero Kit was listed as a dealer option on all cars, painted in body colour for Japan. Coachwork could be finished in Dover White, Pure Red, Arctic Silver Metallic or Tornado Silver Metallic, the latter shade being almost black in reality.

Writing for *Car Graphic*, Paul Frere observed: "Even the Turbo's power does not fully exploit the chassis' potential. Driving the car in pouring rain on the Nishi Nippon circuit, I felt convinced that the example I drove was fitted with the optional limited-slip differential, so good was the traction and the rear end control. But it was not."

In the same month, the Japanese *Motor Magazine* compared a new RX-7 with the Nissan Fairlady 200ZR-II – a two-litre turbocharged Z-car for the home market. From experience, the author can state the ride on the Z is a little harsh, and the turbo is a typical all or nothing installation from the period, but otherwise it is a well-equipped, competent performer. In the end, the journal declared there was little to split the two – both were impressive, although it was noted that the manual gearboxes on both machines could have been better.

Incidentally, 1985 had also seen the introduction of the all-new, front-wheel drive Mazda Familia (323) series in Japan, and although the second generation RX-7 was duly named 1986 'Import Car of the Year' by *Motor Trend* magazine, it could manage only third spot in the Japanese Car of the Year contest. First place went to the new Honda Accord, with the latest 323 in second.

America greets the new model
When the RX-7 arrived in America at the start of the 1986 model year, there were two basic grades – the base model and the luxury GXL. However, the cheaper car could be upgraded via a number of packages and options, although only a normally-aspirated engine was available at this stage. Interestingly, the 2+2 seating was offered in the form of an option in the States, priced at $500, and this could be applied to both vehicles.

With a compression ratio of 9.4:1, the 1308cc 13B unit produced 146bhp and 138lbft of torque. The engine could be linked to the five-speed Type M gearbox, or the optional four-speed automatic.

By normal sports car standards, the entry-level model was far from spartan. In fact, it was very well equipped, with four-wheel disc brakes, 185/70 HR14 tyres on styled steel wheels (the RX-7 now came with a Spacesaver spare), halogen headlights, tinted glass (naturally, with a heater element in the back window), variable speed intermittent wipers, and remote control exterior mirrors.

Inside, there were many features that would have been options in the past. The main items were reclining highback bucket seats in velour, cut-pile carpeting with a fully-trimmed luggage area (including luggage straps), full door trim with velour inserts and lower carpeting, a 40W AM/FM stereo radio with four speakers and an electric aerial, full instrumentation (including an 8000rpm tachometer, an oil pressure gauge, voltmeter, and a comprehensive bank of warning lights and chimes), remote release for the fuel filler door and rear hatch, a quartz digital clock, driver's footrest, a central armrest (with combined storage box and coin tray), and a day/night rearview mirror.

The GXL had such niceties as power steering, larger diameter, ventilated discs all-round, 205/60 VR15 tyres mounted on aluminium alloy wheels, a limited-slip differential, AAS suspension, air conditioning, cruise control, an electric tilt/slide sunroof, better quality seats (with adjustment for the headrests and, on the driver's-side, lumbar and height), a leather-trimmed steering wheel with tilt facility (although it remained basically the same two-spoke design as that found on the cheaper model), power door mirrors, electric windows, central locking, a 100W AM/FM stereo radio/cassette with four speakers, a graphic equalizer and power diversity aerial, higher-quality trim with plush carpets and additional insulation against noise, a graduated windscreen tint, rear wash/wipe, an illuminated ignition barrel and driver's door lock, courtesy door lights, and storage compartments

American brochure announcing the latest RX-7. The tiny headlight window was an inspired idea, giving all the benefits of retractable headlights with none of the traditional shortcomings, such as the loss of passing lights. The arrangement was made possible by the use of a parallelogram linkage, but was not allowed in Japan because of local regulations. Home market vehicles, therefore, had auxiliary lights in place of clear lenses.

The entry level RX-7 for 1986.

Rear view of the base model. All cars came with colour-keyed bumpers with black rubbing strips, the latter perfectly matching the wide body side protection mouldings. Note the high-mounted rear brake light on US cars.

At the time of the American launch, the base model could be upgraded via a Luxury Package or a Sport Package (seen here, at the top of this advert). The other car featured here is the top-of-the-range GXL, with a view of its interior in two-seater guise.

The leather trim option was only available on the GXL, but could be specified on either the 2+2, as seen here, or the two-seater.

behind the seats (on the two-seater, of course) with locks and lights.

At the end of 1985, the top-of-the-range RX-7 GXL was listed at $16,645, whereas the basic model was just $11,995; the standard RX-7 with the Luxury Package came in at $12,795, while the Sport Package was $200 more than that.

By the way, the Luxury Package comprised 14-inch alloys, dual power mirrors, the four-speaker radio/cassette with diversity aerial, a sunroof, and a graduated tint on the windscreen. The Sport Package, meanwhile, included power-assisted steering, a tuned suspension, 205/60 VR15 tyres on five-spoke alloy wheels, uprated disc brakes, a lowered front airdam, aero parts to the rear wheelarch/sill area, and a rear spoiler. Buyers were also given the opportunity to purchase the Sport Package with a sunroof, or without power steering.

Individual options included a tasteful leather trim package (for the two-seater, or 2+2), 14-inch alloys for the base model, a four-speed automatic transmission, air conditioning, an alarm system, various stereo upgrades (including a CD player), cruise control, foglights, a rear window louvre, a front mask, floor mats, and the electric sunroof. There was also an Aero Package, which included a new front spoiler, side skirts, a rear spoiler, lowered rear valance, and a roof trim that made the B-post appear less bulky.

Press reaction

At the time of the car's announcement, *Road & Track* wrote: "The new RX-7 may look different, but one thing about it is thoroughly familiar: the unique sound of its rotary engine. Our sound meter readings don't show it dramatically, but the engine seems much quieter, attesting to the engineers' many sound-reducing measures. It is also a bit smoother and freer-revving, although its rev limit remains at 7000rpm and a buzzer sounds if you exceed it. On the freeway in fifth gear, engine noise drops to a distant hum, and both wind and road noise are low.

"Shifting is pleasant, if not the best in the business, and internal improvements not only shorten the shift throws slightly but promise longer second gear synchronizer life as well. In normal road driving, the only unpleasant characteristic we discovered was a certain drivetrain jerking when getting onto or off of the throttle – something we did not expect given the shock-insulating tube-in-tube (TIT) construction of the driveshaft.

"In our first miles on public roads in the GXL, we were duly impressed by its solidly constructed body, supple suspension (only slightly less supple in the AAS's 'Sport' setting) and excellent steering feel ... Unlike its rather noisy, hard-riding and nervous predecessor, the new RX-7 is an ideal car for a fatigue-free cross-country journey.

"A few laps of the Seattle

An interesting advert from the period, outlining Mazda's commitment to quality.

Another piece of American advertising, this being for the 1986 model year GXL.

International Raceway in the plain-vanilla version with its standard 185/70 HR14 tyres on 5.5-inch rims revealed predictable, stable handling but squealing rubber. Those interested in extracting the handling potential of this car are therefore advised to order either the upmarket GXL, which comes with 205/60 VR15s on six-inch rims, or the optional Sport Package, which is shod the same but includes firmer springs and shocks and an Aero Package. A similar conclusion goes for the non-powered steering, which is a great improvement over the old RX-7's slack recirculating-ball mechanism, and is both adequately quick and manageable in parking; just the same, the exotic new power-assisted steering is so good you just gotta order it. Again, it's standard on the GXL but optional on the base car.

"The four vented discs hauled the fast-moving GXL from speeds in the 80-110mph range to tight-corner speeds repeatedly, and in our fade tests, they also failed to show any fade."

It was with the normally-aspirated, five-speed GXL that *Road & Track* recorded a 0-60 time of 7.9 seconds – that was quicker than both the contemporary 944 and the 300ZX Turbo. The journal described the new 7 as "a sports car of few compromises," with "excellent, tossable handling" and a "responsive engine." On the down side, the magazine felt there was a lack of individuality displayed in the styling, and a degree of disappointment was expressed in some of the interior materials, which were of "no better than average quality."

Summing up, however, the article stated: "Our preliminary conclusion about the new RX-7, then, is that Mazda has raised the standards of sports car performance by a sizable margin."

This, of course, was exactly what Mazda wanted to hear. It should be stressed, however, that praise was not forthcoming from just one source, but was almost universal at the time of the model's launch. Rod Millen, who successfully rallied the old RX-7, said: "I drove this new RX-7 a year ago. It's more chunky feeling. It's more spacious. And anybody can drive faster in this car more easily."

At *Car & Driver*, Larry Griffin wrote:

A left-hand drive car for the European mainland. The sharply raked windscreen was bonded in place, merging with the roof panel to give cleaner aerodynamics, while the windscreen wipers parked below the bonnet line to further aid smooth airflow.

A view of the European interior, complete with its 2+2 seating.

Dashboard of the left-hand drive model. European speedometers were marked up to 150mph or 240kph, depending on the market. Note the three-spoke steering wheel.

"Both the standard model and the GXL share a new rack-and-pinion steering gear designed with high rigidity in mind. To enhance straight-ahead feel, the rack itself has been machined with a 0.5mm (0.019in) bulge at its centre to tighten rack-and-pinion contact at this critical point. To upgrade GXL models, Mazda gives them a special electronically-controlled power steering system. Sensors monitor road speed and steering angle every 0.3 seconds and feed this information to a computer that varies the power steering assist supplied by two tandem hydraulic pumps. The harder you drive, the less the assist. The results are very light, enjoyable steering at low speeds, and firm, stable tracking at high speeds.

"[On the GXL], the heavily-finned,

forged aluminium, four-piston front brakes and the single-piston rears squeeze ventilated discs, and they feel very good through the pedal, producing few doubts either in scorching mountain runs or on the test track, in 186ft [56.7m] stops from 70mph [112kph]. Few cars tell you so clearly that worthy mechanical bits are working in your favour.

"In the cockpit, the shifter and the pedals are sturdier, and they're placed better than ever. The seats are genuine wraparound performance items, multi-adjustable for proper support and reach to the tilt-adjustable wheel ... The instrument layout is first-cabin, but the red-orange markings can be less effective than pure white-on-black markings, especially on a sunny day when sunglasses mask detail in the depths of the instrument pod. The rest of the RX-7's ergonomics are fine. Love those wacky pinball-flipper controls on the dash pod that keep the wipers and the smooth cruise control in play."

Car & Driver concluded: "There are two things we'd get rid of for sure: the two-spoked steering wheel, for a proper three- or four-spoked sport wheel; and our old RX-7, if we had one, for a new RX-7." Enough said.

The latest RX-7 in Europe

The new RX-7 was supposed to be available in the UK from February 1986, although its introduction was then delayed; in fact, the press launch (held in Rome) didn't take place until February!

However, there was no shortage of press coverage in the intervening months leading up to its arrival. In the December 1985 issue of *MotorSport*, it was noted: "From driving experience in both Japan and America, in a variety of specifications, we can say that the new RX-7 is a whole lot better than its predecessor, whose only real claim to advanced technology was its continued use of the rotary engine."

The article went on to say: "In test sessions at Mazda's Miyoshi Global Handling Circuit, and California's doomed Riverside International Raceway, plus during a brief spell on roads from Newport Beach to Riverside, the RX-7 displayed remarkably low wind noise characteristics and a superb ride, even on rough and broken surfaces, while as one would suspect, the European specification cars handle markedly better thanks to firmer damping which dramatically lessens a tendency to roll oversteer evident on the US specification versions.

"At Riverside, we saw a regular indicated 120mph [192kph] before the banked Turn Nine in the Euro cars and as ever the rotary power unit proved more than eager to rev way beyond its 6700rpm warning buzzer, although we weren't over-impressed with its torque beneath 4000rpm.

"It weighs in a fair bit heavier than the older car, mainly because of its upmarket upgrading, but possesses a satisfying feeling of solidity, and is a much more refined vehicle than its forerunner.

"The UK won't get the 180bhp Turbo, nor will it get ABS or power steering, but from our long lead opportunity we'd definitely advise potential Porsche buyers to wait a few more months and try an RX-7 for themselves before making a final decision."

The European models were, in fact, a strange mix of Japanese and American specification, with one or two unique features of their own. All cars sent to the EEC were 2+2s, with a trim level roughly corresponding to America's GXL grade. They eventually went on sale in Britain at the end of March.

As mentioned in the *MotorSport* article, the turbocharged engine was not available in the UK (mainly due to a lack of unleaded fuel in the country at that time, which meant no catalytic converters either), but the fuel-injected RE – which was listed with 148bhp at 6500rpm and 134lbft of torque at 3000rpm in Britain – still managed to represent quite a sizable jump in horsepower over the old 12A unit. Official figures stated a 0-60 time of 8.5 seconds, with a top speed of "around 130mph," which equates to 208kph.

The Type M gearbox was given a 0.758:1 ratio on fifth, and a 4.30:1 final-drive was adopted (an automatic transmission was not available). *Motor* noted that "the gearchange is light and slick, though it can feel a little sticky when cold ... The gear ratios at first seem short, until you realize that the engine has a very usable 7000rpm rev-range. They are sensibly chosen ... putting the 70 motorway limit at a relaxed 3400rpm." As for the chassis details, the AAS was not listed in Britain (although it was available in some mainland European countries). Instead, it came with the standard suspension with firm spring and damper settings – too firm for a number of testers, in fact. The uprated

Rear of the 1986 European (lhd) car. The electrically-operated, tilt-and-slide sunroof was designed in such a way that the steel panel slid outside, rather than between the roof and the headlining, thus saving precious headroom which could have been compromised with the low roofline.

braking system was considered a must, however, and this came as part of the package, along with the home market's five-spoke alloys shod with 205/60 VR15 Bridgestone Potenza tyres as standard fare. The steering was via the manual rack, with 3.5 turns lock-to-lock, but *Motor* described the system as "nicely weighted" and "communicative," so no problems there.

Clothing these mechanical features was a body similar to that found in America, though the front side repeaters were different, rear side markers were deleted, and the European cars came with a colour-keyed rear spoiler. This was the only additional aerodynamic aid, so the vehicle had a Cd of 0.30 instead of 0.29 for one with a full Aero Kit.

The European RX-7 came with cloth trim, a Clarion stereo radio/cassette with four speakers, an electric tilt/slide sunroof, and power windows and mirrors. *Fast Lane* observed: "Both inside and outside Mazda have successfully given the RX-7 a more upmarket feel, with tight and even panel fits, and elegant exterior styling being matched to a well thought out and generally tastefully trimmed interior. They haven't been able to completely avoid the usual Japanese syndrome of over-shiny, tacky plastic and imitation stitching, however, and UK spec cars are also let down by a full-size spare wheel taking up most of the boot space."

This latter gripe wasn't really Mazda's fault, as the manufacturer had to comply with an unfortunate and, frankly, silly law, that was later

Dashboard of the Turbo II. Note the boost gauge and 160mph speedometer.

withdrawn anyway, several years after the rest of Europe had approved the Spacesaver. However, the other complaints regarding the interior were far from unique to this one article, giving the designers an area on which to concentrate further effort.

Priced at £13,995, metallic paint was the only option, and cost £175. This, of course, meant the latest 7 was quite heavy compared to its predecessor, tipping the scales at 1223kg (2691lb). Mazda UK was aiming to sell around 350 cars a year, which seemed a more than reasonable figure to achieve, although the 924S offered some fresh competition at only £1500 more in basic trim.

Mark Gillies compared the RX-7

An interesting cover for the first US catalogue to feature the RX-7 Turbo II. The flap pulled away to reveal a complete photograph.

Interior of the turbocharged car for America.

and the new Porsche in *Autocar*. Both were very evenly matched on paper, the Mazda being 0.1 of a second slower than the 16.1 standing-quarter posted by the Stuttgart machine, although at 134mph (214kph), it had a 1mph higher top speed. The one area where a massive gap developed was fuel consumption: 25.2mpg for the 924S, but only 18.7 for the RX-7.

Gillies was very impressed by the engine, however, and went on to say: "The Mazda's fun factor is enhanced by its road manners. The ride verges on the appalling – it's too harsh by far – and the steering response can be a little woolly at times, but the attempt to blind the driver with science, with the incorporation of 'triaxial floating hubs' and changing toe-in, does actually work ...

"Understeer is the normal trait, becoming pronounced with power-off in tight bends. Boot the throttle, though, and the car puts down its power superbly, only requiring opposite lock under extreme provocation."

The test concluded: "By making the car so similar in looks, the Mazda may suffer from being regarded as a cheap imitation [of the Porsche]. It isn't, and probably comes closer than the Germans would like, but the sad thing is that with a little more attention to detail, with better styling, and a more quality image, Mazda could have shown up the 924S."

Other competitors at the time included the Alfa Romeo GTV, the Mitsubishi Starion, the Ford Capri 2.8i, the Isuzu Piazza Turbo, and, to a

An alternative view of the interior – and everything else, for that matter. (Courtesy Yoshihiro Inomoto)

Early American advertising for the Turbo II; minus the aerodynamic aids.

The tail of an early Turbo II. Strangely, a rear spoiler was not fitted in the early publicity material – even the catalogue failed to mention it in the specifications – although the three-piece aerodynamics kit (a lowered front airdam, rear wheelarch/sill trim, and a rear spoiler) naturally came as standard on the high-speed production turbocharged models.

lesser extent, cars like the Nissan Silvia Turbo, the Honda Prelude, and the new front-wheel drive Toyota Celica. It is interesting to note how much of this market sector was occupied by Japanese manufacturers.

The Turbo in the States

In its February 1986 issue, *Road & Track* put the new RX-7 GXL and the latest 944 head-to-head on the race track. Ignoring the fact that the Mazda was $17,954 (as tested) and the Porsche $29,682 after a few options had been added, the magazine concluded: "The Mazda RX-7 is easier to drive easily, while the Porsche 944 is easier to drive hard.

"So the 944 is still the better sports/ GT car, and Porsche continues to pay what Cadillac used to call the penalty of leadership, ie. the 944 is still the target." However, Mazda had another trick up its sleeve, which it duly produced at the 1986 Chicago Show – the RX-7 Turbo II.

With an 8.5:1 compression ratio, the US specification 13B Turbo developed 182bhp at 6500rpm, and 183lbft of torque at 3500. The rotary unit was linked to the Type R five-speed transmission (initially with a 3.91:1 final-drive – the automatic gearbox was not available on the Turbo), propelling the 1295kg (2850lb) machine from 0-60 in 6.7 seconds, before going on to a top speed of "over 150mph." According to official figures, the standing-quarter could be covered in just 15.2 seconds.

All of these times were later borne out in independent tests. The latest Mazda was thus quicker than the Nissan 300ZX Turbo, the Mitsubishi Starion Turbo (sold as the Dodge Conquest in the States), and even the new three-litre 1986.5 model year Toyota Supra.

To keep this level of performance in check, the Turbo had European suspension settings (no AAS), a limited-slip differential and, of course, the uprated braking system. Oddly, ABS brakes were not offered at this stage, and the chassis was by no means a perfect combination in all conditions. *Road & Track* described the ride as "harsh to the point of jiggly on dots, cracks and bumps." It added: "Although the new rear suspension is heaps better than that of the old RX-7, the extra power and tyres and brakes can overcome it. The rear gets light under full braking, and the wheels judder and tend to lock on bumps going into a corner.

"As a result, the RX-7 Turbo is easy to drive fast, much more difficult to drive faster than that, and demanding to the point of disquiet right on the edge."

In a comparison test with the 944 Turbo and the Chevrolet Corvette, the same magazine mused: "The RX-7 Turbo is in tune and in time, but it's done with synthesizers, those electronic devices that sound like violins or cellos or whatever ... except they don't.

"Mazda's engineers have done their lab work and their proving ground work. What they need to do now is join the Corvette and Porsche engineers, out on the road in the real world." In other words, a little more development was necessary to refine the vehicle's character.

Motor Trend, on the other hand, put forward a different point of view: "On the road circuit, [the RX-7 Turbo] is neutral, predictable, and fast ... To compliment its straight-line speed, the Mazda's advanced DTSS suspension system is exemplary and nearly viceless. Near, or at, the limits of the tyres, the car keeps you informed of what's going on out there between the tyres and the pavement. Step over the limit, and it'll do everything it can to help you gather it back up."

The magazine had no qualms about branding the turbocharged Mazda

Takaharu Kobayakawa became head of the RX-7 project in 1986, and is seen here with Miho, the author's wife, at the RJC Awards Ceremony in December 2000.

Making the infinity mark with the lightweight Anfini model. The infinity symbol appeared on the tail of these special, limited edition machines.

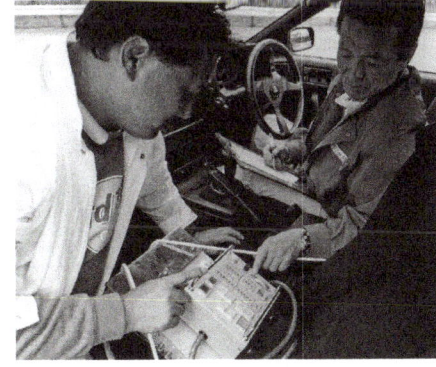

Tamotsu Maeda (left) and Hirotaka Tachibana pictured during Anfini testing.

With the rear seats removed, Anfini models gained illuminated storage boxes in their place.

Cover from the Mazda UK catalogue, dated March 1987.

The new soft-top model, known as the Savanna RX-7 Cabriolet in Japan. This picture was taken at Hakone, near Mount Fuji. (Courtesy Hideo Aoki)

Design sketch for the drophead version of the RX-7.

Interior of the home market Cabriolet; this example has an automatic gearbox. The automatic gear selector suffered from the traditional problems associated with an in-line layout. The only option for secure sporting changes, and now adopted by most manufacturers, was to employ a staggered gate like that found on Mercedes-Benz automatics. (Courtesy Hideo Aoki)

the best Japanese GT available, a view echoed in *Car & Driver*. Tony Assenza wrote: "With the arrival of the Turbo, Mazda has proved that among Japanese sports cars, the RX-7 has no equal ... What you have here is a world-class performance machine that doesn't require a world-class bank balance to own it."

It was easy to spot the Turbo II, due to the bonnet scoop like that found on the Japanese turbocharged models. The American Turbo also featured 16-inch wheels and tyres, which were perhaps the most attractive alloys on offer at that time, and different, colour-keyed door mirrors. Inside, the Turbo came with a GXL level of trim and standard features, although different upholstery was used, it had a 160mph speedometer instead of a 150mph one, a boost gauge replaced the voltmeter, and power-assisted steering was a $450 extra; as a pure sports car, it was decided not to offer the 2+2 seating option on the turbocharged RX.

As the 1986 model year drew to a close, the base two-seater was priced at $13,995, while the GXL started at $18,445. The Turbo II two-seater, classed as an early 1987 car, was listed at $20,195.

Standard coachwork colours included Dover White, Pure Red, Arctic Silver Metallic, Tornado Silver Metallic, Satin Gold Metallic, Royal Maroon Metallic, and Sapphire Blue Metallic. An additional shade – Brilliant Black – was listed for the Turbo.

1987

Before moving on to the 1987 model year, mention should be made of a few changes in Japan. An additional model based on the GT Limited had been announced for the home market in June 1986, with sales starting from 1 July. Known as the GT Limited SE (the SE standing for Special Edition), it

Attractive cover from the first Cabriolet catalogue. Incidentally, the use of European models in Japanese advertising has a long tradition in the motor industry.

Anfini model appeared. As Kobayakawa-san said in a recent interview with the author, the Anfini was introduced "to strengthen the brand's image, and serve as a development vehicle for future products – to enable the RX-7 series to evolve. The chassis work was especially significant, incorporating a great deal of fresh technology."

Priced at 2,788,000 yen, it was a pure two-seater (the first RX-7 to be offered as one in Japan), and featured an aluminium bonnet (like the US Turbo), the optional Aero Kit, forged 6.5J BBS alloys, an uprated suspension (though the AAS system was discarded), different seats, a three-spoke Momo steering wheel, and a matching leather gearknob.

The idea was to save weight, and indeed, the Anfini was some 40kg (88lb) lighter than the GT-X it was based on. According to a *Car Graphic* test, for a number of enthusiasts the Anfini represented a big step forward. The problem, of course, was that only 300 were available!

However, this was obviously a successful formula and, on 23 January, Mazda announced plans to produce another run of 300 Anfini two-seaters. Still priced at 2,788,000 yen, it followed

came with leather trim, a six-speaker stereo with CD player, ABS brakes and a limited-slip differential as standard; it was listed at 3,510,000 yen, while the prices on other grades remained unchanged. At the same time, Pure Red was replaced by Sunrise Red, and Sapphire Blue Metallic augmented the other four shades.

Takaharu Kobayakawa, one of Mazda's original 47 Samurai and a true sports car enthusiast, was one of Yamamoto's most respected engineers, and had been appointed head of the RX-7 programme in January 1986. His preference for lightweight sports cars rather than luxury GTs was about to make itself felt.

In August 1986, the limited edition

A shot of the new Cabriolet with the hood up. Maintaining structural rigidity unfortunately meant employing a high rear sill. However, Kobayakawa-san says it was not so much structural rigidity that caused problems during development, but the hood arrangement that he inherited from his predecessor, which called for three, rather than the conventional two, positions.

the same concept as the original Anfini, with an aluminium bonnet, Aero Kit, BBS wheels (a lightweight alloy Spacesaver spare was employed), bronze tinted glass, and a few interior changes to make it more sporty; a nice touch was the passenger-side footrest, for instance. The Anfini was available in either Noble White or Brilliant Black.

Incidentally, the fifth generation Luce had been launched in the meantime, in September 1986, although the Cosmo would continue in the same form until 1990. The Luce was powered by the 13B RE – by the time the new model reached the showrooms, more than 1,500,000 rotary engines had been built.

For the US market, the 1987 model year saw ABS brakes become available for the first time abroad, but only on the GXL and Turbo II, and even then as a $1250 extra. In addition, cars with a five-speed manual transmission had a starter interlock added, requiring the driver to depress the clutch pedal first before firing the engine. Otherwise, there was very little difference. The base car, GXL and Turbo continued unchanged, the Sport became a proper grade, taking the place of the Sport Package, whilst adding storage boxes behind the seats, floor mats, and a radio/cassette player.

The Luxury Package was deleted, but another new grade – the SE – added power steering, 14-inch alloys, a 100W stereo radio/cassette with diversity aerial, luxury carpets, and storage boxes on the two-seater (the SE could be bought with the optional 2+2 seating, still $500 extra). The SE, in particular, represented very good value, so *Car & Driver* duly put the RX-7 on its 'Ten Best' list, and *Motor Trend* described the Turbo II as "The perfect sports car for the '80s."

By the middle of 1987, the basic two-seater was listed at $14,399 ($200 more than at the start of the season), with the SE commanding an extra $800; the Sport two-seater was $16,649, the GXL $18,699, and the top-of-the-range Turbo, $20,799.

Options included leather trim for the GXL ($720 for a two-seater, $880 for a 2+2), air conditioning ($795), an alarm ($180), various stereo upgrades (including a CD player), cruise control ($200), floor mats ($49), an electric sunroof (for the Sport and SE, priced at $550), power-assisted steering for the base model and Turbo ($450), automatic transmission (for the base, SE, or GXL, at $585), and pepperpot alloys for the base model, listed at $410.

In Britain, the RX-7 entered the 1987 model year at £14,075 (it had been that price since June 1986). *MotorSport* noted: "If the old one was agreeable, the new one is a jump forward in every respect. Still thirsty, but smooth, fast and agile. Handsome and very well-equipped, well worth its price."

In early 1985, AutoAlliance International Inc., a 50/50 venture with Ford, had been established in Flat Rock, Michigan. Having a manufacturing plant in the States would overcome currency fluctuations (MX-6 production began in September 1987, followed shortly by the Ford Probe and later the 626), but it certainly started a lot of gossip.

By this time, there was a certain amount of speculation circulating in the press to the effect that RX-7 production would be moved to Flat Rock, although the rumours were quickly and strongly denied by the Mazda management. Ultimately, it proved to be nothing more than hearsay, and the RX-7 continued to be built at the Ujina factory.

The RX-7 Convertible

The American authorities had failed to pass the much-publicised regulations outlawing the soft-top, but even though the convertible's future seemed assured, surprisingly few manufacturers took the opportunity to build one. It seemed the consensus of opinion was that the convertible market had simply ceased to exist after 1970.

Japan had built very few convertibles since the war; during the early-1980s most were coupés made into cabriolets

A convertible body making its way down the line in Hiroshima.

by third parties. As mentioned in the previous chapter, Avatar did this with the first generation RX-7, but now, with a booming world economy, the time was right for Mazda to bring out its own convertible based on the latest model.

Plans had been laid for the drophead model since the second generation's inception, but it is always a major undertaking converting a coupé into a soft-top. As such, a great deal of reinforcement was necessary to retain structural rigidity, so double-skinned box sections were added to form crossmembers either side of the cockpit, the sills were produced in a heavier gauge steel, extra plates were welded to the floorpan and transmission tunnel, and the door posts were strengthened in a bid to reduce scuttle-shake to an acceptable minimum. With the hood mechanism, this added around 120kg (264lb) to the weight of the vehicle, but it was the only way to achieve the desired results.

Launched in Japan on 21 August 1987 (as the Savanna RX-7 Cabriolet) to commemorate the 20th anniversary of Mazda's rotary-engined automobiles, the novel electrically-operated hood had three positions – fully open, fully closed, or, with the help of a rigid panel that could be stored in the boot when not in use, halfway for a Targa-type opening. Rather than use traditional materials, the hood was produced in SMC (sheet moulding compound) plastic, which proved light, hard-wearing and highly-resistant to fading, a useful feature in the relentless Japanese sunshine. It was fully-lined to reduce noise and hide the mechanism, and the so-called Windblocker kept wind-buffeting to a minimum when it was down.

The Windblocker was Kobayakawa's invention, brought about from his experience of driving with the hood down en route to ski resorts. Developed in the wind tunnel, it was a relatively simple device, but it certainly worked. *Road & Track* observed: "By simply lifting the Windblocker (a small hinged panel behind the seats), turbulence is reduced to the point that it's easy to hold a conversation without shouting; you emerge from a long drive without feeling pummelled by the roundhouse punch of swirling air." Another refinement was the use of a glass backlight, quite unusual at the time, complete with a heater element.

The home market continued to use the turbocharged version of the 13B RE, so the vehicle boasted 185 horses under the aluminium bonnet's air scoop, and came with a choice of either a manual or automatic transmission; the Cabriolet was equipped with the eight-position, manually-adjustable dampers and power-assisted steering as standard.

The traditional five-spoke alloys were adopted, but given a polished finish (as were all RX-7s for 1988), and a unique feature was the high-level brake light in the boot panel – something usually reserved for American models. Incidentally, the Cd was 0.34 on this model, or 0.39 with the top down, which was more than reasonable for an open car.

Luxury features included full leather trim (in black only), a top audio system with radio/cassette and CD player, and cruise control. Priced at 3,720,000 yen, it really was an attractive vehicle (available in either Crystal White or Brilliant Black), made all the more desirable by some excellent publicity material released during that period.

In America, the Cabriolet was known as the Convertible. It was actually quite different to the home market version, having the normally-aspirated engine, and a manual gearbox only (oddly, paired with a 3.91:1 final-drive). Apart from the lack of an air intake on the bonnet (although still shaped in aluminium for the Convertible), an instant distinguishing feature for the US model was adoption of the beautiful 6.5J x 15 BBS alloy wheels previously seen on the Japanese Anfinis.

The Convertible was certainly well-equipped, with an AM/FM stereo radio/cassette with four speakers, cloth trimmed seats (with adjustable headrests, and driver's side lumbar and height adjustment), plush carpets, a graduated windscreen tint, three-spoke steering wheel, courtesy door lights in the map pockets, colour-keyed power mirrors (home market mirrors stayed black), electric windows and, of course, the power hood.

Just for the Convertible, a special (and very expensive) Option Package was put together, adding full leather trim, a CD player, headrest speakers, and cruise control. Air conditioning was listed individually at the standard $849, but a choice of five coachwork colours were available in the States.

Road & Track tested the Convertible in its January 1988 issue, recording a 0-60 time of 9.7 seconds, with the standing-quarter being covered in 17.5. These were respectable figures, and, compared to those taken for the 1986 GXL, only 1.2 and 1.0 down, respectively. Of perhaps more interest was the 0.82g pulled on the skidpan, only 0.01g less than that recorded against the GXL, which proved beyond doubt the rigidity of the structure – and brought into question the need for AAS suspension (the soft-top model came with standard dampers). Braking, via the uprated system, was said to be "very good."

Summing up, the magazine stated: "In total, the RX-7 Convertible is a thoroughly delightful package, from the Windblocker eye-of-the-storm feature to Mazda's pleasing new twist on torsional rigidity. If you're having a mid-life crisis, this is a solution. If you've survived your mid-life crisis, you deserve one of these for your past suffering. And, if your mid-life crisis is still waiting in ambush, consider the RX-7 Convertible as 3030lb of easy-to-swallow preventative medicine."

Other 1988 model year news
At the 1987 Tokyo Show, Mazda displayed the MX-04. The MX-02 and 03 had been practical cars with seating for four, featuring advanced but nonetheless conservative styling. The MX-04 was completely different. Powered by a 150bhp rotary engine, the MX-04 could be fitted with any of three fibreglass body styles: a closed coupé or a choice of two roadsters.

Although the MX-04 was not the prettiest car ever produced by Mazda, some of its features gave a number of clues to the future that few picked up on – independent suspension by unequal-length upper and lower arms, and a backbone chassis developed by Masakatsu Kato.

Apart from the addition of the Cabriolet, the home market RX-7 line-up continued pretty much the same, even down to the pricing. In America,

The polished finish on the alloy wheels was one of the few changes for the home market coupés for the 1988 model year. This is a GT Limited version.

Japanese advertising from 1988, this particular piece featuring the Cabriolet.

however, the whole range was realigned. The SE became the entry-level model, bringing with it a hike in pricing policy, but enhanced equipment levels as standard. The SE itself continued almost unchanged, although an alarm was now part of the package, instead of an optional extra (this was added to all cars).

Other than the alarm, the GXL continued unchanged for 1988, but another grade augmented the normally-aspirated line-up – the GTU. The GTU came with front and side air deflectors, a new rear spoiler, 205/60 VR15 tyres on 6J alloys, a tuned suspension, limited-slip differential, a graduated tint on the windscreen, and colour-keyed power mirrors. There was no 2+2 option listed for the GTU, no power steering, and a distinct lack of electrical gadgets – this was a pure sports car, some 66kg (145lb) lighter than the Turbo.

True to Kobayakawa's philosophy, the GTU was for enthusiasts. "All in all," said *Road & Track*, "the RX-7 GTU is one of today's truly great driving machines, a superb balance of all the things that make a car go without sacrificing any of the qualities that make it nice to be in."

The Turbo II was joined by another turbocharged car – the 10th Anniversary model – celebrating ten years of the RX-7. This had all of the usual Turbo features, with the addition of Crystal White paint, colour-keyed trim and wheels, bronze-tinted glass, special badging, headlamp washers,

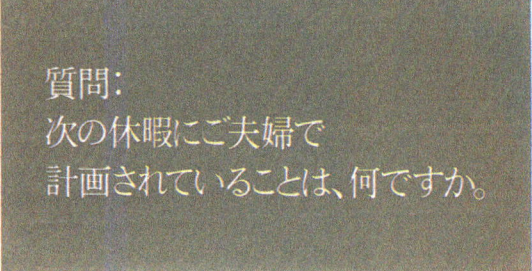

US advertising for the new GTU model, rightfully linking the name with its origin – a celebration of Mazda's success on the race tracks of America. Note the new type rear spoiler, which was carried over onto the Turbo II.

black leather trim (including a leather gearknob and gaiter by Momo), power-assisted steering (with a unique three-spoke steering wheel), commemorative keys, and floor mats.

By the middle of the year, prices had settled down to around $700 more than at the start of the season. The SE was $16,150, with the 2+2 option adding another $500. The new GTU, in five-speed guise only, cost $18,150,

The 10th Anniversary RX-7 for the US market, based on the Turbo II. Only 1500 were produced.

107

American advertising showing the Turbo II model from 1988.

while the GXL started at $20,050. The Convertible, on the other hand, was a very reasonable $21,550, or $24,050 with the Option Package. As for the turbocharged cars, the standard Turbo was $22,750, some $1900 cheaper than the 10th Anniversary model.

Options included leather trim for the GXL ($850 on the two-seater, or $1075 on the 2+2) and Turbo ($1000), air conditioning ($860), ABS braking ($1395), various stereo upgrades, cruise control ($220), floor mats ($55), an electric sunroof ($595), power steering for the Turbo ($500), and automatic transmission for the SE and GXL, priced at $670.

It was now a fine line-up and, in the winter of 1987, *Road & Track* named the RX-7 the 'Best High-Performance Car' in the $17,500-$22,500 price bracket. Sadly, though, despite the introduction of the convertible and a great deal of good publicity, by the end of the year, American figures revealed a 32% drop in RX-7 sales.

Meanwhile, in Europe, nothing much was happening. A new rear spoiler came as standard (like that fitted to the US GTU and Turbo), along with cruise control, central locking, and Mazda's power-assisted steering system, but that was about it, other than swapping tyre suppliers – Dunlop VR-rated rubber was fitted instead of Bridgestones – and giving the same wheels a polished finish.

The adoption of power assistance (and the quicker ratio that came with it) was not liked by all, however. Gordon Cruickshank observed: "Previously, without power steering, Mazda was fielding a car with a really delightful blend of qualities ... Now that well-balanced sensation has been upset; though it takes less physical effort, it needs more concentration to accurately pursue an efficient line through a high-speed corner, because the fat tyres no longer react against the driver's hand over the give and take of an uneven road."

On the other hand, *Autocar* said: "A big improvement over the previous RX-7 is the fitment of speed variable power-assisted steering." The magazine also praised the car's "balanced handling" and "uncanny mechanical smoothness." "Weak mid-range torque" and "poor fuel consumption" were valid criticisms, especially when 16.4mpg was the figure recorded for the test. At the start of the 1988 model year, the RX-7 was priced at £15,555, but this soon rose to £16,499, doing nothing to help the RX-7's case.

It should be noted that in October 1988, Dr Felix Wankel, father of the rotary engine, passed away. Only five years earlier, he'd announced plans to employ two differently-shaped rotors on a new type of RE; sadly, it was not to be. For many Europeans, the rotary concept died with him.

However, in Japan, by this time Mazda was testing a prototype three-rotor RE-powered version of the RX-7 as a possible alternative to the turbocharged twin-rotor unit. Displaying exceptional flexibility, the engine developed 220bhp and 195lbft of almost endless torque, and weighed only 29.5kg (65lb) more than a normally-aspirated 13B powerplant. However, despite encouraging test results, the three-rotor RX-7 failed to enter production.

A new model did make it to the Japanese showrooms, though. In January 1988, a year after the last Anfini appeared, the limited edition Anfini II was launched. Although it followed the same basic concept as its predecessor, and continued to be offered only with a five-speed manual transmission, the final-drive ratio was changed from 4.10 to 4.30:1 to improve low- and mid-range performance, while a new colour-keyed rear spoiler was introduced to enhance overall stability; BBS wheels were still part of the package. The Anfini II could be finished in the new Crystal White shade or Brilliant Black, with the interior changing from its original grey to black. Limited to 300 units, they sold at 2,818,000 yen each.

Incidentally, the Cabriolet gained headrest speakers at the same time, although this was a bonus item, as there was no change in pricing. Seven months later, at the end of August,

Mazda's best-selling lightweight sports car – the MX-5 (Miata) – made its debut in early 1989.

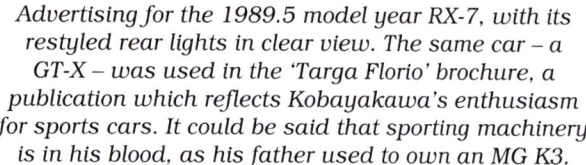

Advertising for the 1989.5 model year RX-7, with its restyled rear lights in clear view. The same car – a GT-X – was used in the 'Targa Florio' brochure, a publication which reflects Kobayakawa's enthusiasm for sports cars. It could be said that sporting machinery is in his blood, as his father used to own an MG K3.

Right, top: The sun setting on one of the facelifted GT-X models. Note the latest ten-spoke alloy wheels.

Right, middle: A look at the luggage space available in the second generation RX-7.

Right, bottom: Interior of the GT-R model from spring 1989.

110

Fascia of the GT Limited from the same period. Note the new instruments and, on this particular example, the latest electronically-controlled automatic transmission – still a very popular option in Japan.

Top right: Studio shot of the contemporary GT Limited.

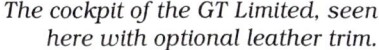

The cockpit of the GT Limited, seen here with optional leather trim.

A beautiful publicity shot of the 1989.5 model year Cabriolet.

another run of Anfini RX-7s came onto the market. This was essentially a second batch of 300 cars based on the Anfini II announced earlier in the year.

Amazingly, model pricing on the standard RX-7 range for the home market was still unchanged from when the second generation was introduced – over 26,000 examples had been sold in Japan during this period. Interestingly, sales had increased in more recent months, almost certainly as a result of the high-profile Anfini specials.

The 1989 season

The Mazda MX-5 was finally unveiled at the 1989 Chicago Auto Show in the States. The event, which opened on 10 February, saw the debut of two other important Japanese cars – the new Nissan 300ZX (the fourth generation Z) and Honda's equally gorgeous NSX supercar.

Mazda promoted its new convertible with the phrase "The return of the affordable sports car." Introduced at $13,800, the MX-5 was indeed cheap; the RX-7 now ranged from around $17,000 to a hefty $26,000. On the other hand, if one looks at the other two Japanese sports cars launched in Chicago, the Z-cars had become progressively more and more expensive (the Z32 type 300ZX was launched at $27,300 in its cheapest form), and the NSX made the Z seem a snip, even at that price.

Changes for the RX-7 were reserved for the 1989.5 model year. In spring 1989, the twin-scroll turbocharger system was refined (including an electronically-controlled wastegate), further improving responsiveness and low-speed torque. A new engine management system allowed a hike in compression ratio – from 8.5 to 9.0:1 – and, as a result, power was increased by 20bhp to 205 (at 6500rpm) on the home market. Consequently, Premium grade fuel was now a necessary requirement, rather than Regular.

Other revisions included electronic control for the automatic transmission, allowing manual selection and hold of all three lower gears, and refinements to the five-speed gearbox linkage (the gearlever design was changed at the same time). In addition, the anti-roll bars were now mounted via ball-joints to reduce NVH levels.

Another picture of the Cabriolet, but this time with its hood in the so-called 'Targa' position. Note the adoption of BBS alloys on the soft-top model. Inset: Interior of the Cabriolet, with leather-bound, three-spoke, Momo steering wheel. The patented Windblocker is in place behind the seats.

Japan's GT-X and Cabriolet pictured together. The facelifted range was announced in mid-March, but didn't go on sale until 1 April.

Styling changes centred around the new rear combination lights (dual circular lamps covered by a one-piece smoked lens, not dissimilar to the quad lights once requested during P747's development), colour-keyed exterior trim (including a new rear spoiler, first seen on the 1988 Anfinis), and a slightly different nose and air intake profile. Although the steel wheel design remained the same, there were attractive new ten-spoke alloys for the top coupés, while the Cabriolet adopted BBS items.

The cockpit featured new Anfini-style seats with added support, and a new fascia layout with circular gauges and different meter markings/needles, bringing the car bang up-to-date. Incidentally, the GT grade was dropped at this point, and the GT-X gained a lightweight aluminium bonnet; a choice of six body colours was available, with interior trim finished in black.

The new RX-7 went on sale on 1 April amid a flurry of PR activity (for instance, a beautiful brochure and video were produced featuring Paul Frere and Nino Vaccarella retracing the route of the Targa Florio in the latest car). Prices, unbelievably, went down, the coupés now ranging from 2,098,000 yen for the manual GT-R to 3,121,000 for the GT Limited SE, whilst the Cabriolet was 3,672,000 yen. An automatic gearbox could be specified on all models for an extra 94,000 yen.

Naturally, all of these changes were carried over to the Stateside models. As well as the styling revisions, normally-aspirated cars gained 14 extra horses and another 2lbft of torque under the bonnet (thanks to a higher 9.7:1 compression ratio, a new ECU, redesigned airflow meter, and a lighter flywheel and rotors), while power jumped up to 200bhp at 6500rpm on the Turbo II (with torque output also enhanced – now quoted as being 196lbft at 3500rpm). At the same time, the chance was taken to realign the range once more. The GTU appellation was now applied to the base car, although, in reality, it was nearer the SE in specification than its earlier namesake. It lost the uprated braking system, reverting back to the basic set-up, and had power-assisted steering, something its sportier predecessor did without. Anyway, it was at least distinctive, with a rear spoiler, a graduated tint on the windscreen, colour-keyed power mirrors, and the home market's ten-spoke alloys shod with 205/ 60 HR-rated rubber. A six-speaker radio/cassette was a standard fitment, with air conditioning, a sunroof, and automatic transmission optional. The GTU was listed at $17,300, incidentally, some $2300 less than the new GTU-S two-seater.

The GTU-S was, in effect, last year's GTU, with a lowered front airdam, side skirts and rear spoiler, vented discs all-round with four-pot front calipers, a limited-slip differential (with a European spec 4.30:1 final-drive), and tuned suspension. Apart

The shortlived GTU-S model for the USA.

American advertising from mid-1989, showing the latest version of the Convertible. From the 1989.5 model year to the end of second generation production, the normally-aspirated US specification rotary engine developed 160bhp at 7000rpm, and 140lbft of torque at 4000rpm.

Cover from the US 1990 model year catalogue. Standard colours for that season included Blaze Red, Brilliant Black, Crystal White, Harbour Blue Metallic and Winning Silver Metallic.

from the use of an aluminium bonnet, another major difference was the adoption of multi-spoke 7J x 16 cast alloy wheels combined with 205/55 VR16 tyres. Inside, in accordance with the back-to-basics theme, the GTU-S had only an AM/FM radio, although the cockpit's sporting flavour was upheld with a leather-covered steering wheel, gearknob and handbrake grip (strangely, the column tilt facility was not available on the GTU).

After around 100 had been sold, the GTU-S was dropped. *Road & Track* tested one before it disappeared from the price lists, and, having recorded a 16.7 second standing-quarter, concluded: "Although it won't be embarrassed in the daily traffic nip-and-tuck, the GTU-S is happiest on an open stretch of road with its tachometer needle spinning in the upper third of its rev range. At 7000rpm, the rotary engine doesn't even seem to be breaking a sweat, because each rotor is turning at only one-third the speed of the flywheel. And the smoothness is uncanny; the engine's mechanical pitch and exhaust note ferocity increase as the revs climb, but the low level of vibration stays nearly constant."

With an 8000rpm red-line, it was

The superb Anfini III, with 215bhp on tap, thanks to a different exhaust system. (Courtesy Hideo Aoki)

stated: "A better revver than bruiser, the GTU-S can require a tricky blend of revs and clutch timing off the line, but stopping is a total pleasure, the pedal being superbly sensitive and communicative." It was also noted: "Steered smoothly into a bend, the RX-7 moderately understeers, but if you saw at the steering wheel, the tail will dance out – never truly threatening, but sometimes unexpected."

Interior of the Anfini III, with its special Momo steering wheel.

while the GTU-S model's wheel and tyre combination gave the car a very purposeful stance. Standard features included an lsd, the uprated braking system (with ABS), power-assisted steering, and AAS, while inside, there were GTU-style seats, and a leather Momo steering wheel.

Jack Nerad at *Car & Driver* said: "The Turbo II will put the hurt on many European cars costing thousands more." Indeed, during testing, it recorded a 0-60 time of 6.4 seconds,

The tail of the Anfini III. Note the use of the 'infinity' symbol, used on all of the Anfini models from introduction. (Courtesy Hideo Aoki)

The $21,600 GXL continued almost as before, although it did acquire the latest ten-spoke alloys with VR-rated tyres, a rear spoiler, front foglights and a luggage cover, and the gearknob and handbrake grip were now trimmed in leather to match the steering wheel. The GXL became the only model with the option of fold-down 2+2 rear seats – still very reasonable at just $500.

At $25,950, the Turbo was more aggressive-looking than ever. A new aerodynamics package included a lower front airdam with integrated foglights, side skirts, and a rear spoiler,

115

The home market GT-R of June 1990, now sporting wider rubber on 16-inch rims. The high-level rear brake light was introduced on Japanese specification coupés as part of the earlier, mid-1989 facelift.

Interior of the GT Limited SE, which came with leather trim and a whole host of other extras included in the price.

Fascia of the GT-X, complete with CD player as standard.

and could demolish the standing-quarter in a shade over 15 seconds – highly-impressive figures.

The Convertible, priced at $25,600, was a different beast, with the emphasis on Grand Touring in style. Cruise control, central locking, a 100W radio/cassette with eight speakers and a CD player, full leather trim (including the steering wheel, gearknob and handbrake grip), electric windows, the patented Windblocker device, power steering, 205/60 VR15 tyres on 6.5J BBS alloys, and halogen foglamps, all came as standard. The only items missing were the dual map lights (no roof to fix them to), storage compartments (no room), and rear spoiler. Although the Convertible was now the only RX-7 not to have this latter feature, a rear spoiler had never been fitted to the soft-top model anyway.

At last, Americans could buy the Convertible with an automatic transmission, and it was in this guise that *Car & Driver* tested the model in its August 1989 issue. The reporter felt that with this gearbox, which admittedly took a lot of hassle out of the daily commute to work, too much of the performance was blunted. Indeed, a 10.7 second 0-60 time was a little on the slow side.

But perhaps buyers of the drophead RX-7 were quite different to buyers of the Turbo II, and this was something which was acknowledged in the article. Jeff Karr observed: "This pair of Mazdas shows just how wide a personality spread can be between two basically similar cars. With a turbo panting under the hood and sporting rubber wedged under the fenders, you have a marvellously capable sports car. The Turbo II's motor is strong, flexible, and just plain fun. It begged me to wring its little rotary neck, and I obliged. I have very little willpower when it comes to this car.

"The Convertible, on the other hand, is a completely different animal. I think it might be better to be seen in the Convertible than to actually be in it. Though it's quite comfortable and pleasant, my strongest recollection of trips in the car are dim images of women I made eye contact with or pleasant sunny places where I stopped for frozen yogurt.

"But what happens if it's raining, all the women are safely at home, and the frozen yogurt stores are closed? That would be a sad day indeed to be strapped into the Convertible. For me, at least, it's better to feel good than to look good. And I always feel good in the Turbo II."

The 1990 model year

In America, the US 1990 model year, naturally enough, saw few changes following the mid-1989 update. A driver's side airbag became standard on the soft-top variant, housed in a rather attractive, four-spoke steering wheel.

Incidentally, fifth gear had changed to 0.719:1 on the US spec Type R 'box as part of the 1989.5 model year revisions, while fifth went to 0.697 on the Type M. On both transmissions, the final-drive ratio remained unchanged for the coupés, as it did for the automatic. There is always an exception to every rule, however, and, on the Convertible, the final-drive became 4.10:1 for 1990, regardless of whether the owner chose the five-speed unit or the four-speed ECT.

Otherwise, that was about it, apart from the fact that prices had gone up since April 1989 by between

In June 1990 it became possible to specify a tan interior for the home market Cabriolet model, at least on black and dark green cars, the latter being a new coachwork colour.

The GT Limited SE model of mid-1990. The multi-spoke alloys look superb, and give the car a far more sporting appearance.

117

A rare Anfini advert. Kobayakawa-san explained that because of the financial climate and low numbers involved, only a very small advertising budget was allocated to the project. Instead, he had to rely on press reports to let people know a new model was available. This is the Anfini IV, by the way.

Japanese advertising from mid-1990.

$580 and $930, depending on the model. Nevertheless, in 1990 the RX-7 accounted for 9743 of the 226,000 Mazdas sold in the States that year.

Meanwhile, in Japan, on 16 September 1989, the GT-X-based Anfini III went on sale. The biggest news was a 10bhp increase in power, taking the total to a healthy 215bhp; maximum torque output had also increased, from 199 to 202lbft, despite the engine having the same compression ratio.

The Anfini III featured a Torsen limited-slip differential, and the familiar BBS alloys, but now 7J x 16 in size and shod with Pirelli P Zero 55-section tyres. Suspension bushes and shock absorber values were changed once more, a strut bar was added, and a larger brake master cylinder was adopted, along with new pads. Inside, there were new bucket seats, kneepads, and a leather-trimmed Momo steering wheel. Limited to 600 units, it was priced at 2,843,000 yen. Having recorded a 14.6 second standing-quarter time, and been generally impressed with the changes, *Car Graphic* described it as "wasteful" that such a small number were being built, convinced that demand for the vehicle would far outstrip supply.

All Savanna RX-7 grades became available in black for 1990, and on 20 February that year a special 70th Anniversary model was added. Finished in Shade Green, the Anfini series was used as the basis to add a little kudos to the machine, priced at 2,714,000 yen.

The all-new Eunos Cosmo was introduced in April 1990, with a three-rotor RE (the Type 20B-REW) and a sequential twin-turbo arrangement. This system employed two turbochargers, but the second unit would only come into operation at higher revs – a clever, effective design, and a definite sign of the future. Styled as a 2+2 coupé, the latest Cosmo was an elegant blend of leading-edge technology and luxury.

Two months later the Savanna RX-7 range adopted the 205/55 VR16 tyres first introduced on the Anfini series and, for the GT-X grade and above, the multi-spoke 7J x 16 alloys employed on last year's Turbo in the States; the GT-X also gained a CD player.

The turbocharged RX-7 arrived in the UK for the first time in July 1989.

Although the GT-R stayed the same price at 2,098,000 yen, the higher specification GT-X, the GT Limited and the SE model all went up slightly, to 2,486,000, 2,920,000 and 3,136,000 yen respectively.

On the Cabriolet, the list price remained at 3,672,000 yen, but the Crystal White option was deleted in favour of Shade Green. On the latter coachwork colour (and Brilliant Black), it was now possible to specify an interior trimmed in tan.

A few days after on 22 June, the 215bhp Anfini IV made its debut. Limited to 600 units, it followed the same proven formula as the previous Anfini, with BBS alloys, Pirelli P Zero tyres, a Torsen differential and strut bar, but the suspension and the braking system were subtly revised once again. Inside, to continue the sporting theme, the new lightweight bucket seats (developed with Recaro) were augmented by kneepads, and a Momo leather-trimmed steering wheel. The Anfini IV was priced at 2,843,000 yen, and worth every last bit of it if contemporary reports are anything to go by. Although the Anfini range was for the home market only, one was shipped to the States to allow journalists to try it.

Road & Track observed an exceptional 0.91g on the skidpan, and declared: "This engine and chassis work together with an ease that's surely not accidental. Where the stock RX-7 Turbo takes a noticeable understeering set when pushed to its limits, the Infini seems as neutral as Switzerland." (Note that the US article says 'Infini' – this is a difficult point, because the real Mazda word begins with 'E' but is impossible to spell on a standard typewriter. It sounds like 'Infini', because it originates from the French word, but Mazda PR spells it 'Anfini', so this is the style I have adopted.) By the way, mention should be made of the Eunos and Anfini sales channels established in Japan during this period.

European update

In the UK, like Japan and America, there was no real change for the 1989 model year proper (the solitary RX-7 listed for Britain was priced at £16,999 in October 1988, incidentally), but there were significant alterations to the line-up in July.

With unleaded fuel becoming more readily available (therefore making catalyst-equipped vehicles easier to sell), Mazda UK decided it was time to drop the normally-aspirated RX-7, and replace it with two turbocharged models – a coupé and the soft-top version. These were similar to the Stateside Turbo II and Japan's Cabriolet models, but for Europe were called the RX-7 Turbo and the RX-7 Turbo Cabriolet.

In UK trim, the 13B Turbo unit, running on Super Unleaded, produced 200bhp at 6500rpm and 195lbft of torque at 3500. This was enough power to fully justify the term 'rotary rocket' – official figures quoted a sub-seven second 0-60 time, despite the coupé weighing in at 1360kg (2992lb), and the Cabriolet 60kg (132lb) more than that.

The Type R gearbox was used, but with a 0.719:1 fifth gear, combined with a 4.10:1 final-drive. The £21,999 coupé

Interior of the British specification RX-7 Turbo of late 1989.

was equipped with the multi-spoke 7J x 16 alloys found on the US Turbo (shod with ZR-rated 205/55 Bridgestone rubber), while the Cabriolet came with 205/60 Bridgestone tyres mounted on 6.5J x 15 BBS alloys. Naturally, the uprated suspension and braking system was adopted, and the variable-assist power steering was a standard feature.

Like previous European spec vehicles, both models were fully equipped, with electric everything, and leather on the steering wheel, gearknob and handbrake grip. There were some subtle differences, though. The coupé was trimmed in velour rather than leather (as found in the drophead model), but gained ABS brakes, an Aero

The summer of 1989 not only saw the turbocharged engine arrive in Britain, but also marked the debut of the soft-top model for that country. A high-level rear brake light was still not a legal requirement in the UK at that time.

For 1991, the American range was simplified to take in three basic models – the Coupé (seen at the back in this picture), the Turbo (up front) and the Convertible.

Kit and a power sunroof – of course, the Cabriolet hardly needed the latter item! Whichever way one looks at it, about the only option was air conditioning.

Mazda occupied Stand C5 at the 1989 Earls Court Show. While the MX-5 – which made its UK debut at the event – was undoubtedly the main attraction, the £23,000 RX-7 Turbo Cabriolet was also there. Kevin Blick tried the drophead versions of the RX-7 Turbo and 944 S2 for *Performance Car*, and found that the Porsche's hood was perhaps the best of the two; rear three-quarter vision was a problem with both cars when the hood was erected (something often criticised on the standard RX-7 coupé due to the heavy B-post), but the Mazda lost its rear seats because of the framework and Windblocker.

Apart from the heater struggling to cope with the British winter weather (the test was conducted in December!), Blick also noted: "Inside, the RX-7 is a lot fussier than the Porsche – but that's the Japanese way. Even so, the rotary switches and stubby, flipper-like stalks are unnecessary gimmicks and detract from what could be a good cabin. The seats, certainly, are grippier and more supportive than the Porsche's."

There was no shortage of speed either (the Mazda clocked 145mph, or 232kph, on the test track), and Blick was obviously delighted with the engine, but a major concern was fuel consumption – an average of just 18.1mpg, compared with 23.0mpg for the three-litre Stuttgart machine. Ultimately, he preferred the 944.

On the other hand, *MotorSport* tested an earlier press car and was far more complimentary. One of the few criticisms it did have, however, was the vehicle's poor economy – "it shows little sympathy for fossil fuels," was how the magazine put it. In Britain, where petrol is notoriously expensive, these things have to be considered.

The Cabriolet soon went up to £23,999, while the official Mazda UK price list dated 5 September 1990 listed the turbocharged RX-7 coupé at £22,599 and the Cabriolet at £24,999. Air conditioning added £1395 to the invoice, and mica paint was an extra £175.

At this time, £14,899 was quoted for the basic MX-5, while the most expensive 323 was £13,279 (prices in that range starting at just £8469), so the rotary-engined car wasn't exactly

The US specification RX-7 Coupé for the 1991 model year.

Interior of the Coupé, this one with a manual transmission, although an automatic gearbox was available for those who preferred driving with only two pedals.

cheap. But in terms of performance and value-for-money, the RX-7 did offer an interesting alternative.

For those who thought the Sierra Cosworth too common, the Alfa Romeo SZ was supposed to be around £40,000 (about the starting price of the contemporary Porsche range), Nissan's latest 300ZX was £34,500, the Ferrari Mondial was over £60,000 in its cheapest form, as was the blisteringly quick Honda NSX, the BMW Z1 was £36,925, and both the entry-level Jaguar XJ-S and Maserati Biturbo cost about the same as the Munich machine. Along with the sporty Toyotas, Renault-Alpine and TVR, Lotus was one of the few companies that could offer a competitive package at a similar price. There was always the Lancia Delta Integrale – assuming you could find one!

The US market in 1991

One would have thought that Mazda would be content to leave the RX-7 range alone in its final year, but it was realigned yet again. With prices starting from $19,614, mechanically the car was unchanged, but there were now three basic models – the Coupé, the Turbo and the Convertible.

All were equipped with air conditioning, speed-sensing power steering (including a leather-trimmed wheel), an AM/FM stereo radio/cassette with six speakers, central locking and electric windows with tinted glass as standard.

The Coupé came with 205/60 VR15 tyres on new 6J five-spoke alloy wheels, and could be upgraded via a couple of option packages. Package A included a power sunroof (also available separately), a rear wash/wipe facility, cruise control, a tilt steering column, foglights, upgraded cloth trim, thigh and lumbar adjustment on the driver's seat, uprated disc brakes (standard on the Turbo and Convertible), ignition barrel illumination, an illuminated entry system, cargo tie-down straps and a noise insulation pack. If the owner specified Package A, he could then add Package B, which listed leather trim, a CD player and a cargo area cover. Automatic transmission was available as an individual option.

The Turbo had the usual

wash/wipe. The Package B upgrade was available on the turbocharged car, although the cargo cover was already a standard fitment.

The Convertible carried on virtually unchanged, with the four-speed ECT gearbox about the only option listed. Standard coachwork colours (on all models), included Blaze Red, Brilliant Black, Crystal White and Brave Blue; trim came in either black or blue.

By spring 1991, the basic Coupé was priced at $20,000, with the Turbo at $27,100 and the Convertible commanding a further $1050. Package A was $1700, whilst Package B was listed at $2000, or $1875 for the Turbo; the four-speed automatic transmission (not available on the Turbo) cost $750.

Unfortunately, Mazda's sales in America fell by around 4000 units on the previous year, with the RX-7 responsible for a lot of the downturn – only 6986 were sold Stateside in 1991. As its replacement had been predicted for some time (most magazines were favouring a 1991 Tokyo Show debut, which ultimately turned out to be correct), this lower figure was hardly surprising.

Japanese specials

From March 1991, another run of Anfini IV models became available. Only 300 were built this time, finished in either Shade Green or Brilliant Black. Naturally, the Torsen limited-

Interior of the Turbo.

The Turbo was just made for roads like this ...

refinements one associates with the model, including an Aerodynamic Package, 205/55 VR16 tyres on alloy wheels, ABS braking, a limited-slip differential, foglights, a power sunroof, illuminated entry system, a tilt facility on the steering column and a rear

The Convertible, as sold during America's 1991 model year.

slip differential, BBS alloys and Pirelli P Zero rubber continued as leading features – Kobayakawa was particularly fond of these Italian tyres, describing them as "wonderful" even ten years on. While the Anfini cost 2,704,000 yen, prices on the standard range remained unchanged from June 1990.

In June 1991 the author was lucky enough to witness a Mazda 787B (car number 55) take an historic victory at Le Mans. Two months later, Mazda launched the Savanna RX-7 'Winning Limited' model to commemorate the occasion. Based on the GT-R, the 'Winning Limited' model was an Anfini lookalike, with 16-inch BBS alloy wheels shod with 205/55 tyres, a full aerodynamics package, strut tower bar and Momo leather-rimmed steering wheel. Finished in either Shade Green or Blaze Red, 1000 were built, priced at 2,298,000 yen each.

End of another era

In America, there wasn't a 1992 model year RX-7. Instead, last year's cars were sold unchanged until the last few examples disappeared from stock, making way for the third generation vehicles, classed as early 1993 models.

The 1991 Earls Court Show saw the British debut of the MX-6. This elegant Grand Tourer (which eventually went on sale in the UK during February 1992), was joined on the Mazda stand by the recently-launched MX-3 coupé (known as the Eunos Presso in Japan), the top version being powered by the world's smallest V6 engine. The sporting theme was continued with the RX-7 Turbo Cabriolet and, of course, the MX-5, two of which were displayed. Apart from the usual 121, 323 and 626 models, the stand was completed by the Mazdaspeed 787B that had won at Le Mans earlier in the year, and the Group A 323 rally car that Hannu Mikkola had campaigned during the 1991 WRC season.

By this time, Mazda UK was selling cars with the same three-year warranty as its counterpart in the States (six years on body corrosion), and managed to sell 22,416 vehicles during 1991 – sadly, very few of these were RX-7s, though. The turbocharged coupé was now priced at £23,090, with the drophead model costing £25,542.

In Japan, with no plans to make the third generation into a convertible, a limited edition of 150 'Final Version' Cabriolets was announced as late as August 1992. Finished in Brilliant Black or Shade Green with gold BBS alloys and beige hoods (instead of black), these 3,700,000 yen machines would commemorate the end of the soft-top model and, indeed, the end of the second generation RX-7. Up to this point, Mazda had built a total of 22,268 drophead models during a five-year run.

Looking towards the future

The respected Japanese journalist, Jack Yamaguchi, had interviewed Mazda's Kenichi Yamamoto in 1988. Having asked the question whether all future RX-7s would have rotary power, the reply came back: "Of course, without equivocation. Mazda and the rotary are inseparable; it's the image of the company. Naturally, Mazda's power unit choices are not limited to the RE, but we seek distinctiveness in the pursuit of technology. To forsake

A British poster proclaiming Mazda's historic win at Le Mans in 1991. The author was there, and can still remember that wonderful exhaust note! The car was later displayed at Earls Court for the 1991 Motor Show. By the time the event had finished, a new RX-7 had made its debut in Japan.

the rotary is like losing one's identity. The RX-7 could not and would not exist without the rotary."

With formal confirmation that a replacement was in the pipeline, there was little doubt about what would power it. A while later, the March 1991 issue of *MotorSport* gave a good indication of the state of the contemporary sports car market, as well as what to expect with the new Mazda model. It said: "Mazda's next generation RX-7 will follow the continuing Japanese trend toward visible muscle and concealed power. Oriental factories are now waging a struggle to gain an edge over their rivals in a desperately competitive sports car market where Japan is setting the benchmarks instead of following European leads. Nissan's powerful and exceedingly handsome 300ZX has made itself the current darling of western magazines, while Mitsubishi plans to leap-frog the Starion name from the previous coarse Capri-type coupé to an ultra-sophisticated all-electronic wonder called the 3000GT.

"In its climb upmarket (inexorable for any model replacement), the RX-7 now faces this upper mid-range pair plus Toyota's forthcoming new Supra, as well as its current rival, the Supra's turbocharged 4wd smaller brother, the Celica [GT-Four]. Power available for the reborn RX-7 jumps to 250bhp, through a bi-turbo conversion of the faithful and very sweet twin-rotor Wankel motor. Performance can be expected to be impressive, with 0-60mph on tap in under six seconds.

"Extensive use of aluminium, for example in suspension components, will keep weight low even though the new design is bigger all-round ... Four-wheel drive is not envisaged – Mazda's existing all-drive system is based on a transverse engine layout, as opposed to the RX-7's traditional in-line plan.

"But in case the car is overtaken by rivals to come, Mazda has something up its corporate sleeve. Last year, for the Japanese market only, Mazda created the Cosmo, a 626-based coupé equipped with the first three-rotor Wankel sold for the road. Fed by two sequential turbos, it was 'detuned' to 280bhp, but it is said to be able to churn out 360 if required. With somewhere between these two figures, a triple-rotor RX-7 could take another performance leap."

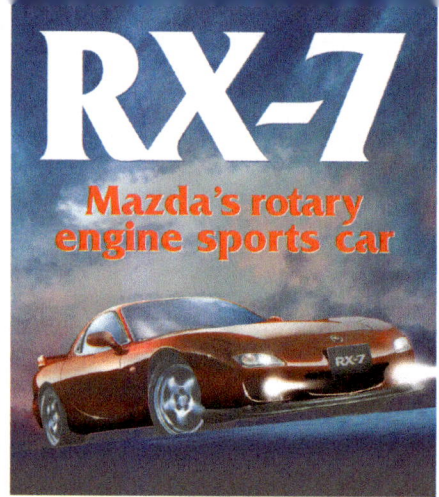

5

The third generation

The Anfini IV was perhaps the ultimate expression of Takaharu Kobayakawa's vision of what the RX-7 should represent. Having seen what he did with the second generation model, gradually shifting it away from 'boulevard GT' towards a truer interpretation of the oft-abused GT moniker, it was fairly obvious what he had in mind for its replacement.

A clean sheet of paper

Like so many great automobiles, the third generation RX-7 project started with a clean sheet of paper. The first question Kobayakawa asked his team was what was their image of a sports car, and what did they want from it? This may seem a fairly simplistic thing to ask, but it's amazing how many different answers one receives nowadays. In the 1950s and '60s, it was perhaps much easier to get a clear-cut definition, but times change, and people's expectations change with them.

The team had also to consider the other cars in the line-up; the MX-5 would soon provide an entry-level sports car, whilst the MX-6 was a modern interpretation of the GT theme. The new RX-7's role would have to be significantly different to justify its existence. There was no other sports car in the Mazda range when the original RX-7 was launched, so there wasn't a clash. A basic specification and strong sales, the result of good looks and a superb value-for-money package, ensured the RX-7 returned a profit and fulfilled its objective – to boost the image of the rotary engine, then at an all-time low.

When the second generation came along, it was still the only sporting machine Mazda had to offer, but it took on a more upmarket stance and, as a consequence, went up in price, while production volumes reduced (ultimately, 272,027 were built, compared with 471,018 first generation models). In Japanese terms at least the RX-7 had suddenly become a specialist vehicle.

With the MX-5 becoming Mazda's bread-and-butter sports car in the near future, and the public no longer perceiving the RX-7 as a cheap GT, this was an ideal opportunity to make it into a low-volume flagship model. As such, this new machine could not be built up from the existing Mazda parts bin – it was a question of enhancing company prestige, of raising brand image after several decades of carefully laying a strong foundation.

Establishing a concept

Having analyzed replies to the question of what a sports car meant, Kobayakawa-san then arranged for each of the team members to attend the Jim Russell high-performance driving school in California, and the equivalent school at Miyoshi. This was to allow them to develop a feeling of communication with a vehicle under extreme conditions, to better gauge the way a car reacts at high speeds in a safe environment. He then introduced them to the world of racing karts – a perfect arena for teaching the value of a low centre of gravity, a low moment of inertia, good weight distribution, and, most of all, the importance of a favourable power-to-weight ratio.

With this knowledge, and a strong bond already forming between the team members, comparison testing began. A massive range of vehicles was assessed, not just sporting GTs. Naturally, cars

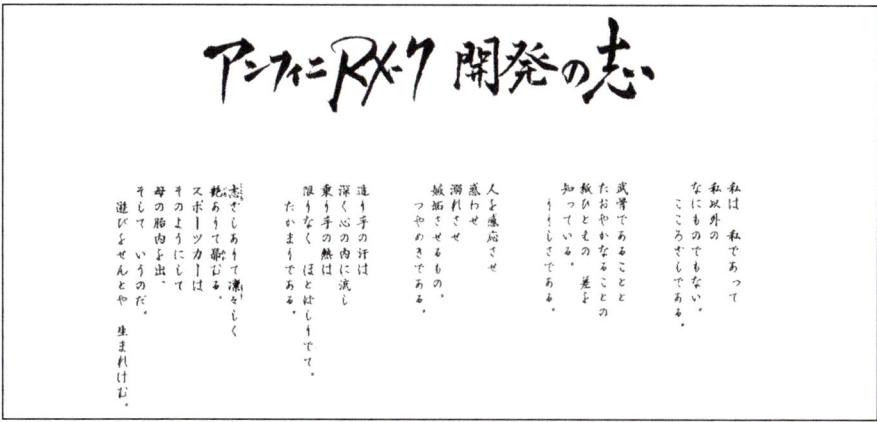

The poem, The Spirit Of The RX-7, that was commissioned to give the development team inspiration. (Courtesy Takaharu Kobayakawa)

like the Corvette, Ferrari 308GTB and the Porsche range were evaluated, but the Caterham Super Seven was also included; family saloons were brought into the equation to clarify where the difference between sports cars and more mundane machinery lay, and even luxury marques like Rolls-Royce and Jaguar were given the once-over.

It was an all-encompassing exercise which enabled the engineers and designers to forge ideas and come up with a basic concept. The design had to be full of originality and panache, with no doubt about its pure sporting nature. It could not possibly be perceived as simply a sporty coupé; it had to set new standards in dynamic performance, and provide the driver with a feeling of pleasure and oneness with the car.

A catchphrase of 'RE Best Pure Sports' was duly adopted, and a poem called 'The Spirit Of The RX-7' was commissioned to provide inspiration. To further focus the minds of the engineers, a mock-up set of press and publicity material was put together, outlining the leading features of the vehicle: size had to be optimized, with weight kept to a minimum throughout the design, and then distributed evenly using an FR layout and rotary engine; it would boast a low centre of gravity, and an equally low yaw inertia moment to provide the driver with the ultimate in sports car handling.

In August 1987, nine months after the P732 (J65H) project started, the new RX-7 got the green light. The key members of Kobayakawa's team were Takao Kijima (Chief of Engineering), Nobuhiro Yamamoto (powertrain), Takashi Mizuma (the man responsible for the basic layout design) and Akihiro Kashiwagi (chassis design) on the mechanical side, with Yoichi Sato (Chief Designer) and Yasuhisa Kochi (Interior Designer) providing input on the design and styling elements. Shoji Oda was responsible for chassis testing, whilst Hiroyoshi Moriyama covered vehicle testing.

The powertrain

Thoughts about using the Cosmo's three-rotor engine were quickly dismissed, as it would necessitate a bigger car than Kobayakawa and his team wanted. It would fit, but meeting crash regulations would have increased bulk and weight, and made it harder to balance the car's handling due to the extra length of the 20B. Cost and worries about fuel consumption also played a part; although one can perhaps justify marginal economy in a heavy luxury saloon, it's impossible to do so in a lightweight sports car. On the other hand, it was felt that more power was required if the car was to compete effectively at a world class standard. Enter the 13B-REW ...

The fuel-injected 13B-REW (654cc x 2) employed the sequential twin-turbo (STT) system first seen on the new Cosmo. At that time, apart from the Cosmo, the only other production car to feature the STT arrangement was the Porsche 959 supercar. But its advantages were beyond doubt.

The first turbo, driven by the exhaust gases from both chambers, added boost from low revs, with the pre-spun secondary unit cutting in at 4500rpm to give a maximum of 10psi. Smaller, lighter turbochargers can accelerate faster than an equivalent single turbo system, so throttle response was much quicker, and low rpm torque (an area where so many engines with forced induction are disappointing) was enhanced because of the constant boost provided by the

The 13B-REW rotary engine at the heart of the third generation RX-7. The five-speed Type R gearbox can clearly be seen in this shot; power was delivered to the rear wheels.

primary turbo. Indeed, up to 90% of the 13B's torque was available from as low as 2500rpm.

Naturally, a drawback of this system is the transition from one to two turbos. Mazda engineers overcame the problem by allowing a portion of gas from the primary boost stage to be led into the second turbocharger, allowing it to spin before it was required to provide boost. As such, prior to full use, the second turbo was spinning at around 100,000rpm, but this was still not enough to eliminate poor transition. To make it accelerate harder, a by-pass valve was closed, allowing the second turbo to spin at 140,000rpm. Once this speed is achieved, a control valve opens allowing exhaust gases in, and the second turbo spins into operation. This ensured smooth and precise power delivery throughout the rev range, rather than the all-or-nothing scenario often experienced with traditional installations.

In addition, engine electronics were improved and the induction system refined. Like many of the more prestigious Japanese cars from the period, the distributor was discarded in favour of mini coils, which provided a spark for two platinum-tipped plugs per chamber. The Bosch D-Jetronic fuel-injection now employed air density measurement instead of airflow metering. Eliminating the metering system made the power unit more responsive and smoother running, while the air density system offered precise fuel management, thus enhancing the RE's economy.

The engine was not only designed to use less fuel but less oil as well – a crucial element in rotary cooling efficiency. Air intakes in the nose, situated each side of the main central orifice, fed air onto one or two oil coolers (depending on the model). The heated air was then directed around the wheelwell in order to avoid the brakes, and let out through the sculpted vents in the front wings. On the subject of cooling, the compact and lightweight radiator was mounted at an angle to keep the bonnetline low, and fitted with twin variable-speed electric fans.

A single exhaust pipe (as opposed to the dual system adopted on P747) was employed to save weight (8kg, or 17.6lb, to be precise), with back pressure control enhanced thanks to a new, lightweight metal bed being used to hold the catalyst materials together.

Determined to maintain the rotary's hard-won reliability record, Mazda engineers ran one test RE at 8000rpm for six months, and another from tickover to 7000rpm and back again for three months. In addition, the company realized that few owners let turbocharged engines cool down gently (as they should), so a different test involved running at the equivalent to Japan's national speed limit for extended periods, and immediately shutting the unit down to deliberately abuse the Hitachi HT12 turbos.

Ultimately, with a 9.0:1 compression ratio, combined with a front-mounted, air-to-air intercooler and reduced friction in both the engine and its ancillary components, this latest version of the 13B twin-rotor RE produced 255bhp at 6500rpm (the maximum rev limit was set at 8000rpm) and a torque figure of 217lbft at 5000rpm. The same basic powerplant would be employed in all markets.

The five-speed transmission was a development of the Type R unit, and featured double-cone synchronizers on the lower gears to enable the 'box to handle the engine's extra torque and improve change quality. Ratios for Japan were 3.483:1 on first, 2.015 on second, 1.391 on third, fourth was direct, and fifth was 0.806. However, as with previous generations of RX-7, fifth gear ratios would change depending on the car's destination. One thing that did remain constant this time, though, was the final-drive – 4.10:1 for all markets. The clutch, incidentally, was a new design, being 263mm (10.3in) in diameter.

Some countries could specify a four-speed, electronically-controlled automatic gearbox. This came with three shift modes ('Normal', 'Sport' and 'Hold'), and was linked to the engine's ECU to enable it to momentarily retard the ignition before gearchanges, thus ensuring smooth progress.

On the automatic transmission, the ratios were 3.027 on first, 1.619 on second, 1.000 on third, with fourth listed at 0.694; the final-drive on two pedal cars was 3.91:1. These were the same for all markets where the ECT was sold.

The PPF (Power Plant Frame) was first seen on the MX-5, although it was actually originally developed for the RX-7. Made from high-tensile steel, the PPF was a novel way of bracing the driveline, in effect making the engine/gearbox and back axle (complete with standard Torsen differential) into an integral unit, and thereby refining power delivery. The PPF also offered a less obvious benefit – a crush area to prevent the differential housing from making contact with the 76 litre (16.7 Imperial gallon) fuel tank in the event of an accident. Amazingly, the RE, drivetrain and PPF weighed in at only 370kg (814lb).

Chassis details
In view of the new RX-7's pure sports car role, there was no real option for the suspension – it had to be double-wishbones all-round. The front upper A-arm was in cast aluminium alloy, whilst the lower arm was forged, mounted on pick-up points on the subframe structure. This lower arm carried the concentric shock absorber and coil spring, as well as the anti-roll bar, the latter being tubular to save weight; some models also received a tower bar.

Bushes and suspension pivots played an important part in the car's handling. Mazda used a system with sliding rubber bushes. Each bush's rubber body enclosed a sliding metal collar which prevented deformation, but allowed the suspension to be tuned for optimum lateral rigidity. At the rear, a double-wishbone arrangement was employed again, with the aluminium A-arms mounted on the rear subframe via sliding rubber bushes. The lower wishbone was formed by a trailing link and a transverse arm; not surprisingly, Mazda opted to retain its twin trapezoidal link suspension system to improve high-speed stability by toe control, but in a much simpler form. A rear anti-roll bar was fitted across the range, with gas-filled shock absorbers and coil springs completing the picture underneath. Up top, a rear tower bar was standard, compromising luggage space somewhat, but adding greatly to the vehicle's rigidity.

Front suspension for the new RX-7, complete with braking system and steering rack.

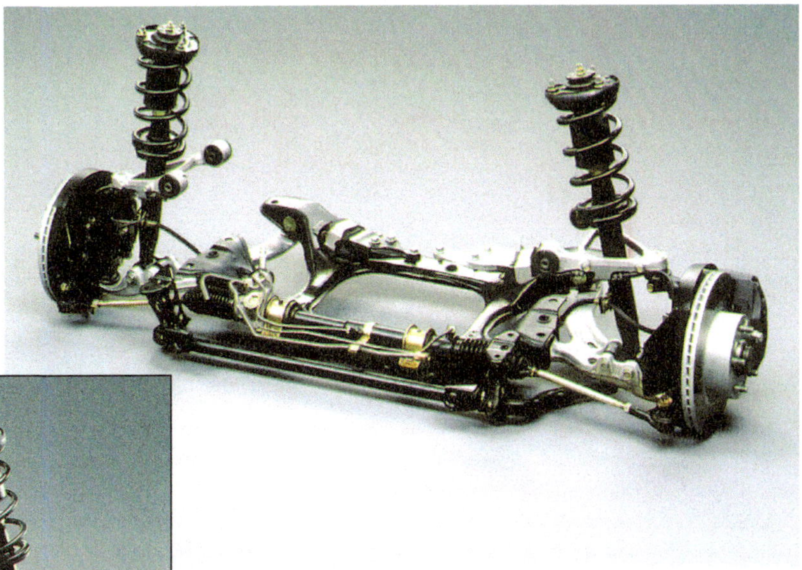

Rear suspension, brakes and final-drive. Note the strut brace in this picture.

Fantastic cutaway drawing of the new RX-7, showing the location of all major chassis components and the stunning lines of the car's body. Pop-up headlights were retained – a feature on all RX-7s since 1978. (Courtesy Yoshihiro Inomoto)

Early design sketch, with the Jaguar D-type providing inspiration. Shades of the E-type and XK8 are very evident.

Steering on the new RX-7 was by power-assisted rack-and-pinion. The computer that monitors engine speed to provide the variable assistance was made more responsive; in fact, reaction times were cut to correspond with those of a human brain. The 15.0:1 steering ratio was quicker than before, calling for just 2.9 turns lock-to-lock. For improved rigidity, the rack mounting bracket was integrated with the subframe that supported the engine and suspension, and by employing a double-jointed steering column, the engineers avoided sharp kinks to ensure smooth operation. The column also incorporated a telescopic section

Styling proposal for the tail of the new car, aping that of a modernized Alfa Romeo TZ1.

Another early design drawing, this time full-sized and obviously based on the MX-03 concept car.

The third generation RX-7 is starting to show through now, but the tail is rounded at this point. This design came from the Yokohama studio, and was duly taken to the scale model stage.

which could collapse in two stages in the event of an accident; an additional safety feature was the fitment of a driver's side SRS airbag as standard on most models.

The new RX 7 came equipped with ventilated discs all-round, 294mm (11.6in) in diameter, both at the front and the rear. Four-pot calipers were used up front, with single-piston floating calipers at the back. An electronically-controlled, four-wheel ABS system came as standard, it being the four-sensor, three-channel type, enabling the front brakes to be controlled individually and the rear brakes as a pair. The handbrake was mechanical, operating on the rear discs.

Newly-designed, five-spoke 'squeeze cast' alloys were adopted, 8J x 16 in size. This manufacturing process, pioneered by the aviation industry, enabled the wheels to be extremely strong yet exceptionally light. In fact, each wheel weighed a mere 7kg (15.4lb), comparable to an average 14-inch aluminium wheel that would not have allowed such large brakes to be fitted. They came shod with 225/50-section tyres, with a VR or ZR rating depending on the model; a Spacesaver spare was standard in all markets. This combination, augmented by a centre of gravity a full 25mm (1in) lower than before, and an ideal 50/50 weight distribution made possible through the careful placing of components (including 'front-midship' mounting of the engine), endowed the new RX-7 with a tremendous capacity to change direction quickly. Some quarters of the press rated the handling as superior to that of the Porsche 968, the replacement for the 944, and the car which most contemporary reports held up as being the best in the world in the chassis department.

prepared for a final decision to be made in California during May 1988. Kenichi Yamamoto and a group of executives flew to the States, and duly declared Chin's design the winning proposal. However, all were impressed with the Hiroshima mock-up, and it was stressed that elements of that model should also be incorporated into the final styling. The project's Chief Designer, Yoichi Sato, said: "While the American proposal had presence and massiveness, the Hiroshima design was advanced yet simple, embodying a feeling of forward propulsion."

Above & right: Two proposals from Hiroshima, seen here as scale models. Both had long tails.

A styling competition

Like most Mazdas in recent years, the initial design was given to several studios. Teams from Hiroshima, the recently-completed Yokohama office, and the stylists at MANA in the States, all submitted proposals based on the outline concept supplied. In addition, John Shute's IAD concern in England (a company involved in the early development of the MX-5 as well), was also approached.

In November 1987, around six months after design work began, nine of the original styling sketches were reviewed and narrowed down to just two – one from Hiroshima (put forward by Jun Okazaki), and one from America. These two designs were then refined and duly taken to the clay model stage in the Hiroshima studio in the following months. Wu-Huang Chin, a talented young designer who had also been involved in the initial stages of MX-5 development, had submitted the Irvine proposal, and was flown over to Japan to ensure the correct interpretation of his sketches.

Eventually, resin models were produced of both designs, and

Development continued in California, with the ultimate result being a car with very pure lines. There were no styling gimmicks whatsoever. Every single feature had to justify its existence through functionality – pop-up headlights, the front and rear spoilers, the aerodynamic shapes

An interesting scale model from MANA in the States – a modern interpretation of the Cosmo Sport 110S.

A scale model from Yokohama. This was a truly beautiful design that, thankfully, wasn't wasted – elements of it can be seen in the MX-3 coupé.

Another of the MANA models; ultimately, this was chosen for further development.

Various scale models being reviewed. On the far right is Shigenori Fukuda (Director of the Design Department), seen here with Yoichi Sato (appointed RX-7 Chief Designer) in the background, and Tomatsu 'Tom' Matano (in his signature black attire). All were heavily involved with the MX-5, too.

Above: Some familiar features were starting to show through in this full-size clay, but there was still a lot of work to do on the nose. Another model produced at this time looked like it was wearing a big smile!

A full-size model from Hiroshima.

Tail styling of the Hiroshima proposal.

The MRA model, put forward by Wu-Huang Chin, brought up to life-size.

Full-size mock-up of the RX-7.

The distinctive tail graphics taking shape. Note the lack of a rear badge at this time (a triangular motif was added shortly after), and the V705 registration plate – the MX-5 was developed under this number in its initial design stages.

One of the last prototypes, seen here with the lights in the raised position. Ultimately, rectangular headlamps would be adopted for production cars.

The final prototype, with its 'Aero Wave' roofline. Surely, this has to rank as one of the design classics of the modern era?

The new Mazda rotary sports car in the wind tunnel, where it displayed a Cd of just 0.29.

found in the 'Aero Wave' roofline and the mirrors, the vents in the front wings, a flat underfloor tray (to lower drag and produce a venturi effect, thereby reducing lift), and the flush door handles and mouldings. It was also wider than the original proposal, which would mean owners having to pay higher tax in Japan. This was considered necessary to balance the car's voluptuous curves and give it an aggressive stance on the road. Displaying a Cd of 0.29 in its cleanest form, this brave design was duly passed in January 1989.

As *Classic & Sportscar* observed:

"Youthful jaws hit pavement whenever this new RX-7 comes into vision. Lithe, spare and organically muscular, its low, fat-tyred presence looks other-worldly. This is Mazda's wildest shape yet and as a head-turner it works every time."

The galvanised steel bodyshell was new from the floorpan up, and exceptionally rigid, employing what Mazda termed 'space monocoque' technology. This combined the best features of a conventional unit-body and a spaceframe – the lightweight chassis used mainly on racing cars. Large-section longitudinal frame members ran as straight as the

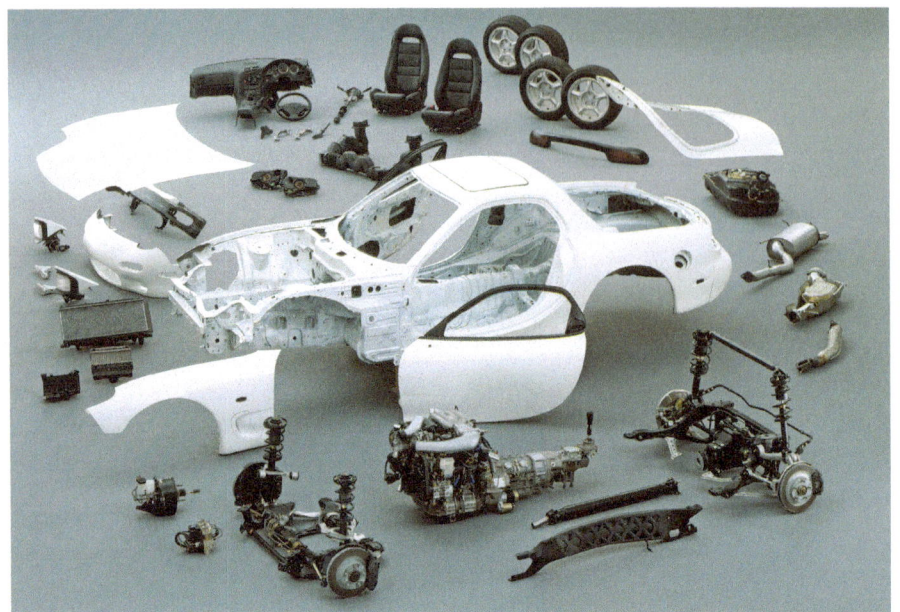

The bodyshell was exceptionally strong for safety reasons and in order to provide the engineers with a suitable platform on which to fine tune chassis components. Before going into production, each aspect of the whole vehicle was reviewed to see if any weight could be saved – no less than six times!

the upper body. Computer analysis played an important part in the RX-7's body design to ensure that, although it would be lightweight, it would also be strong and safe. As a further safety measure, side-impact door beams were fitted as standard.

Meanwhile, work on the cockpit was taking place simultaneously. In spring 1988, the decision was taken to refine a Hiroshima proposal. Of course, driver comfort was of great importance, but the design also placed function and a sense of driver/machine unity high on the agenda. The dashboard flowed around the side of the car in a continuous sweep, providing occupants with a cosy, wraparound feel. All dials and gauges were simple, round and separate, with white on black markings and red needles. Chrome rings around the meters added a sporting flavour to the instrument cluster, a theme reinforced by the central positioning of the tachometer; there was no boost gauge at this stage.

Bucket seats were employed (cloth upholstery was standard in most markets, although some received leather trim – usually an option), and

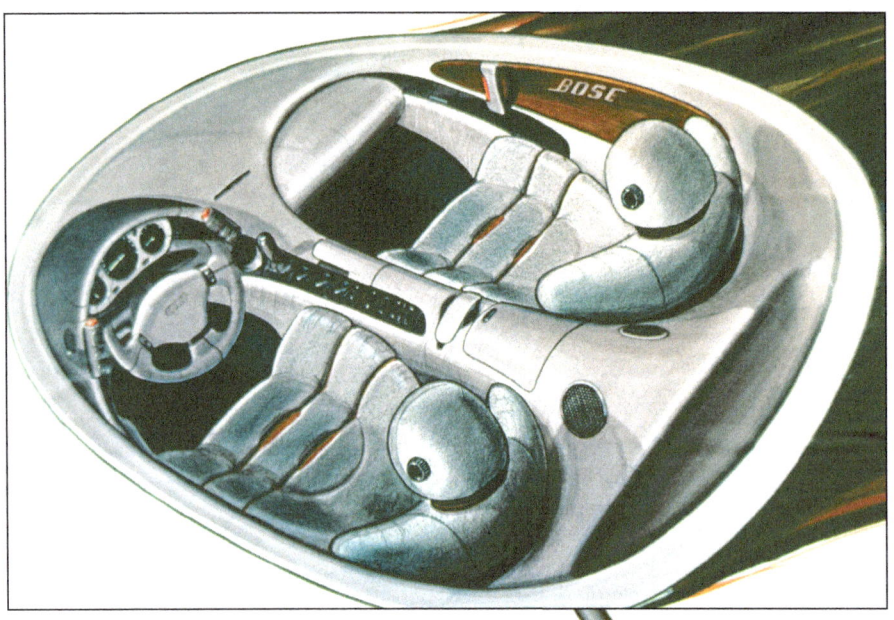

Above & right: Early design proposals for the interior.

underbody layout would permit, while the broad transmission tunnel helped strengthen the centre of the body; five crossmembers ran the length of the car to add support and strength to the longitudinal members. The front and rear subframes also played a part in the vehicle's overall rigidity.

Surrounding the passengers was a strong cage-like structure that formed

Fukuda-san trying an interior buck for size. Note the theme of individual cockpits being followed through from early sketches, and the resultant handbrake location.

Another early interior styling buck.

Almost there. The smooth organic lines have merged with true sports car overtones. The perfect environment for hard driving.

Left & below: A production dashboard and interior, this being a home market model from the time of the new car's launch. Note the kneepad on the driver's side of the transmission tunnel.

all controls were positioned with driver ergonomics in mind. Like the MX-5, the gearlever was ideally situated and had a very short throw, while the pedals were laid out to enable racing types to easily carry out heel-and-toeing; naturally, a driver's footrest (or dead pedal) was also provided.

The RX-7 was the first car to feature Bose Acoustic Wave technology, which provided enhanced bass response, although, it has to be said, at the cost of valuable luggage space. It was usually an option anyway, so those owners who preferred to listen to the exhaust note

Tamotsu Maeda smiling for the camera (just as a good PR man should!) during S-1 testing in Arizona. At the other extreme, the new Mazda was also tested in deep snow in Hokkaido, Japan's northernmost island. On both occasions, the car was run in disguise.

Below, left: A convoy in Palmdale, California, the S-1 prototype leading the way ahead of competitors' cars (and an earlier RX-7), gathered together to establish how the latest Mazda performed.

Below: Testing in Germany, where Paul Frere was asked to take part to give his opinion on the prototype. An older RX-7 and a Nissan 300ZX were also driven for comparison purposes.

The S-1 at speed through the desert.

got a larger cargo area. This could be accessed from the beautifully-shaped rear hatchback, or from inside the car. Japan continued to adopt a 2+2 configuration, with a fold-down rear seat, whilst export markets had a two-seater version.

'Operation Zero'

When one talks with Kobayakawa-san, it becomes obvious that this usually mild-mannered gentleman has a passionate dislike for something – weight. If weight were an animal, it would definitely be extinct by now! But as Mazda's motorsport boss, he knew as well as anyone that weight was indeed an enemy of sports and racing car designers.

Kobayakawa-san's philosophy is simple: design a part, analyze it, reduce its mass to a bare minimum, then redesign it to make it look as elegant as possible without losing its primary function, strength, or putting any weight back on. It is a beautiful engineering concept, and one that, fortunately, is possible to uphold on a low-volume, expensive model, where cost is not such a consideration.

Takaharu 'Koby' Kobayakawa (right) pictured with legendary Le Mans driver Jacky Ickx, who also gave his valuable opinion on the new Mazda. Ickx was involved with the Hiroshima concern's racing efforts, too.

High-speed endurance testing at the Miyoshi Proving Ground.

A final prototype emerging from the darkness to clock up the last few miles of testing.

A lot of inspiration came from the Mitsubishi Zero fighter of WWII fame, not only from a styling point of view, with its lean, minimalistic looks, but from that of weight reduction measures, too. The Mazda team flew to Los Angeles to see the last one in service first-hand, and were then lucky enough to inspect several wreckages prior to restoration back in Japan. Everyone was impressed with the attention to detail, and the RX-7 weight reduction programme was duly named 'Operation Zero'.

The second generation RX-7 and Porsche 944 had already been stripped down and inspected by the time Operation Zero was initiated in October 1988. In the early stages, drawings were

A press photograph introducing the RX-7 (this is the home market's Type R version, with its deeper front airdam skirt and standard rear spoiler). Mazda's hard work certainly paid off. In addition to receiving the RJC 'Car of the Year' award, Motor Magazine voted the new RX-7 'The Best of the Best' shortly after its debut. The Japanese monthly admired the maker's pure approach to the project, resulting in a lightweight sports car with sure handling and bold styling. It said the RX-7 was unusual for a Japanese vehicle – one that appealed to all five senses.

scrutinized to see where weight could be lost, but, as the project progressed, the actual parts were analyzed. By the time the S-1 prototype (built in the spring of 1990) had completed its test programme, the engineers had reviewed the design no less than six times, often calling on other Mazda employees along the way to give their input.

Thermoplastics were used on much of the car's bodywork, smaller glass areas were adopted (saving 9kg, or 19.8lb), and plastic was used to form the seat frame and headlight housings in order to save an extra few grammes. Aluminium was used for many of the major components, such as the bonnet (8kg or 18lb lighter than the equivalent steel item), the double-wishbone suspension systems and rear bumper reinforcing, as well as the wheel hubs. An aluminium jack and handle was specified, and the drilled pedal assembly was one of the lightest on the market.

Mazda even went as far as using flange welding instead of spot welds. Flange welding had previously been considered too expensive for production cars, but robotics ultimately made it viable. Thinner metal could be employed, thus cutting weight, with the strength regained through the new

The Anfini RX-7 at the 1991 Tokyo Motor Show. This is the Type X model. Note the standard depth skirt on the front airdam, compared with that of the Type R. Interior of the Type X (centre), complete with leather trim. Note the token rear seats provided for occasional use in the back. Also, a rear view of the car displayed at the Tokyo Show. (Courtesy Hideo Aoki)

Interior of the Type S, the entry level model in the new RX-7 range.

Luggage compartment of the new model. Note the strut brace (or tower bar), which enhanced vehicle rigidity but also compromised its load-carrying abilities. The Bose stereo system further encroached on valuable cargo space, although the back seats offered extra space if there were no passengers, of course.

manufacturing techniques. The end result was an exceptionally strong, lightweight machine that was capable of passing all of the safety regulations known at that time. It has been said that Operation Zero reduced the weight of the vehicle by as much as 110kg (242lb), compared to what it would have been before the exercise, allowing Mazda the rare honour of being able to say that the new RX-7 was actually lighter than the model it replaced. The power-to-weight ratio was ultimately within 2% of that recorded for the Ferrari 348, and 2% better than that of the aluminium-bodied Honda NSX.

The first S-2 prototype (the final version) was completed in winter 1990. With a wheelbase of 2425mm (95.5in), the new RX-7 was 4295mm (169.1in) long, 1760mm (69.3in) wide and 1230mm (48.4in) high; the track was 1460mm (57.5in) front and rear. As such, the latest model was lower, wider and shorter than its predecessor, with considerably less overhang at either end, and 20% more torsional rigidity.

Original production schedules set a target of 1200 units a month, with chassis numbers starting at FD3S-100001. Meanwhile, Kobayakawa had guided Mazda to its first (indeed, Japan's first) win at Le Mans. Driven by Johnny Herbert, Bertrand Gachot and Volker Weidler, the 787B won the famous event by two laps, putting the Hiroshima company in the forefront of the minds of motorsport enthusiasts. The timing for launching the new RX-7, at least from a publicity point of view, could not have been better.

The new model in Japan

The all-new RX-7 was announced on 16 October 1991. Nine days later, it

Rear view of the Type R. Note the unusual smoked cover over the back lights, which also served to hide the high-mounted rear brake light, standard in Japan and America. Different badges (front and rear) were used for home and export markets.

made its debut at the Tokyo Show (by now firmly established at the current Makuhari Messe site), the Mazda stand featured a Vintage Red RX-7 on a highly-symbolic, rotor-shaped revolving stand.

The Savanna name was gone, and the new model was referred to as the Anfini RX-7. The Type S was the cheapest in the range, priced at 3,600,000 yen, or 3,700,000 yen with automatic transmission. A limited-slip differential was standard, even on this base version, as were alloy wheels, ABS, and power steering. It also came with power windows and mirrors, an AM/FM stereo radio/cassette with five speakers and an electrically-operated diversity aerial, central locking, leather trim on the steering wheel, gearknob and handbrake, a rear wash/wipe (in addition to the heated rear window), halogen headlights, illuminated door locks and ignition barrel, and air conditioning.

The Type R offered suede seating surfaces in place of fabric, projector-style halogen foglights, a different front airdam skirt incorporating brake cooling ducts, and a rear spoiler. As the sportiest option, it was shod with ZR-rated tyres instead of VR rubber as found on the other models (although all came with the same 8J x 16 alloys and a Spacesaver spare). It also featured harder dampers, a front strut bar to add to the standard item fitted at the rear, and dual oil coolers. Available in manual guise only (priced at 3,850,000 yen), the Type R weighed in at 1260kg (2772lb).

The Type X was the top specification model, with Hi-Reflex paint, an SRS driver's-side airbag, leather trim, uprated fully-automatic air conditioning, an electric sunroof, cruise

control, the Bose Acoustic Wave stereo system, and additional soundproofing. The Type X was listed at 4,340,000 yen; an automatic gearbox added 100,000 yen to the price, with the Type R-style spoiler option adding a further 60,000.

Sales started on 1 December through the Anfini sales channel. A few days later, it was announced that the RX-7 had been voted the RJC 'Car of the Year'. At the same time, the RJC (a body of journalists and followers of the industry) named Kenichi Yamamoto as winner of the coveted 'Person of the Year' title. The highly-prized RJC title was the first of many accolades bestowed upon the new Mazda. Similar awards came from *Motor Magazine* and *Best Car*, while *Car Styling* gave the design its 'Golden Marker' trophy. Unfortunately, storm clouds were gathering on the horizon ...

The recession that followed the boom of the late-1980s naturally hurt Japanese car manufacturers, but a change in local taxation laws and unfavourable exchange rates only added to the problem. It was the latter that was holding Mazda back; a luxury car division (called Amati) was planned to compete with the Lexus, Infiniti and Acura organisations but, in view of the economic situation, the idea was eventually binned. Yoshihiro Wada, Mazda's President since December 1991, didn't seem overly worried,

Left & below: A couple of pictures from the first Japanese catalogue, showing a Type R model on French registration plates. In fact, the car was photographed all over Europe.

Part of a 'Sneak Preview' brochure produced in the States. "If you've longed for the return of the pure sports car, take heart," it said.

although it came as no surprise that Ford's involvement with the company grew ever stronger.

It was a particularly cruel situation, as the RX-7 was a definite hit with the motoring press. *Car Graphic* compared the Type R with the Nissan Skyline GT-R in early 1992, the venue – the only suitable place for this clash of the titans – was the race track. The magazine was unanimously in favour of the Mazda, but when the 'bubble' eventually burst in Japan, the repercussions were both swift and crippling. Supercars like the new 7, the Nissan 300ZX, the Honda NSX, and so on, would have a very hard time selling in a market that seemed to shrink overnight.

The American scene

In America, the new RX-7 went on sale in spring of 1992. There was a basic two-seater model (priced at $31,300), with two packages enabling the owner to tailor the vehicle to individual taste. The $1000 'R-1' option was performance orientated and the $3000 'Touring' alternative gave the car a more civilised GT character.

Mechanically, US specification cars were very similar to their counterparts in Japan, with the 13B-REW delivering exactly the same 255bhp. In fact, this figure was later confirmed as being spot-on by *Motor Trend* magazine, which checked the unit on a dynamometer. As for the gearing, only the manual 'box's fifth gear ratio was different, with a 0.719 cog being adopted; the Torsen limited-slip differential was also carried over.

The ABS braking system was standard, along with power-assisted steering, and the home market's 8J x 16 five-spoke alloy wheels shod with 225/50 rubber – usually VR rated, but ZRs for the R-1. Anti-roll bar diameters were 30mm (1.18in) up front and 17mm (0.67in) at the rear, incidentally.

All cars came with air conditioning, a leather-trimmed steering wheel (complete with SRS airbag), gearknob and handbrake grip, colour-keyed

143

Rear of the new RX-7 in American trim, complete with the Touring Package.

Interior of the Touring Package model, with leather trim coming as standard (it was an option on the base model, and not available on the R-1). The tachometer was marked up to 9000rpm! However, the red-line was at 8000, or 7000 for the automatic model. The speedometer was calibrated to 180mph, and all instruments were angled down slightly to reduce glare.

power mirrors, electric windows, a five-speaker AM/FM radio/cassette with electric aerial (a CD player and autochanger was available as a dealer option), an alarm, central locking, tinted glass, remote fuel door and hatch releases, storage compartments behind the seats, and cloth trim. Cruise control was thrown in for good measure, with the most commonly used operating switches mounted on the steering wheel, although, strangely, this was deleted if the owner chose the R-1 option.

The R-1 Package listed a rear spoiler, dual engine oil coolers, a tuned suspension, front tower bar, and ZR-rated tyres. The manual only R-1 also came with dedicated front brake cooling ducts in the front airdam skirt, but the model's aerodynamics aids were available separately as options, so the owner could make his or her car look like an R-1 without the harsher ride. In addition, like the Type R in Japan, a different material was used for the seat upholstery, finished in black, while the

For 1993 model year US specification cars, the rotary engine produced 255bhp at 6500rpm (or 6200 with automatic transmission), plus 217lbft of torque at 5000rpm. Four people were involved in building a turbocharged RE.

exterior could be painted in red, black, or yellow only on this model.

The Touring Package comprised leather trim, the Bose Acoustic Wave stereo system with CD player, halogen foglights, a rear wash/wipe facility, power tilt and slide sunroof, Hi-Reflex paint, better sound insulation, and a luggage cover. Leather trim (in black, tan or red, depending on body paintwork) and the four-speed automatic transmission were listed as individual options, priced at $800 and $850 respectively, although both were not available if the owner specified the R-1 Package. As well as those mentioned earlier, dealer accessories

This shot was used in early American advertising, as was a similar one with a silver car. The latter can be seen reproduced in full on the next page.

The R-1 Package was for those who liked driving hard, but some testers felt it was perhaps too performance orientated, at least for the average owner. Several journalists complained about the harsh ride in everyday situations. On the track, however, it was a different story ...

American advertising from mid-1992, "Announcing the return of the pure sports car."

ANNOUNCING THE RETURN OF THE PURE SPORTS CAR. This is the kind of sports car manufacturers stopped making years ago. The all-new 1993 Mazda RX-7 is specially designed for a handful of uncompromising individuals. Those who believe in the simple thrill that only comes from driving a lightweight car with a lot of power. ♡ What makes the RX-7 lightweight is also what makes it powerful. The world's only sequential twin-turbo rotary engine. More compact, and hundreds of pounds lighter than a comparable piston engine, it powers the RX-7 from 0-60 in 4.9 seconds and offers unique design advantages including perfect weight distribution. It even inspires the car's fluid shape. ♡ No gimmicks. No gadgets. No compromises. The all-new Mazda RX-7. Unless you race, you've never felt anything like it.

THE 1993 MAZDA RX-7 Sequential twin-turbo rotary engine. 255 horsepower. Independent double-wishbone suspension. 11.6-inch, ventilated 4-wheel disc brakes with ABS. Torsen® limited-slip differential. 36-month/50,000-mile, no-deductible, "bumper-to-bumper" warranty. Free roadside assistance. See dealer for limited-warranty details. For a free RX-7 brochure call 1-800-639-1000.

included items such as rear mudguards and stainless steel treadplates.

Coachwork colours initially included Silver Stone Metallic, Montego Blue Mica, Vintage Red, Brilliant Black and Competition Yellow Mica, the latter hue for the R-1 only.

In its preview of the RX-7, *Motor Trend* noted: "It's a great-looking car. The skin stretches tightly over big tyres mounted on wide alloy wheels stuck way out at the edges. The roofline dictates only two people go inside. There's a sense of the muscular but minimalist purposefulness of early Ferraris and Cobras, and the pumped-up, rounded fenders and tapering tail define space in the same way as a D-Jag. It enters the wind with a drag co-efficient of 0.30. It enters the showroom with a lot of sass.

"The interior follows the current organic fashion, full of rounded, partially ovoidal and semi-elliptical forms. Still, the flowing, wraparound feel is inviting, and function was a high priority. Directly in front of the driver is a big 9000rpm tach, red-lined at 8000rpm. Not many production cars in that category.

"The seats are deep, supportive buckets, just the ticket to hold you in place for road-bound acrobatics. A stubby little shift lever sprouts from the console. The three-spoke steering wheel with airbag has the desired thick rim. The cast aluminium brake and clutch pedals look racier than a Formula One team jacket."

Dennis Simanaitis tried an early R-1 for *Road & Track* and observed the following: "A first impression already noted is of the car's compactness. It's smaller than the Nissan ZX or Mitsubishi 3000GT, more curvaceous than the former, less rococo than the latter. Inside, there's a definite cockpit feel, the high centre console focusing the driver's responsibilities. Its control panel sweeps around to the left defining the instrument cluster and then into the door panel with its integrated heat/vent/air conditioning outlet. Oversize gauges are white-on-black with classic chrome bezels. The stubby shifter is almost, but not quite, Miata-like in its short positive throws. Clutch and brake pedals are plated and perforated, the brake well positioned for heel-and-toe operation. The airbag-equipped steering wheel is especially thick-rimmed, with perforated material to encourage proper hand placement.

"Underway, the car's rotary powerplant continues to amaze and delight, seemingly getting smoother and smoother with increased revs. The sequential twin-turbos give excellent performance, especially in mid- and top-end operation. It's not the sort of powerplant offering jackrabbit launches at throttle tip-in, however. Also, now and again, our early prototype exhibited the slightest of transitions around 4000rpm, a mini-flatspot that coincided with the second turbo's entry.

"Overall, the car's road feel belies its lightweight construction. In our mind's eye, we were reminded more of Nissan 300ZX or Mitsubishi 3000GT

American advertising from the latter part of 1992, outlining just some of the lengths Mazda engineers went to in the quest to save weight.

A brilliant piece of advertising announcing the new RX-7 in Britain.

than of Porsche 944 or Mazda Miata. Its handling felt predictable on rough road or smooth, its steering exhibiting crispness on input and good communication in response. The ride most definitely emphasized the sporty side of the car's Sports/GT nature. No complaints here.

"Probing limits around Willow Springs' sinuous asphalt, this new RX-7 exhibited excellent turn-in, plenty of grip and a commendable ability to invoke or not invoke its ABS under heavy braking. Through the Rabbit's Ear (Turn Two), a giant half-circle skidpan of 137m (450ft) radius, the car pushed predictably, with maybe a bit less off-throttle tuck-in than some of us would have liked. This same benign control felt just fine on the high-speed sweeper (flat out for some, 'tis said) leading into Turn Nine. And the car displayed nary a twitch over the circuit's several changes in elevation.

"Understandably missing from our early prototype drives were two crucial aspects: mixing it up for real, everyday traffic and granting our trusty *Road Test* Editor his computer-quantified track time. We're eager for both of these experiences with this significant new sports car, from a company that is not afraid of looking back as well as forward." *Automobile Magazine* said: "The first thing we noticed was the effortless, swelling low-rev urge available in the new Mazda. The second thing we noticed was the wonderful high-fidelity steering. With the front end securely planted by its double-wishbone suspension and its tyres' wide footprints, the RX-7 snakes into corners like a shark turning toward a meal."

The basic five-speed model weighed in at 1265kg (2783lb), but even the Touring with automatic transmission was hardly a heavyweight, tipping the scales at 1326kg (2917lb). Mazda quoted a top speed of 156mph (250kph), with 0-60 in 4.9 seconds, and 0.93g on the skidpan – the last two figures superior to those recorded for the Honda NSX. Independent tests later confirmed them to be accurate, with *Car & Driver* seeing 159mph (254kph), 0-60 in five seconds dead, and an amazingly high 0.97g. The same magazine compared the new RX-7 (in R-1 guise) with the Chevrolet Corvette, Nissan's 300ZX Turbo and the Lotus Elan to find the best two-seater in the world. The RX was declared the "raciest of the speedsters," while the ZX was "the suavest" of the breed. The Mazda scored 90 points, earning it second place; the Nissan won on 92, with the 'Vette coming in on 82, and the British car trailing on 68. Looking at the results, an improvement in ride quality could just as easily have swung the verdict in favour of the Hiroshima machine.

Trying to find the best-handling car in America, racer Danny Sullivan tried an R-1 model for *Road & Track* at the Willow Springs circuit, and stated: "It's like a big Miata, in that it has similar handling characteristics. You have to be careful, though, because if you are too hard on the throttle, it can get light at the rear. But with this turbo set-up, the power hit is very consistent. The steering effort is very light. It turned in real well, and once the car is pointed, the tail comes out a bit and the car handles nicely. It doesn't have as much power as some of the others [in this test], but I'm really impressed with the engine's kick."

Kobayakawa would have been very pleased with the result: "The new Mazda RX-7 shines brightest, with three of the six editors giving it the nod as the best handler. The car is so incredibly well-balanced that it makes going fast easy. Yet, it's fun, never boring – or frightening. It feels connected to the driver's senses. Mazda's weight reduction has paid big dividends." For the other three editors, it was a toss-up between the Porsche 911 Turbo and the Honda NSX; Sullivan went for the Stuttgart machine, incidentally.

Not long after, *Motor Trend* conducted a similar test to the *Car & Driver* one, except the Lotus was replaced by a Mitsubishi 3000GT VR-4, and a Honda (Acura) NSX was also thrown into the equation. On the track, the RX-7 set fastest time of the day – by quite some margin – but it was the Nissan that ultimately won the battle. Had price not been a factor, the NSX would have taken the top spot; whatever, it still wasn't the Mazda. Mac DeMere, author of the *Motor Trend* article, made an interesting observation: "The RX-7, especially its R-1 variant, is like Cajun cooking: though a devoted cadre will love its laissez les bon temp roulet personality, many will find it too spicy. With no low-powered, normally-

PERFORMANCE
THE PURE SPORTS CAR

RX-7

The pleasure of driving a real sports car lies not only in impressive performance, but the true feeling of oneness between car and driver. It is a sensation felt only when the movement of the car precisely reflects the driver's input.

The new powerplant for the RX-7 is based upon the proven twin rotor 13B, and is basically identical to the R26B that powered the 1991 Le Mans winning race car, except for the number of rotors. The rotary engine has no reciprocating parts and is thus inherently smooth at speed, with twin sequential turbos controlled to provide a seamless flow of power throughout the rev range.

High levels of safety and comfort are also required in a modern sports car. In the RX-7, besides ABS, you'll find a driver's side airbag as standard and side impact bars located in both doors. Windows and door locks are power operated, as is the tilt and slide sunroof.

Air conditioning and cruise control are also standard as is leather upholstery.

The new RX-7. A pure sports car, designed and equipped to offer an unmatched combination of performance and refinement in one unique package.

The first press photograph of the UK specification RX-7. The badging was the same as that for the American market.

aspirated version available, the RX-7 comes only in Extra Hot and the Tabasco-flavoured R-1. And that jives with Mazda's new philosophy to build cars that some people love rather than a lot of people like."

This statement was perhaps reflected in Mazda sales for 1992. Of the 248,000 cars sold in the States that year, only 6006 (or 2%) of them were RX-7s.

The car's arrival in Europe
A Mazda UK press release read: "In recent years, the Mazda marque has become synonymous with stunning and individualistic sports cars. Now with the launch of the outstanding all-new Mazda RX-7 Turbo, the Hiroshima-based manufacturer is set to become a major contender in the exclusive world of high-performance cars.

The RX-7 page from a Mazda UK range brochure, dated October 1992. It shows the new car in full flight, and the leather-trimmed interior. The same steering wheel was used in America and on the Type X model in Japan. Incidentally, RX-7 exports shot up from 3409 units worldwide in 1991 to 11,495 in 1992. However, the figures fell dramatically the following year to less than 2000.

Tail of the European specification RX-7.

"Mazda Motor Corporation can justifiably claim to have continued the legend with the new RX-7 Turbo, not only for its distinctive and elegant lines, but also by the fact that it's still the world's only sports car to use a rotary engine.

"The latest version of the Mazda RX-7 Turbo is a radical and totally new car, as right from the initial design stages the engineers were given a completely free brief to build the ultimate high-performance sports car from Mazda. The result is a car that has been designed to appeal to sports enthusiasts throughout the world."

The RX-7 Turbo was launched in the UK on 27 June 1992, initially priced at £34,000. It was now a pure two-seater, with no 2+2 option whatsoever. Due to the different measurement system, the European spec RE was quoted as having 237bhp at 6500rpm, with 218lbft of torque being developed 1500rpm lower down the rev range; the compression ratio remained at 9.0:1. Oddly, European versions were redlined at 7000rpm.

Official fuel consumption figures for the new RX-7 quoted 17.7mpg for the urban cycle, with 37.2 at a steady 56mph (90kph) and 29.4 at 75 (120). Although not as frugal around town as the 2.5 litre MX-6, it was not so different to the V6 coupé on the open road, which just goes to show how much progress had been made with the rotary powerplant over the years. In reality, though, it was so tempting to revel in the delight of extending the RE, that few drivers ever got much above 20mpg on average.

Gearing was virtually the same as that found in other markets, with only fifth being different, listed at 0.702; factory figures quoted a 5.3 second 0-60 time and a 156mph (250kph) top speed. The steering and braking system was carried over from Japanese models, while the suspension tuning was somewhere between the two US packages, with the R-1's ZR-rated Bridgestones coming as standard, along with the front tower bar (in addition to the standard rear one) and twin-oil coolers.

The body resembled the R-1, too, with the rear spoiler and brake cooling ducts in the front skirt. However, the mudguards that were offered as an accessory in the States were standard in the UK and other EEC countries, finished in black instead of body colour. The Cd was 0.31 for Europe, although rear end lift was virtually zero, thanks to the aerodynamic appendages.

Some of the cars on display at the 1992 Motor Show held at the NEC, on the outskirts of Birmingham. Nearest the camera and to the left is the Xedos 6, with the new third generation RX-7 next to it. A 626 is behind the RX-7, and the elegant MX-6 makes up the foursome.

The European model certainly came fully loaded, with leather trim, power steering (with an SRS airbag incorporated into the three-spoke steering wheel), air conditioning, cruise control, a 100W Panasonic five-speaker radio/cassette with electric aerial and integral digital clock, colour-keyed power door mirrors, electric windows, central locking, headlight washers and levelling facility, a rear wash/wipe, power tilt/slide sunroof, remote releases for the bootlid and fuel flap, illuminated ignition barrel and driver's door lock, storage boxes behind the seats, and security window coding.

Strangely, given the level of car crime in the UK, an alarm was listed as an accessory, along with treadplates, a sunroof visor and various mats and roofracks. Standard colours were the same as those for America, except the yellow shade was not available, and the interior came in black leather only. Having tried the new model, *MotorSport* observed: "Cabin noise levels were notably low, even under hard acceleration, and the ride was excellent at all but town speeds on poor surfaces.[However], the interior itself is not a £34,000 class act. Too many cheap trims are on display, particularly in the doors: was the priority low weight or low cost in this area?"

But despite this – and experiencing the odd flatspot during part throttle – the magazine summed up the new Mazda with the following words: "It is not often that a pure production car loses weight as the generations develop around extra standard equipment. Nor is it often that such a popular car impresses us just as much on the track as on the road.

"The RX-7 suavely achieves both objectives and sets new benchmarks in many areas, standards that others will struggle to emulate at any cost."

Autocar was perhaps less enamoured. It said: "The car has already displayed its mettle to us in the US where, in a group test that included the [Porsche] 968 and Mitsubishi's soon to appear here 3000GT, it breezed a win without ever raising so much as a sweat.

"There are changes to the car we get here, though. It's heavier, for starters, because Mazda UK has, unsurprisingly perhaps, taken the opportunity to load it with profit-making extras – a move which goes against the car's fundamental principles of lightness and clarity of purpose."

Indeed, the UK specification car weighed in at 1310kg (2882lb), but with only one model being listed, there was no opportunity to buy a purer sporting machine. On the other hand, the suspension was tuned for European-style driving, which led some testers to call the ride harsh – there was no facility to opt for softer settings. In this respect, the USA offered the best packages, but then sales volumes would be completely different for the two markets.

Whatever, *Autocar* admired the car's styling, its level of handling ("grip is superb, poise on the limit extraordinary"), the RE – "there is almost something surreal about the smoothness of the RX-7's rotary engine at high revs" – along with the "fabulously quick and deliciously mechanical-feeling gearshift" it was linked to, and its performance (with the standard 4.10:1 final-drive, a 0-60 time of six seconds and a top speed of 156mph, or 250kph was recorded). However, it criticised the poor fuel economy (just 15.5 miles for each gallon of 95 RON unleaded; a later *MotorSport* test got 16.7, but it's not that much better in reality), the ride, lack of space, and "boring engine note." It was also stated: "The RX-7 cabin fits like a glove for normally sized drivers but lacks head-and legroom for taller occupants. Doesn't feel special to be in, unlike a 968, despite faultless ergonomic design and good visibility."

At least when the *Autocar* compared it to its rivals, which included cars like the £34,945 Porsche 968, the Nissan 300ZX (£32,775), Renault-Alpine's A610 (£37,980) and the £28,940 Audi Coupé S2, the staff voted for the RX-7. In UK trim, "the 'edge' has been softened but it's still sharp enough to get our vote here," they said.

The Mazda stand at the 1992 Motor Show (held at the NEC between 24

Kijima's first project was the RZ. His only regret was that so few were built, and that sales were limited to Japan.

Takao Kijima pictured at the 2003 Tokyo Show. In a recent interview, the author's wife asked him what his aims were when he took over as head of the RX-7 project. He told her that his main aim was to lighten the car still further, which represented a major challenge, as he could still remember the sleepless nights Operation Zero caused. He also wanted to improve the vehicle's stability.

October and 1 November), had the new RX-7 as star attraction. As the press release stated: "One of the highlights of the stand will be the Mazda RX-7 Turbo. This stunning new sports model created a sensation at its international debut in Tokyo at the end of 1991. The RX-7 has just gone on sale in the UK, but with only 120 cars available this year, it is set to be a very exclusive sports car."

The RX-7 joined a distinctly sporting line-up, including the MX-3, MX-5 and MX-6, as well as the 323, 626, and luxury Xedos 6 range. To reinforce Mazda's desired image, the 323F used by Patrick Watts in the 1992 British Touring Car Championship was also on display.

Before the end of the year, the price was reduced slightly. While a number of Mazdas were subjected to increases in January (the Mazda MX-3 1.8i now cost £15,729, the standard MX-5 was £15,780, while the MX-6 started at £18,519), the RX-7 remained at £32,536; an automatic transmission was not available, although mica paint could be specified as a no-cost option.

Before leaving Europe for the time being, these apt words from *Classic & Sportscar* perhaps sum up the feelings of most people: "The way today's teenagers lust after the RX-7, its future classic status is assured. By then its bumpy ride and tight accommodation will be endearing character flaws, not obvious failings in an otherwise superb driving machine."

News from Japan

Takao Kijima became chief of the RX-7 project in 1992, and headed the MX-5's development three years later. Kijima, who had been with Mazda since 1967, was highly-respected for his work on the RX-7, which stretched back well over a decade, and he was also an important part of the team which had developed the first Miata.

On 1 October 1992, the limited edition Type RZ was announced. Based on the Type R, the 'Z' suffix was supposed to represent 'Mugen' or 'infinity', as in the Datsun Z-cars, but in this context, it can be taken to mean the ultimate bond between man and machine.

Limited to just 300 units, the leading features included larger, uprated Showa shock absorbers, new coil springs and bump-stops, special lightweight 225/60 ZR16 Pirelli tyres, a 4.30 final-drive ratio, a unique 0.762 fifth gear, and new seats jointly developed with the famous Recaro concern.

This was the first two-seater offered in Japan, its sporting pedigree further enhanced by having air conditioning and audio equipment as options, and adding a kneepad on the driver's door and a drilled alloy footrest for the passenger; storage bins were included behind the ultra-light seats.

Offered with manual transmission only, it weighed 30kg (66lb) less than the Type R, and was finished in Brilliant Black with the alloy wheels sprayed in Gunmetal Grey. Whilst the price of the standard 1993 model year RX-7 range was unchanged from launch, the Type RZ was listed at 4,050,000 yen.

Ironically, in view of the new car's purposeful image, the company announced it was no longer going to field a team at Le Mans, and predicted that this would be the last generation of RX-7s. Mazda had been hit very hard when the 'bubble' burst in Japan, so the launch timing on the rotary-engined model was especially unfortunate. Had it come out a few years earlier, the story could have been very different ...

American update

The American *Road & Track* magazine had an RX-7 on long-term loan. After some 33,000 miles, it had this to say:

"When the RX-7 Touring model began its long-term test last year, we knew from the road test that its abilities as a grand tourer were limited. The cockpit was cramped and cargo space virtually non-existent – thanks to mammoth speaker tubes in the rear compartment. Also, ride quality was dreadfully harsh. But despite this, we were convinced that the RX-7 would prove itself to be a capable long-termer. And we were right.

"The RX-7 was usually our first choice for trips that took us north, where narrow, secluded roads snaked through dense woods or clung to cliff edges above the crashing waves of the Pacific. These picturesque highways begged us to press the RX-7's accelerator pedal to the floor and unleash the 255 horses residing in the twin-turbocharged two-rotor Wankel. Power came on immediately, and the car's sudden forward acceleration never failed to snap our heads back and press our spines into the seats.

"The RX-7's handling was equally impressive. On all kinds of corners – from tight 90 degree right-handers to long sweepers – it was amazingly stable."

Despite the need for oil changes every 3000 miles (4800km), "the delicacy of the RX-7's exterior and interior finishes," and the odd unexpected trip to the dealer, Sam Mitani described it as "an affair to remember ... We give the 1993 RX-7's overall performance a hearty thumbs up."

Douglas Kott reinforced this viewpoint in another article in which each editor chose their favourite sporting machinery: "Apologies to the staff's romanticists, but racing heritage, history and related drivel play no great part in my definition of a sports car ... What does head my personal priority list of sports car 'must haves' is responsive and agile handling, followed closely by power and a strong dose of style. My pick, Mazda's latest RX-7, has each by the shovelful."

Specifications and options remained unchanged for the 1993 model year proper, although prices were destined to rise. By the start of the season, the basic RX-7 was $1200 more than it had been at the time of its launch, and by spring 1993 it commanded $32,900;

A nice piece of Mazda advertising describing Hi-Reflex paint. Both Pirelli and Michelin used the RX-7 in much of their 1993 US publicity campaigns.

the R-1 Package was listed at $1500, while the Touring option added $3500.

With falling sports car sales, timing could certainly have been better for the launch of Toyota's fourth generation Supra. However, it quickly made an impression, with *Car & Driver* ranking it first in a six-way battle (interestingly, four of the top sports cars included in this particular test were Japanese), and a similar conclusion was drawn in a *Motor Trend* article.

Nevertheless, considering the financial climate and increased competition, the RX-7 sold quite well, accounting for 5062 of the 260,000 Mazda's sold in the States during 1993, and was duly voted 'Import Car of the Year' by *Motor Trend*. It was also declared 'Car of the Year' by *Playboy*, in addition to appearing in the *Car & Driver* 'Ten Best' listing for 1993, '94 and '95.

For those who felt 159mph (254kph) – a figure recorded by *Motor Trend* – was a little timid, there was certainly no shortage of tuning companies willing to give the car even better performance. *Road & Track* was full of praise for the Rod Millen Motorsport RX-7, which boasted 350bhp, 17-inch BBS wheels with BF Goodrich tyres, and uprated brakes and suspension for around $15,000 more than the standard model; Maryland-based Peter Farrell, another Mazda racer, also

A series of shots showing the home market's Touring X model of August 1993. Note the glass sunroof in place of the previous steel item, and the white foglights instead of yellow ones.

Above & right: The home market's Touring X model of August 1993.

offered a conversion, known as the PFS RX-7. This $50,000 machine featured a 330bhp engine, 17-inch OZ wheels and BF Goodrich rubber, uprated brakes and suspension, and a new nose and rear spoiler. Perhaps the boldest conversion came from HKS, which not only gave the rotary engine 485bhp, but also reduced vehicle weight by some 100kg (220lb)!

Changes for 1994

Almost 16,000 FD3S models had been sold by the summer of 1993, but Mazda needed to sell more. The changes for the 1994 season were introduced in mid-August in Japan, and included a complete reshuffle of the home market's line-up. The manual-only Type R was 3,910,000 yen, but it was joined by the new R-II, a two-seater version of the car, priced at 3,380,000 yen. The automatic Touring S and Touring X models were listed at 3,740,000 and 4,230,000 yen respectively.

All cars received suspension changes: the front bump-stops were longer, and those at the back changed from rubber to urethane; shock absorber size was also increased. The front strut tower bar, previously fitted to performance models only, became standard on all grades, augmenting the already standard rear one, and the rear crossmember was modified. These latter revisions resulted in an even stronger bodyshell.

Inside, the appearance of the fascia was improved with a more chip-resistant finish, a new speedometer was employed, and the gauge trim rings changed from chrome to black (although the Touring S and X models retained the original style). A bigger armrest was specified, while an ashtray became listed as a dealer option. On the environmental side, ozone-friendly R134a gas was now used in the air conditioning.

When fitted, the sunroof was made of glass and the foglights changed from yellow to white, but otherwise the exterior was much the same. However, from 1 October, a limited edition model was available with 17-inch wheels and tyres, and these could be specified as an option on the Type R from this date.

The special edition model was the Type RZ. Based on the Type R and limited to just 150 units, it was launched to commemorate the 15th anniversary of the RX-7. Finished in Brilliant Black, it carried over the best points of the first RZ, and featured full bucket seats by Recaro, Bilstein dampers, and a 17-inch wheel and tyre combination (8J BBS alloys with 235/45 Bridgestones, with 8.5J rims shod with 255/40-section rubber at the rear); audio equipment was listed as an option on this 4,350,000 yen machine.

Naturally, the production changes were applied to America's 1994 model year cars, with the suspension refinements being at the top of the list. Even the R-1 was made to ride slightly softer, and renamed the R-2 in the process, although it was only this model with the front strut bar in the States.

The basic car, which now came with dual airbags and map pockets added to the seatbacks, was priced at $36,395. The Touring Package was pretty much the same, except the sunroof was now made of glass, and the price had gone up to $4200. Likewise, the $2000 R-2 Package carried over all the features of the former R-1 option, although the tyres were now Pirelli P Zeros. A new option package, called the Popular Equipment Group and priced at $1800, included leather trim (no longer available separately), a steel tilt/slide sunroof and a luggage cover. The alternative automatic transmission was now listed at $900.

Motor Trend was certainly pleased with the new R-2 Package: "The new R-2 chassis package combines all the agility of the old R-1 set-up, but with much more livable suspension calibrations. Even between test venues, drivers were raving about the car. On the racetrack, they lapsed into giddy delirium." Sadly, though, despite Mazda's Stateside sales in general increasing by quite some margin, the RX-7 continued to struggle, with only 2212 of them finding new homes during 1994.

In the UK, the 1993 Earls Court Show catalogue said: "The Mazda sports range is led by the 150mph Mazda RX-7 – the world's only rotary-engined sports car. Hailed as a true challenger to some of the most established sports

Interior of the R-2 model.

The R-2 at speed. Compared with the old R-1, most testers agreed the ride/roadholding compromise had been achieved far more satisfactorily.

America's 1994 model year RX-7 with the R-2 Package.

An American 1994 model year RX-7 with the Touring Package. Note the new glass sunroof.

cars available, the Mazda RX-7 is set to become a classic."

However, the price was slashed in September 1993 to just £25,950. The Mazda people in Britain should perhaps have realized that the RX-7 was always going to sell in very small numbers, and priced it even higher at the start, rather like Honda's NSX – after all, the cars were in a similar class, but the NSX was £57,000 during this period. At the end of the day, there's a lot to be said for rarity value, and to devalue the flagship model was certainly not a good idea.

The *Daily Express* Guide to World Cars noted: "Everything works smoothly and crisply, and the result is a car that is easy to drive at any speed. All things considered, the RX-7 is astonishing value for money." On the other hand, it went on to say: "The only problem is petrol consumption – however smooth and reliable the Wankel may now be, it's still a thirsty engine."

Japanese specials

In April 1994, Mazda had won the Bathurst 12-hour Race for the third year in succession. To commemorate the occasion, in August a limited edition Type R-II 'Bathurst' model was launched in Japan. Based on the R-II two-seater, it featured special decals and blue-tinted glass. 350 were built, priced at a very reasonable 2,998,000 yen each.

A few months later, in February 1995, Mazda announced the Type R 'Bathurst', naturally based on the Type R, but without an audio system to make it cheaper. However, on 22 March, the whole range was realigned once again. The Type R 'Bathurst' proved popular, so became listed as a standard model, priced at 3,285,000 yen. The RZ also joined the line-up, continuing the previous RZ format but also incorporating an uprated braking system (with 314mm, or 12.4in, diameter discs), a new adjustable rear spoiler, and a Momo steering wheel. Available in black only, it was listed at 3,960,000 yen. The Type R was deleted, but, with 17-inch wheels and the RZ's spoiler and Momo wheel, it became the 3,890,000 yen R-S.

In the last part of the reshuffle, the Touring S was merged with the Touring X, so that only the latter appeared on the lists. At 3,815,000 yen, it was now the only automatic model, and, whilst it featured the new rear spoiler, the leather trim previously employed was replaced by suede, which went some way towards explaining the cheaper sticker price – down 415,000 yen on the old Touring X grade.

Standard colours included Chaste White, Vintage Red, Brilliant Black and Silver Stone Metallic. The limited edition Type R 'Bathurst' X of July 1995 was available in all these shades except silver, and was given contrasting leather trim in either red or black. For the 3,350,000 yen asking price, the proud owner also got the new rear spoiler, a dark grey finish for the alloy wheels (rather like the first RZ in appearance), grey-tinted glass, a Momo steering wheel and unique badging. Only 777 were built.

The US 1995 model year

The RX-7 line was simplified in America, too. The Touring Package disappeared, leaving only the $37,500 basic car, and the R-2 and Popular Equipment Group options (both the same price as in 1994, but the latter now including foglights). The ABS unit was lighter and more compact, and the suspension settings received attention yet again.

The press release read: "Mazda's award-winning RX-7 sports car enters 1995 with a smoother, more

Japan's Type R 'Bathurst' of February 1995.

A dramatic shot of the Type RZ of March 1995.

Interior of the Type R 'Bathurst' shortly after it became a standard model.

comfortable ride and a revised line-up of model offerings. The RX-7's virtues of a strong, lightweight body, exceptional handling and dramatic performance remain unchanged.

"Revised suspension tuning for all RX-7 models, except the competition-tuned R-2 package, delivers a smoother, more comfortable ride in day-to-day driving while retaining the car's quick reflexes and agile handling. To achieve this, the diameter of the rear stabilizer bar has been reduced and softer suspension bushes are used."

The M2 organisation was established in November 1990 as a point of direct contact between the factory and enthusiastic end users. Four Mazda workers were involved, including Hirotaka Tachibana and Masanori Mizuochi (now Chairman of the Roadster Club of Japan. A number of exciting projects were instigated, including this one based on the RX-7 – the 1995 M2-1020.
Inset: Tail of the M2-1020, showing the much sought-after M2 badge. Several MX-5 derivatives made it to market, but, sadly, this RX-7 was destined not to. (Courtesy Masanori Mizuochi)

The 265bhp M2-1020 at speed. The main features included a more powerful RE (the extra horses coming from a different ECU and a Mazdaspeed main silencer), better engine cooling, improved aerodynamics, an uprated suspension (with 40-position dampers) and braking system, a stronger lsd, and 17-inch BBS alloys with Bridgestone Expedia tyres; lightweight Recaro seats were used inside. (Courtesy Masanori Mizuochi)

The M2-1020 was due to be launched in April 1995, but, two months beforehand, the decision was taken to close down the M2 operation in May. The project was cancelled because of worries regarding aftersales care. However, M2's Kobashi-san joined the mainstream development team, and some of the features were duly carried over to the 280bhp production model. (Courtesy Masanori Mizuochi)

While anti-roll bar diameters were 30mm (1.18in) up front and 16mm (0.63in) at the rear on the R-2, the other models now had bars of 28.5mm (1.12in) and 14mm (0.55in), respectively.

Standard colours included Montego Blue Mica, Brilliant Black, Vintage Red, White and Silver Stone Metallic, with trim coming in either black cloth, or black or tan leather (the red leather option was deleted). The R-2 was not available in the blue or white shades, incidentally.

A July 1995 *Motor Trend* article clocked an R-2 at an impressive 160mph (256kph), but its performance in the showrooms was nowhere near as spectacular. Unfortunately, Mazda's US sales fell quite dramatically in 1995, with the RX-7 accounting for just 1399 of the 223,000 units sold. The writing was definitely on the wall ...

The RX-01

At the 1995 Tokyo Show, Mazda displayed the stunning RX-01 concept car. Literature handed out at the event revealed that the ultra-compact engine was mounted very low down and behind the front axle line. In addition to giving the vehicle a low centre of gravity, this gave the engineers the opportunity to adopt a completely straight driveline back to the driven wheels. To get weight distribution perfect and aid traction, the fuel tank and battery were situated over the rear axle. The newly-developed, multi-sideport rotary unit produced a healthy 220bhp and, combined with a lightweight body, the car's performance was almost as exceptional as its styling.

Aerodynamics played a major part in the RX-01's development. The positioning of the engine allowed a short and low bonnet line, but the integrated rear wing and underbody spoilers were, perhaps, the most interesting features. Although overall dimensions were not that dissimilar to the RX-7, by employing years of weight-saving

A US specification RX-7 for 1995, this being an R-2 model. Sadly, time was running out in the States for the 'rotary rocket.'

The RX-01 concept car displayed at the 1995 Tokyo Show. Many were hoping that this would be the next RX-7 ...

technology acquired via Mazda's racing programme (even the 17-inch wheels were in magnesium alloy to save a few grammes), the vehicle tipped the scales at just 1100kg, or 2420lb.

In January 1996, Mazda gave the rotary another 10bhp, and took the opportunity to make some minor modifications and change the line-up once more. The Type R 'Bathurst' was killed off and replaced by two new models – the Type RB and the Type RB 'Bathurst'. The RB, priced at 3,200,000 yen, was the basic grade, and easily distinguished from the 3,400,000 yen Bathurst variant by its lack of a rear spoiler. All cars gained new rear combination lights and green on black markings for the instruments, and all bar the Touring X had 265bhp engines and a Momo steering wheel as standard (the Touring X, still the only model with automatic transmission, retained its 255bhp rotary and its price). The 3,975,000 yen RZ continued pretty much the same except for the production changes, of course, but the R-S became even more performance orientated. Priced at 3,665,000 yen, it adopted new 17-inch, ultra-light, five-spoke alloy wheels, and the uprated brakes and lower 4.30:1 final-drive from the RZ. In the process, the model became known as the Type RS (minus the hyphen), but the Type RZ remained the only two-seater.

A sad situation

In the *Road & Track* guide to the 1996 model year, it was noted: "The company's performance-flagship RX-7 goes into 1996 unchanged, but Mazda has us anticipating a 'mid-year announcement' about the fate of this rotary-engine rocket. The early rumblings are ominous, but we're keeping our fingers crossed for an 11th-hour reprieve for this sports car."

The RX-7 was dropped from US price lists in spring 1996. The American magazine, *Motor Trend*, said in the November 1994 issue: "The RX-7 R-2 isn't a lifestyle choice. It isn't a 'Grand Tourer'. It's a $36,000, 0-60mph in 5.3 seconds, take-it-out-and-play-with-it adult toy. It rewards the aggressive with deft reflexes. It punishes the hedonist with a stiff ride, an austere interior, and no damned drink holders." In reality, the writer had knocked the nail on the head: the RX-7, like the new Toyota Supra, was a rich man's plaything and, in the post-Black Monday era, there simply weren't many rich men left ... It was inevitable that so many of the Japanese supercars would fall by the wayside as people opted for more practical forms of transportation.

Only 369 RX-7s were sold in 1996 (all 1995 models), with the final 12 finding homes in the following year. Early reports pointed towards "something new for 1997" – indeed the RX-01 was "still under consideration," but, sadly, it was not to be. For both the RX-7 and the rotary engine, a long and eventful era had come to a premature end.

In Europe, it was a similar picture. The price had been allowed to creep back up, to £29,400 for the 1995 season, and on to £35,299 by the summer of that year. However, *Complete Car* noted: "Mazda's RX-7 is disappearing at the end of the year, because the rotary-engined car will not meet noise emission regulations. So far this year the car attracted just a handful of buyers, and is available now on special order only. Mazda's most powerful sports car could return in the form of the RX-01, the sports coupé shown at the Tokyo Show. But Mazda – which is facing serious financial problems – has yet to decide whether to commit itself to the pricey project."

In the early part of March 1996, Mazda UK stopped listing the RX-7. Now, it's not very often I put forward my personal point of view in a book; as a historian I feel it is better to quote several sources from the contemporary press and let the reader judge. However, this important event was allowed to pass virtually unnoticed (on both sides of the Atlantic, as it happens), and deserves some further examination. As far as not being able to meet regulations goes, I find it very hard to believe that a minimum of investment wouldn't have put things right. If Mazda's enthusiastic engineers could make the RE pass the world's strictest gas emissions tests time and time again, they could certainly make a car a touch quieter. The reality is that Europe was in the depths of a recession and, for the majority of people, paying the mortgage took priority over buying expensive two-seater sports cars. Period.

Note the round lights behind the smoked lens, which replaced the earlier square items in January 1996. This is the new RS model.

Left: The new Momo three-spoke steering wheel which was fitted to all models except the luxury Touring X.

Interior of the RS. Incidentally, the Type RB and RB 'Bathurst' lost their rear strut bars at this time, while the Touring X grade came with a rear brace only; the Type RS and RZ had tower bars at both front and rear.

Interior of the Type RZ, with its lightweight Recaro seats. Note the storage bins in place of the +2 seating behind them. The RZ remained the only two-seater for the home market.

This picture, along with a whole series of high-speed driving shots, was reproduced in black and white for the Japanese catalogue.

A 1995 model year RX-7 for the British market. Sadly, exports had fallen to disastrous levels, and the rotary-engined model was discontinued outside Japan during spring 1996.

In Britain, in particular, it was a big mistake to reduce the RX-7's price shortly after launch: it took away all of the model's credibility, and, naturally, made a lot of earlier buyers unhappy, because they could have saved a fortune if they'd waited a little while, and the trade-in value of the vehicle they had bought was a fraction of what it should have been. Add in ridiculous insurance premiums and the high cost of petrol, and no matter how good the car it was doomed.

The new Supra went the same way, along with the Nissan Z-car and Mitsubishi's 3000GT, to name but a few. In my opinion, the noise, exhaust and whatever other regulations were thrown into the arena had nothing to do with their departure; they were simply selling in too small a volume to justify importation. That's not necessarily anyone's fault, it was a sign of the times as much as anything, but blaming the new regulations allowed the concessionaires to opt out without losing face.

The legend continues

In Japan, at least, the RX-7 legend was allowed to continue. *Car Graphic* looked at the RZ in its June 1996 issue: the magazine felt that the Mazda had far more punch at higher revs than either the Toyota Supra or the Nissan Skyline GT-R, with power available right the way up to the 8000rpm redline. It was also noted that the Type RZ was the perfect car for drifting around corners!

More changes were announced in December 1996, with the driver's airbag becoming standard again, although a 40,000 yen hike on all models except the Touring X – the only car with the SRS system included in the sticker price last season – is probably more than just a coincidence. Anyway, all RX-7s now had the same four-spoke Momo steering wheel.

The special edition Type RB 'Bathurst' X was announced at the same time. Available in either black or white, and based on the basic Type RB, it came with red leather trim, a front and rear spoiler, foglights, a rear wash/wipe and unique decals. Priced at 3,370,000 yen, it was limited to just 700 units.

Corporate news

Ford had increased its share in the Japanese company to 33.4% on 12 April 1996, thereby achieving a controlling interest. Mazda is quite unusual for a Japanese company in that, of the top 35 positions at the end of 1997, eight were held by foreigners, due mainly to Ford's involvement. One of these foreigners, Henry Wallace, joined the Mazda board in 1993, along with two other Ford executives, and became President three years later after Wada was appointed Chairman. Wallace became the first gaijin to hold the presidency of a Japanese car company.

Meanwhile, in summer 1997, news leaked out that, instead of abandoning the rotary, Mazda was still working to improve the RE. Reduced friction helped the engineers extract 280bhp from the unit, and fuel consumption

Advertising for the limited edition Type RS-R, introduced in October 1997.

Cover of the catalogue for the Type RS-R.

figures were also said to be enhanced. However, by the end of the year, its future was once again open to question.

Wallace went on record saying: "Today, our priority is the recreational segment. We have prioritised the SUV market, which is strong in the USA and Japan, and now growing in Europe. We have placed these vehicles ahead of our sports car strategy, which had been a priority. For the moment, we haven't decided about the rotary engine; it's an open issue we will have to resolve in the future. Although development work continues, it's at a low level."

The 1998 model year

Despite the Anfini name disappearing (the car was now known as the Mazda RX-7) and the adoption of a new badge on the nose and tail, the 1997 catalogue was re-issued with a new cover and touched-in photographs depicting the latest insignia. Prices were unchanged from the previous season, as were the colour options, so the owner still had a choice of black, white, red or silver hues.

The only difference was the addition of the 500-off Type RS-R in October 1997. Priced at 3,625,000 yen, it was launched to celebrate the 30th anniversary of the rotary engine. As the name implies, it was based on the RS, but it came with Bilstein dampers from the RZ, chrome trim on the instruments, special fabric trim, an aluminium footrest for the passenger and a door-mounted kneepad for the driver; foglights and the audio system were passed onto the option list. Finished in either Brilliant Black or Sunburst Yellow, the Bridgestone-shod wheels were painted dark grey.

Apart from the new, second generation MX-5s and a solitary RX-7, the theme of the 1997 Tokyo Show stand very much reflected the fashions of the time, with MPVs and estate cars dominating. No-one could blame the management, though, as this was the strongest sector of the market in Japan as the millennium loomed, while sports cars were in danger of becoming a dying breed. Japanese sales figures released for December 1997 confirmed the growing trend in utility vehicles and MPVs in preference to sports cars and coupés. The best-seller in the sporting line-up was the Toyota Corolla Levin with 722 units for the month; the Celica managed 464 sales, while the Supra clocked up just 145 – the MR2 recorded a disappointing 91 sales.

Mazda was also struggling with

An RX-7 in service with the Chiba Police Force, used for highway patrol duties. Interestingly, from 1992, the VAZ factory modified a number of Russian Police Ladas to take RE engines. (Courtesy Chiba Police Force)

The 1998 model year saw the adoption of 'wing-type' badges after the loss of the Anfini name. This is the Mazda RX-7 Type RS ...

sales of 206 Eunos Roadsters (the MX-5) and 202 RX-7s. The Nissan 300ZX and rest of the Fairlady Z range found just 40 customers, though this was quite a lot compared to Honda's NSX supercar, sales of which amounted to only 13 units.

By comparison, Honda sold 4230 of its CR-V and no fewer than 11,123 of the StepWgn people mover. In the smaller MPV class, Suzuki sold over 16,000 of the Wagon R models. Even executive cars were outselling sporting machines at a rate of almost ten to one! As the world's most dedicated followers of fashion, the Japanese were clearly telling manufacturers that the sports car era was well and truly over unless they were offering something new.

... and this is the Type RB 'Bathurst' from the same period.

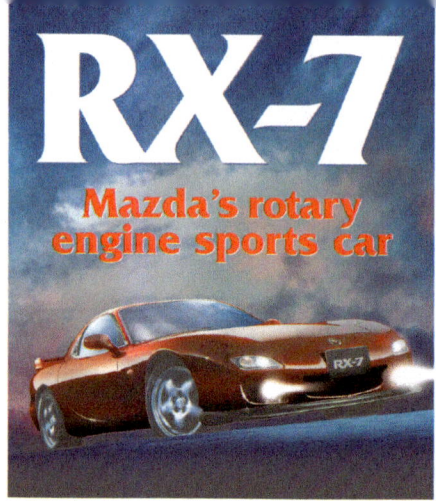

6

The RX-7 in competition

Over the years, the RX-7 has built up an enviable record in the field of motorsport. From Japan to America and the race tracks of Europe, the rotary-engined machine has claimed numerous victories. It has even left its mark in rallying, in both the US SCCA series and the prestigious World Rally Championship. One could easily write an entire book on just the competition exploits of the model, but space dictates otherwise. Nevertheless, below is a comprehensive review of the RX-7's lengthy motorsport career.

IMSA racing

The professional, and therefore highly-competitive, International Motor Sports Association (IMSA) racing series was founded at the start of the 1970s. There were essentially four classes – GTU (GT Under 2.5 litres), GTO (GT Over 2.5 litres), RS (Racing Stock) and AAGT (All-American GT).

Mazda planned to campaign the RX-7 in the 1979 IMSA season, so, in order to be fully prepared, two works cars were sent over from Japan to compete in the 1978 Daytona 24-hour Race. In addition to the American drivers, Walt Bohren, Jim Downing, Stu Fisher and Roger Mandeville, there were two Japanese racers, Yoshimi Katayama and Yojiro Terada.

Yoshimi Katayama was a private racing enthusiast specializing in Mazda machinery. He had been part of the team that campaigned the Cosmo Sport at the 1968 Marathon de la Route, and continued to be heavily involved with the marque for decades to come. Terada, too, would also establish strong links with the Hiroshima company, making a number of appearances behind the wheel of a Mazda at Le Mans.

Anyway, this attempt was not particularly successful, but it did give the Mazda team a lot of useful experience in this important season opener. In 1979, two race cars and a spare were once again sent from Japan, with Katayama, Terada and Takashi Yorino allocated one machine (number 7), and Bohren, Downing and Mandeville the other (number 77). Having applied all the lessons learnt from the previous year, at its first Daytona 24-hour Race, the RX-7 easily took GTU honours. After 46 of the 68 starters fell by the wayside, the Japanese team finished fifth overall (first in Class), while the American drivers came home in sixth (second in Class). It was a fine result, the best placings recorded by GTU models in the history of the event, setting the standard for the new Mazda sports car in IMSA competition.

The three cars were later campaigned by Bohren, Downing and Ed Parks. Ironically, this convincing victory backfired, as the RX-7s were made to run heavier in the future to bring them closer to their competitors. This decision was later reversed, but the damage was done and the '79 GTU crown went to Datsun racer, Don Devendorf. Bob Bergstrom, whose vehicle was prepared by Dave Kent's Creative Car Craft workshops in Hawthorne, California, came second, as did Mazda in the manufacturers title chase.

The top runners were using fuel-injection in 1980, taking horsepower up from around 270 to well over 300bhp. Walt Bohren, driving a Racing Beat-prepared RX-7, won six rounds to claim the GTU title, while other wins from Brad Frisselle and Jeff Kline ensured that Mazda took the manufacturers championship.

The Class-winning RX-7 pictured at Daytona. The 1979 IMSA cars, with a twin-choke Weber carburettor and standard 9.4:1 compression ratio, produced 270bhp at 9000rpm.

Fuel-injection was banned for 1981, but the Kent Racing models were still producing around 300bhp. Another interesting development was the introduction of the BF Goodrich team, which ran RX-7s on standard road tyres. Dave Kent's racers won 11 out of the 16 rounds, with ex-BL man Lee Mueller taking the spoils and Walt

The sister car that came home sixth overall (second in Class) in the pit lane at Daytona in 1979.

Bohren second. Their performances were enough to give Mazda a well-deserved second GTU trophy.

With Kent Racing changing alliance to Toyota and BF Goodrich moving across to Porsche for 1982, the majority of factory support went to Jim Downing and Roger Mandeville. Meanwhile, a works car powered by the 13B engine was sent to contest the GTO category in the Daytona 24-hour Race. Driven by Katayama, Terada and Yorino, it finished fourth overall and easily won the GTO Class – a Dave Kent-prepared model took GTU honours in the team's last Mazda foray, followed by five other 'rotary rockets'. RX-7 drivers gained 13 other IMSA GTU victories that year to secure the title for Mazda for the third consecutive year; Downing was declared GTU Champion.

The Californian Racing Beat organisation, based in Anaheim, Los Angeles, moved into the GTO arena in 1983, winning at Daytona (third overall) and Mosport. In the GTU category, the RX-7 was still the dominant machine. Mazda claimed the title again, with RX-7 drivers taking the flag at 11 events; it was Roger Mandeville who came out on top on this occasion.

Mandeville contested the GTO Class in 1984, modifying his GTU car to suit, and giving it a new 13B peripheral port power unit. He won only two

The 1979 Daytona car pictured at Laguna Seca in October 2002 after a full restoration by the factory. The original driver, Yoshimi Katayama, was again in the hot seat (in red overalls), with Mazda's Le Mans hero Takaharu Kobayakawa (in chinos, with his back to the camera), overseeing operations. (Courtesy Ken Hoyle)

After the RX-7's highly-successful debut at Daytona in February, the Competitions Department in the US was quick to offer reproduction panels, both for racers, and enthusiasts who wanted to give their road car a distinctive look. A replica of the GTU Class winner was later displayed at the 1979 Tokyo Show. (Courtesy Hideo Aoki)

A Kent Racing GTU model from 1980.

Top & above: The successful Katayama, Terada and Yorino team took the GTO spoils at Daytona in 1982, repeating their GTU victory of three years earlier.

Jim Downing, the IMSA GTU Champion for 1982.

The Racing Beat GTO car from 1983.

Roger Mandeville had to settle for second place in the GTU category in 1982, but this is his winning car from 1983.

Mazda's racing successes in the States were used to good effect in promoting the brand at home, whilst the company's Le Mans campaign continued in the background. The pure racer on the right is the 717C.

Mazda action at Sears Point in 1983.

Jack Baldwin on his way to a second consecutive GTU title in 1985.

This Savanna RX-7 'GTO' mock-up was displayed at the 1985 Tokyo Show, when the second generation model made its debut. Note the Group B rally car behind it, and the nose of the 737C Le Mans car just visible on the right. (Courtesy Hideo Aoki)

rounds, at Riverside and Lime Rock, but consistent finishes in the other events gave him the title. Jack Baldwin, an experienced racer but relative newcomer to the IMSA scene, took the GTU title, with Jack Dunham (another RX-7 driver) taking second. Needless to say, with RX-7s taking seven of the 17 rounds that season, Mazda secured its fifth GTU title.

Although the GTO campaign was not as successful as it had been in the previous year, by 1985, thanks to continued dominance in the GTU Class, the RX-7 had broken the IMSA victory record for a single model, and was still going strong. Both Baldwin and Mazda retained their respective titles.

In 1986, the RX won 13 of the 17 GTU rounds that season, giving Mazda yet another championship. Although Mandeville took the flag no less than eight times, it was a fellow RX-7 driver, youngster Tom Kendall, who walked away with the title. Kendall won again in the following season, his particular car having now taken GTU honours five times with three different drivers! With 11 race wins to its credit, amazingly, Mazda had won the GTU series for an unprecedented eight consecutive years, from 1980 to 1987. Unfortunately, the company's bid for the GTO title wasn't strong enough against the might of Ford, Chevrolet and Toyota.

Mazda at Le Mans

Mazda was the first Japanese manufacturer to tackle the legendary French 24-hour event, by supplying a 10A engine to a team of Belgian privateers to power a Chevron B16. It

Mazda at Le Mans in 1981. This is the car shared by Win Percy, Hiroshi Fushida and Yojiro Terada. Sadly, both RX-7's entered that year were destined to retire. (Courtesy Win Percy)

was not particularly successful, but did at least signify the RE's debut at the Sarthe. As racing driver Yojiro Terada said in a recent interview: "To prove a design at Le Mans is far more beneficial in terms of publicity than any amount of advertising. No matter how many professors and critics recommend an automobile, this is the ultimate test."

The Mazdaspeed Type 254 that finished 14th at Le Mans in 1982.

Left & right: Two views of the competition rotary engine prepared by Racing Services of Twickenham.

Main pic: Tom Walkinshaw on his way to a Class victory (second overall) in the 1979 British Saloon Car Championship – forerunner of the BTCC.

Inset, below: Win Percy at Mallory Park in 1980. Percy not only took the flag on this occasion, but also claimed the BTCC at the end of the year. (Courtesy Win Percy)

Three years later, the Japanese Sigma concern tried its luck at Le Mans, although the Sigma MC73-Mazda was destined to retire with electrical problems. The same team entered another rotary-engined machine in 1974 but, despite reaching the end, due to a shortage in the number of full laps, was not classified in the final results. A private French team entered an RX-3 in 1975, paving the way for Mazda's new sports car. As Mazda's finances improved, Terada managed to convince the company to send a team. A long-tailed RX-7, known as the Type 252i, was spotted at the 1979 event, but the 285bhp car (entered by the motorsports section of Mazda Auto Tokyo – forerunner of the Mazdaspeed concern – and wearing the number 77) failed to qualify due to problems with the fuel-injected engine and suspension.

Although still a low-budget affair, the following year saw a far more successful assault on this most famous of all endurance races. Built by Holman Moody and entered by an American firm, ZW Enterprises, the white RX-7 (number 86) driven by Ernesto Soto, Pierre Honegger and Mark Hutchins beat off a lot of stiff competition to finish 21st overall in the final standings. From an historic point of view, it was the first rotary-engined car to officially complete the 24-hour race.

Mazdaspeed entered two of the so-called Type 253 long-tail RX-7s in 1981 (like the 252 before it, this model was designed by Takuya Yura). Car number 37, which was predominantly red and white, was piloted by Tetsu Ikusawa, Tom Walkinshaw (of TWR fame) and Peter Lovett, while number 38 (finished in black and gold) was handled by Win Percy, Hiroshi Fushida and Yojiro Terada. Sadly, both 290bhp vehicles went out with transmission maladies, the Percy machine in the third hour, and the Ikusawa car in the 11th.

Mazdaspeed returned to Le Mans the following year with two improved Type 254 models, featuring a long tail and reprofiled nose section. After problems 20 minutes from the end, car number 82 (campaigned by Allan Moffat, Yojiro Terada and Takashi Yorino) held on to take a noble 14th (sixth in the IMSA-GTX Class), but number 83 (also finished in white, and driven by Tom Walkinshaw, Peter Lovett and 'Chuck Nicholson', aka Charles Nickerson) was destined to retire in the 15th hour with engine trouble.

Yasuo Tatsutomi, one of the original Mazda Samurai, then approached the Board and convinced it that what amounted to a half-hearted assault on Le Mans was doing little for company image. He duly managed to get 1000 people assigned to the racing project and, with the coming of the Group C era, Mazdaspeed took a rather more serious approach – the 717C of 1983 vintage being the result. Mazda was rewarded with first and second in Class at Le Mans that year, but the series was quickly developed over the following years until the ultimate weapon – the 700bhp 787B – appeared in 1991.

The author was at Le Mans in 1991, and can clearly remember the winning 787B, both for its glorious exhaust note and its rather striking paint scheme. Although I was there cheering on the Jaguar team, at least witnessing the first ever win at the Sarthe for a car from the Land of the Rising Sun helped to deepen my respect for Japanese automobiles, which I had all too easily dismissed until the advent of the Lexus LS400.

Having seen his beloved rotary engine win this most demanding event, Kenichi Yamamoto cried with joy and opened a bottle of wine to celebrate. A plaque was duly unveiled at Miyoshi with Yamamoto's inscription: "Never grow tired of the challenge!"

After a change in the regulations, Mazda tackled the 1992 event with the TWR-built MXR-01, but fourth was the best it could muster; the French Peugeot team took the flag and then won again the following year. However, 1994 saw the welcome return at Le Mans of an RX-7. Driven by Mazda veteran Yojiro Terada, Pierre de Thoisy and Franck Freon, it finished 15th, sandwiched between two NSXs. The fact that the rotary-engined machine could compete on equal terms with the Honda supercar says an awful lot for its engineering integrity. However, this was to be the model's last appearance at the French track.

Racing in Britain

Due to the interior's dimensions and seating configuration, the RX-7 managed to qualify for the RAC British Saloon Car Championship (forerunner of the BTCC). Looking forward to the 1979 season, *MotorSport* observed: "Tom Walkinshaw should also cheer things up in this Class by running a Mazda RX-7 twin-rotor sports car of 2.3 litres against the [Triumph] Dolomites and some Vauxhall Magnums which are serving out their last homologation year. The Mazda weighs under 1000kg and should have some 190bhp from the Racing Services of Twickenham rotary. Walkinshaw says there is no conflict with his BMW activities as he has formed a separate company to develop and race the five-speed Mazda. The Japanese car could well mean the Dolomites give up their traditional domination of the Class, for the RX-7 also has a good aerodynamic drag factor – certainly rather better than that of an elderly four-door saloon!"

The car didn't go on sale in the UK until September 1979, but the Tom Walkinshaw racer

The combination of Win Percy's driving, Tom Walkinshaw's management and Mazda's 'rotary rocket' proved virtually unbeatable. TWR made the most of the situation, as these two pieces of advertising show.

competed nonetheless. Sure enough, Walkinshaw's RX was quick enough to trouble the three-litre Capris, let alone the cars in its 1600-2300cc category, which he duly won with ease. The overall title, however, went to Richard Longman, who was driving a 1275GT Mini in the Under-1300cc Class, with the Flying Scotsman second.

1980 and 1981 were Win Percy's years, although the Walkinshaw link remained as he was driving a TWR-prepared RX-7. Breathing through a twin-choke Weber (like the works machines), the rotary produced around 210bhp in racing trim, though as Roger Bell found out in a 1980 *Motor* article, the competition RX-7 was nowhere near as forgiving as the road car when driven close to the limit. Bell commented: "Easy? Win Percy makes it look that way, but I believe he worked a lot harder than it seemed to clinch the title."

In a letter to the author, Win wrote: "One thing I had drilled into me by TWR was never to use the engine to assist with braking but, due to the regulations, we had to use drum brakes on the rear. With this set-up, and in effect no help from the engine, it really was a huge test for the driver.

"I remember that I was limited to 9200rpm, but I always seemed to manage to go over once during a race – just the once, honest! So, on the slowing down lap, I used to slacken off my belts, reach up under the dash, trip the tachometer back and blip the throttle until the tell-tale hit exactly 9200! This worked well for some time, but then Tom found out. The tachometer back was duly covered over and a very small hole drilled in the front glass, allowing it to be reset with a long, thin screwdriver. But the ingenious driver quickly found a way around it, by hiding a piece of wire in my race suit. Sure enough, 9200rpm was always recorded after the final lap!"

Percy won his Class in ten of the 11 rounds in 1980, and can clearly remember crossing the line at Thruxton to take the BTCC title. He recalled: "Tom Walkinshaw came on the radio, and said 'Well done, Champ! Let's do it again next year!' I agreed to give it my best shot."

Win had a faster, better-handling RX-7 for 1981, and he duly won his Class in nine of the ten rounds – enough to earn him the BTCC crown yet again. Two races at Donington and Oulton Park were outright victories, beating the factory Rovers, Capris and BMWs.

Win has many fond memories of the RX-7: "In April 1981, I won a two-heat race at Zolder in Belgium. The Mazda

Win Percy's RX-7 led the BTCC pack again in 1981. This picture shows the Dorset man leading into the first bend at Donington Park. (Courtesy Win Percy)

British advertising from late-1981 celebrating Win Percy's retention of the BTCC title.

was so good to drive around such a tight, twisty circuit. I have great respect for the RE – such a smooth, deceptively powerful engine. Two wonderful years with a car I still enjoy driving today."

As well as racing Mazdas, he used to sell them, too, at one time owning a dealership in Weymouth; he was also the boss of Mazda UK's motorsport arm in 1994, heading the Xedos 6 BTCC programme. A true gentleman and a magnificent ambassador for the sport, the author considers it a great honour that Win is godfather to his son, Louis.

Other European races

An RX-7, entered as a joint venture between Mazdaspeed and TWR, won the 1981 Spa-Francorchamps 24-hour Race. This could have happened

Japanese poster outlining Mazda's high-profile competition exploits. Success would elude Mazda at the 24-hours of Daytona and Le Mans, but the RX-7 victory at Spa was well-deserved, with Tom Walkinshaw and Pierre Dieudonne taking the chequered flag.

a year earlier when Win Percy and Peter Lovett were leading their Class, until a rear wheel broke away just after the last pitstop. Percy said: "I can certainly remember the engine noise that year. There were four cars entered with megaphone exhausts – I had a headache for a week after the event!"

The rotary-engined model was also starting to feature in the top three in the highly-competitive European Touring Car Championship (ETCC) for Group 2 saloons. At the final round in the 1980 series (the Zolder three-hour event), Tom Walkinshaw and Pierre Dieudonne took third place on the podium after a sterling battle with the BMWs.

Action from Spa in 1981.

Tom Walkinshaw (with Tippet and Palmer) during the 1979 Tourist Trophy event. He retired after holding fifth place on this occasion, but revenge would be sweet ...

The 1981 Silverstone six-hour event, with Win Percy and Yojiro Terada in the Le Mans car. It was a wet race, and Win actually took the lead towards the end, but was later shunted off the track by the very Porsche he had just demoted to second! (Courtesy Win Percy)

In the following season, the RX-7 came good, and Walkinshaw (this time with 'Chuck Nicholson') managed to win the TT race at Silverstone, beating off a strong challenge from the works-backed 3.5 litre BMW coupés. A second Mazda, driven by Heinz Kunhe-Weiss and Fritz Muller, also featured in the 1981 results, with a third at Vallelunga, and a third at Zolder.

Following a change in the regulations, the RX-7's assault on the ETCC faded away after that. Walkinshaw and 'Nicholson' repeated their success in the next Tourist Trophy, but by now with a Jaguar XJ-S.

SCCA racing

In the States, the Sports Car Club of America (SCCA) races, although supposedly amateur, have proved of great importance from a publicity point of view. For this reason, manufacturers have always been keen to support the series.

The RX-7 didn't feature in the results of the SCCA Run-Offs in 1979 (or the years running up to it), nor did its main rival, the Porsche 924, for that matter, although the German company came good in the following season. At the 1981 Road Atlanta Run-Offs, Porsche again took D-Production honours, although John Hogdal took his RX-7 to the runner-up slot in the C-Production category (a Triumph TR8 won, with a Datsun 280ZX in third).

C-Production victory at last went to the Mazda marque in 1982, with Robert Reed taking the flag ahead of Morris Clement (280ZX); John Finger, another RX-7 campaigner, came home third. The same three drivers fought it out again the following year, when the cars were transferred into the newly-formed GT-2 Class. Having led from start to finish, Reed won once more, with Finger second and Clement third.

The 1984 Run-Offs saw the same familiar names heading the GT-2 results, but this time it was Clement who restored Nissan/Datsun honour, followed home by Hogdal and Reed (both still racing the rotary-engined machine with a great deal of success).

The Mazda-versus-Datsun battle continued in 1985, with John Hogdal taking the GT-2 spoils on this occasion,

Robert Reed's SCCA racer.

ahead of two 280ZXs. Meanwhile, in the *Playboy* (later Escort) Endurance series, Scott Grissom, Tom Start, Tom Mankin and Joe Estrada won the Showroom Stock A category.

Hogdal was leading the GT-2 finale in 1986, but was forced to retire. It wasn't until 1990 that an RX-7 driver took the top step on the winner's rostrum again, when Matt Mnich won the GT-2 Class for Mazda.

The RX-7's WRC record

The RX-7 made its World Rally Championship debut on the 1979 Monte Carlo Rally. Starting from Monte Carlo itself (one of nine starting points entrants could chose from that year), Hajime Nakagawa and Osamu Morikawa took car number 157 to a Group 2 Class win based on engine capacity and 73rd overall – about halfway down the field – by the time the event came to an end on 26 January.

Significant WRC appearances were then few and far between, until 1981, that is, when Rod Millen tackled the gruelling RAC Rally – the last event of the season. Although some way behind the winning ex-works Audi Quattro, he finished in a highly creditable 11th place in a TWR-entered model (number 26, registration UKL 970X).

Millen then entered the 1982 Motogard Rally of New Zealand with a Group 2 RX-7. Millen had been based in America for a long time (indeed, the Mazda had been prepared in his California workshop), but he is a Kiwi by birth, so this was something of a local rally for him. Partnered by John

1983 Swedish Rally. Danielsson/Eklind finished sixth on one of the stages, but the Mazda wasn't really suited to the event.

Bellefleur, Millen took a Class victory and fifth overall, finishing only 26 minutes behind the winning Toyota of Bjorn Waldegard.

The New Zealander also returned to Britain for the 1982 RAC Rally with the TWR-sponsored car. Bryan Harris was his co-driver on this occasion, but an accident forced them to retire after completing 48 of the 68 stages. Incidentally, 1982 saw the change from the old Group system (ie. 1 to 4 for most rally cars – Group 2 being the tuned saloons, with Group 4 being modified GTs) to the new Group A, B and N. A run of 5000 units was necessary for Group A cars, but only 200 were required for the more-specialized Group B machines; there was also a Group B Evolution category that allowed just 20 full competition models to be produced. Group N, meanwhile, was for cars in near-standard trim.

For now, the older machines were allowed to compete alongside the Group A, B and N cars, but they were not permitted to enter sanctioned events after 1983. With the birth of the Group

B supercars, the face – and pace – of rallying was changing, and changing fast.

On the 1983 RAC Rally, Chris Lord and Kevin Gormley used the same RX-7 that Millen had driven the previous two years, but engine failure towards the end of the event put paid to their chances. In the meantime, Lord had entered the 1983 British Championship with UKL, although he had a troubled season with one problem after another. He did, however, manage to take Group A honours on the Circuit of Ireland, finishing sixth overall.

Group B capers

Following Millen's performance with the RX, in May 1983, Mazda Rallye Team Europe was created to mount a serious assault on the World Rally Championship. Run by the experienced Achim Warmbold from Mazda's European headquarters in Brussels, the team's first entry on the WRC scene was the 1983 Acropolis Rally (starting at number 100, the blue and white machine carried the Swiss registration

GE 103915). Harri Toivonen finished well down the field (third in Group 2), but the Greek event was nothing more than a trial run in reality. MRTE was looking towards the 1984 season ...

The RX-7 was the first rotary-engined car to be homologated in Group B (it was actually built in basic and evolution trim), and was the most powerful of all the contemporary normally-aspirated rally cars. With the papers stamped on 1 February 1984 (reference B255), improvements in the Group B car compared to the old Group 2 machine included the use of rack-and-pinion steering, and a more powerful 2616cc version of the 13B engine.

Introduced three months later, the 990kg (2178lb) Evolution models went a stage further by having the 300bhp engine mounted slightly nearer the bulkhead to improve weight distribution, and by employing a number of lightweight plastic panels, an oil cooler in the rear wing, a rear-mounted dry sump tank and parallel rear axle links. Maximum power was produced at a heady 8200rpm, incidentally, whilst the 196lbft of torque peaked at an equally high 7500rpm.

The 1984 Acropolis Rally, which ran from 28 to 31 May, saw Mazda Rallye Team Europe enter two Group B RX-7s – one for Achim Warmbold and 'Biche' ('Biche' was the girl who was Jean-Claude Andruet's co-driver when he won the very first WRC round, the 1973 Monte Carlo Rally), and another for Ingvar Carlsson and Benny Melander. Warmbold was in car number 17 (with the Belgian registration CRJ 130) and managed to finish ninth, while Carlsson (car number 20, registration CJH 710) retired with differential problems on the first day. It is interesting to note that these were classed as works entries, and there were rumours of a four-wheel drive version to follow.

In July, the Carlsson/Melander pairing won the 1984 Polish Rally, and took second place on the Skoda Rally of Czechoslovakia a week after. These European Championship rounds were ideal preparation for the RAC Rally later that year. On the famous British WRC event, Philippe Wambergue and Michel Vial took over CRJ 130 (number 21 on the rally), but they lost a wheel on the second day and had to retire. Carlsson was again piloting CJH 710 (number 26), but, unfortunately, the rear axle gave way in sight of the finish.

On the 1985 Swedish Rally, Carlsson and Melander drove the Group B Mazda Rallye Team Europe RX-7 (registration CJH 710) to a creditable eighth; creditable because it was the top two-wheel drive car to finish the snowy event.

A couple of months later, Carlsson was out again in CJH 710, this time for the Acropolis Rally. On this occasion, he scored his – and the RX-7's – most impressive result to date on a WRC event: third place overall, behind a Peugeot 205 T16 and an Audi Sport Quattro. Moreover, Achim Warmbold and 'Biche' took another works car (CCA 771) to sixth. Although a long way off the scorching pace of the winning Peugeot, this was nevertheless a brilliant achievement.

For the 1985 RAC, MRTE invited Rod Millen over from the USA to drive the second RX-7. Paired with Bryan Rainbow in CRJ 130, Millen started at number 25 but managed to finish ninth overall. Carlsson and Melander, as usual in CJH 710, although seeded at number nine, were to finish 18

1984 Acropolis Rally. Team Manager, Achim Warmbold, on his way to ninth place in the Group B RX-7. The Carlsson/Melander sister car retired after 16 of the 47 stages (in fact, only 32 of the 104 starters managed to finish!).

seconds and one place behind the Kiwi. With these extra points, Mazda finished tenth in the World Championship, with Ingvar Carlsson 16th.

The flamboyant Marc Duez took a Group B RX-7 to second place on the Boucles de Spa in the 1985 European Championship, and Carlsson once again tackled the Skoda Rally in 1965 – he also finished second.

Rallying in America

Whilst attracting massive crowds in Europe, strangely, rallying has never had the same kind of enthusiastic following in the States. However, during 1980, Rod Millen brought the RX-7 to the attention of the growing band of rally fans in the USA. In the SCCA Championship, Millen scored no less than five wins and two second places with the RX-7, and was very unlucky not to take the title – although level on points at the end of the season, John Buffum (driving a Triumph TR8) was declared champion yet again.

Millen's main sponsor for 1981 was Tokico shock absorbers, with additional support coming from Hella and BF Goodrich. His car was beautifully-prepared as always and, at last, it was to be his year. With Bob Kraushaar as co-driver, Millen won eight of the 13 rounds to take the SCCA title; fellow RX-7 driver, John Woolf was declared runner-up, having claimed victory on the Susquehannock Trail and second place no less than three times, finishing behind Rod Millen on each occasion. Not surprisingly, Mazda took the manufacturer's crown.

The 1982 SCCA Championships saw Millen and Buffum fighting it out neck and neck once more. Millen again had Kraushaar in the seat beside him, but Buffum campaigned the mighty Audi Quattro this year. At the end of the season, Millen had won four of the 13 rounds, with Buffum taking the other nine, often with Millen in second place. John Buffum was declared champion, with 135 points to Millen's 125.

During the 1983 SCCA season, Rod Millen developed a four-wheel drive version of the RX-7. Four months' work resulted in a 626 fwd set-up being employed at the front, designed to work in conjunction with a standard RX rear. Making its debut on the Nor'wester Rally

Rod Millen in action during the SCCA Championships.

in April, the switchable transmission proved a little on the weak side, although with 300bhp on tap in a car weighing just 1050kg (2310lb), when reliable, the Mazda was more than quick enough to take victory, as it did on the Olympus and Sno-Drift rounds. However, in 1983, John Buffum and the Audi Quattro were far too strong a combination, and Millen was destined to finish second once more.

In the 1984 SCCA Championships, John Buffum again took the title in his Audi Quattro. Of the nine rounds, Buffum won five, with Millen taking three. Again, the margin was only ten points, but it was enough to prove the superiority of the German machine. This was confirmed when Millen took the RX-7 up Pike's Peak – although he recorded the second fastest time, he was beaten by the works Quattro of Michele Mouton. However, in the newly-introduced Production GT category, RX-7 driver and Millen employee, Richard Kelsey, finished ahead of the rest of the field at the end of the season.

Of the eight rounds held in 1985, Rod Millen won three, with John Buffum taking the remaining five. It was becoming a familiar situation, with Millen losing the title to Buffum once again by the narrowest of margins, although, as some consolation, manufacturer's honours went to Mazda.

Facing reality

On its few WRC appearances the RX-7 had looked and sounded great, but it was never going to be a top-line rally car. It was obvious that a lot more development work would be necessary before the Mazda could compete with the other Group B supercars and take the winner's laurels. With the 323 needing an image boost, it was time to turn to more conventional machinery.

The 1986 Monte Carlo Rally saw the debut of the lighter and eminently more suitable Group A Mazda Familia 4WD, thus bringing the RX-7's era to an end. This first event saw both works cars retire, but the little 323s had shown great promise. Their time would come.

The 323 proved to be a much better rally car than the RX-7, but the rotary-engined machine was still a powerful contender on the track.

Meanwhile, the rotary-engined car could still be spotted occasionally. On the 1986 Rally of New Zealand, Neil Allport and Rodger Freeth persisted with the Group B RX-7, and were rewarded with sixth place on the event; later in the year, Allport was declared New Zealand's National Rally Champion.

In America, Rod Millen won only

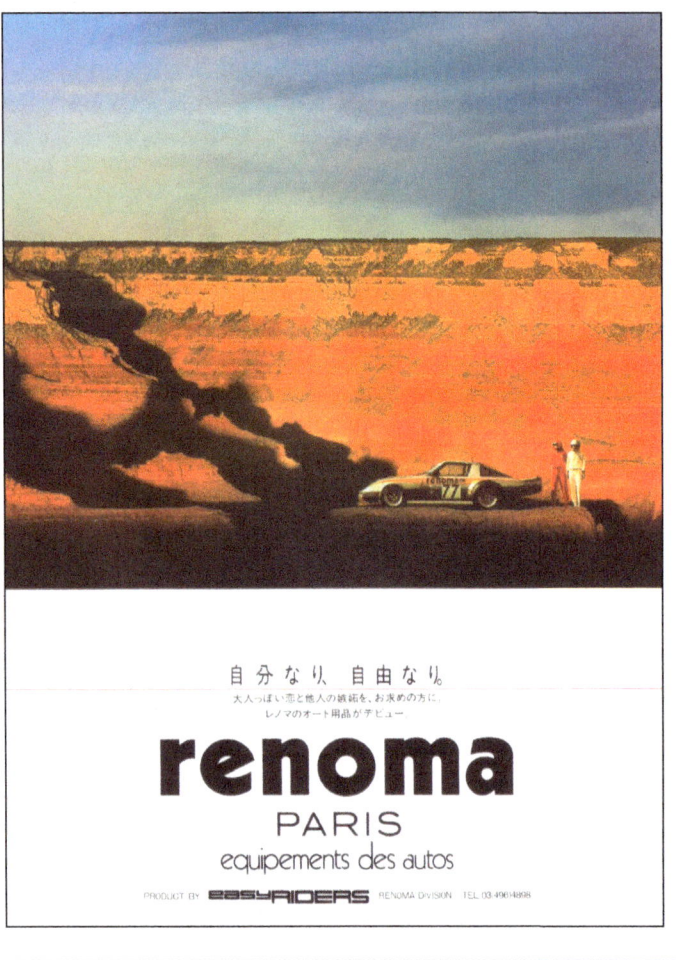

Japanese advertising from Renoma, released during the spring of 1983.

one SCCA round with his RX-7 (the Budweiser Sunriser in September); once again the title went to John Buffum. In 1987, Millen at last turned to the 323, although he continued to tackle the Pike's Peak hillclimb in the rotary-engined car. Eventually, the Millen/RX-7 combination took the flag in 1991, winning by a full minute.

Racing in Japan & Australia

In more recent years, the rotary-engined machine has competed in the All-Japan GT Championship, but, surprisingly, has made little impact on home territory beforehand, probably because Mazda was more interested in directing efforts towards American and European programmes.

1994 saw the first full year of the JGTC, and a second generation model finished fifth in GT2. In the following season, Haruhiko Matsumoto and Hironori Takeuchi took a third generation model to second place in the GT2 category. The rotary-powered machine also came fifth in GT300 (what was GT2) in 1999 and 2000. Fortunately, greater success was to be found in the Antipodes.

A wet Bathurst in 1992. The RX-7 won on its debut in the 12-hour Enduro.

On the starting grid for the 1994 James Hardie 12-hour Enduro at Bathurst. This event saw a third consecutive win for the rotary-engined machine, leading to a number of home market road cars being named after it.

When the RX-7 made its first appearance at Australia's legendary Mount Panorama Circuit in Bathurst, it was badly in need of development, and Mazda relied on the RX-3 to save face. However, the third generation RX-7 won the James Hardie 12-hour Enduro (not the Toohey's 1000, incidentally, held later in the year at the same track) on its debut in 1992, taking an easy victory ahead of a BMW M3 and Saab 9000. This success was repeated in '93 and, with Allan Horsley as Team Manager, he guided Gregg Hansford and Neil Crompton to a third victory in a row, fending off a strong Porsche challenge in the process. In recognition, Mazda used the 'Bathurst' appellation on a number of production models.

LSR attempts

Using a highly-tuned but otherwise virtually standard model (except for a lowered suspension, disc wheel trims and a rollcage), Don Sherman – a regular visitor to the Bonneville Salt Flats, but perhaps best known as a *Car & Driver* staff writer – set a new Class E/GT record of 183.90mph (294.2kph) at the end of 1978. It was the first of many LSR attempts for the RX-7 in the Utah desert.

Seven years later, another record was set, this time by Nick van Nugteren in Class E/Modified. Driving a 367bhp turbocharged RX, he was timed at a very impressive 190.98mph (305.5kph). In 1986, the Racing Beat-prepared RX-7 of Don Sherman set a new Bonneville National Speed Trial record of 238.44mph (383.7kph) in the SCTA's C/GT category. Racing Beat moved the target again in 1995, achieving 242.00mph (387.2kph) with a third generation model.

IMSA update

The 1988 GTU season was disappointing by Mazda standards, and there was little improvement in the company's fortunes in the GTO category. Although the GTU title went to Tom Kendall for the third time in a row, he was driving for Chevrolet that year, and it was the American marque which took the manufacturer's trophy. Mazda had won only two GTU races, at Daytona and Sebring.

1989 signalled something of a revival, with Mazda restoring its position as the one to beat in GTU. However, of the five wins that helped clinch the manufacturer's title, three were taken by MX-6 drivers. Roger Mandeville's GTO programme was

Don Sherman pictured at the Bonneville Salt Flats in 1978.

Pete Halsmer at speed in the new four-rotor GTO car. The defending champion came third in the 1990 season.

A Japanese advert celebrating Mazda's 100th IMSA victory.

The starting grid at San Antonio in 1990, when Pete Halsmer chalked up Mazda's 100th win in IMSA racing.

One of the IMSA GTO cars photographed at Laguna Seca in 2002. (Courtesy Ken Hoyle)

Every RX-7 Comes With The Power To Make History.

Rotary power. It's made the RX-7 the winningest car in IMSA history with over 100 victories. And most recently, it has made Mazda the first Japanese manufacturer to win the world's most prestigious car race – the 24 hours of Le Mans.

With only three primary moving parts, the rotary engine offers unmatched reliability. So astonishingly efficient, it produces race-winning horsepower from an engine half the size and displacement of the competition. So compact, it changes the rules of automotive design. Allowing us to build cars lighter, better balanced and with better handling.

Best of all, unlike most of the exotic technology you'll find at race tracks from here to Le Mans, rotary power is available to you. Just tell your Mazda Dealer you want to test-drive an RX-7. Because what good is a car that can make history unless it can be part of your future?

For a free brochure on the RX-7, call toll free 1-800-345-3799.

mazda
IT JUST FEELS RIGHT.

still not bringing the desired results, and was abandoned halfway through the season, while the other main GTO contender, CCR Racing, had already moved across to Nissan.

For 1990, it was announced that Mazda was going to withdraw from the Camel Lights series and support two four-rotor RX-7s in the GTO category – one for Jim Downing, the other for defending champion, Pete Halsmer. The reason was simple – it was much easier to relate to an RX-7 than a Group C-style racer, and was therefore of more benefit from a marketing point of view.

Lee Dykstra designed the new GTO model, which was powered by the 600bhp 13J RE. Dykstra had almost 30 years' experience in designing and building successful competition cars, so was perhaps the ideal man for the job. Halsmer won at Topeka, Mid-Ohio and San Antonio (the latter being the RX-7's 100th IMSA victory), giving him third in the 1990 Championship.

The only GTU win for the RX was at Daytona, a situation repeated in 1991 when the rotary-engined machines took the first three places. Although the RX-7 was at last starting to lose its grip

American advertising from the end of 1991. Although a regular winner in the GTU category, Mazda took its first GTO title that year. However, for 1992, with confidence at an all-time high following this, and the win at Le Mans, the company decided to concentrate its efforts on a GTP programme.

The RX-792P, designed to give Mazda the GTP title. Sadly, it didn't. However, Mazda's contribution to motorsport has been wide-ranging and highly-successful. The inset picture of the 787B is testament to this.

on the IMSA GTU series, it had now taken Class honours at Florida's 24-hour classic for the tenth consecutive year.

Meanwhile, with Pete Halsmer and Price Cobb campaigning the two works-supported cars in the GTO category, Mazda's perseverance paid off. Although disappointing at Daytona, wins came in New Orleans, Laguna Seca, West Palm Beach, Miami and Mosport – enough to give the Hiroshima firm the manufacturer's title for the first time, and Halsmer his second GTO Championship.

The RX-7s were retired at the end of the 1991 season, with Mazda concentrating future efforts on the GTP series. As Mazda Motorsports boss, Dick St Yves, said at the time: "Mazda will use all of the experience we've gathered over these 12 years of motorsports success in North America as a stepping stone for our involvement in the pinnacle of sports car racing. It will be our biggest challenge yet."

Halsmer and Cobb duly gave the RX-792P GTP car its debut at the Daytona 24-hour race, but while that failed to impress, Dick Greer, Al Bacon, Peter Uria and Mike Mees combined to take GTU honours, thus repeating their success of the previous year. In 1993, they did it again, making three consecutive wins at Daytona for this dream team. By 1994, however, Porsche had arrived on the GTU scene ...

In the meantime, Peter Farrell campaigned the RX-7 in the Bridgestone Supercar Championships from 1992, with Willy Lewis at the wheel of a sister car. Mazda was allowed to reduce the weight of the rotary-powered machine to make it more competitive with the Corvettes and 911 Turbos, but the series turned out to be a Porsche

benefit. Farrell also did a few races in Europe, and went on to develop the PFS RX-7 for the road.

SCCA news

Michael Lewis took the GT-3 title in the 1992 Run-Offs, after leading the race for only one lap. But it was the one that mattered – the one before the flag! In 1994, when the finals moved to Mid-Ohio (they had been held at Road Atlanta since 1970), Duane Ablamis regained GT-3 honours for the RX-7 after briefly losing them to a Honda CRX driver. 1995 was disappointing for Mazda fans, but Michael Lewis won the GT-3 category in his RX-7 in 1996 and 1997.

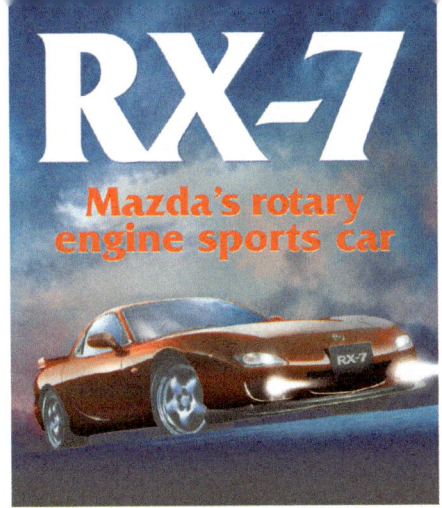

7

The twilight years

By 1998, James E. Miller had become the latest President of the MMC. Thankfully, he realized how important the RX-7 was to the company's image, and on December 15 that year a number of minor changes were announced that would enable the rotary-powered model to continue into the 21st Century. These revisions could well represent the last major modifications for the RX-7 as we know it.

Presumably in an attempt to confuse historians, the model grades were

The Type RB, with and without a rear spoiler, pictured at the end of 1998. The rear spoiler came as part of the S-Package, available on the five-speed RB, but not on the automatic (the third Type RB variant).

Interior of the Type RB with S-Package.

Dashboard and controls of the Type RS. All models came with the same steering wheel, and the usually white markings on the gauges glowed green on black when the lights were switched on. Note the six o'clock start position on the tachometer.

The 280bhp RE fitted to the Type R and RS. Kijima-san recently told the author's wife, Miho, that it would have been easy to extract more power from the rotary, but it was not possible due to Japanese regulations that restricted the maximum figure for showroom models.

changed once more. In effect, the old Type RS became the new Type R, whilst the RZ became the latest Type RS; the Touring X was dropped completely, as was the 'Bathurst' version, with the new Type RB covering these, and its original specification, by coming in three variations. However, in a return to 1991, all cars became 2+2s.

The big news for enthusiasts was the increase in engine output for the Type R and RS. Subtle refinements in the turbocharger – as well as in the exhaust, lubrication and cooling systems – released a few more horses, taking the total to 280bhp at 6500rpm. Maximum torque output was also

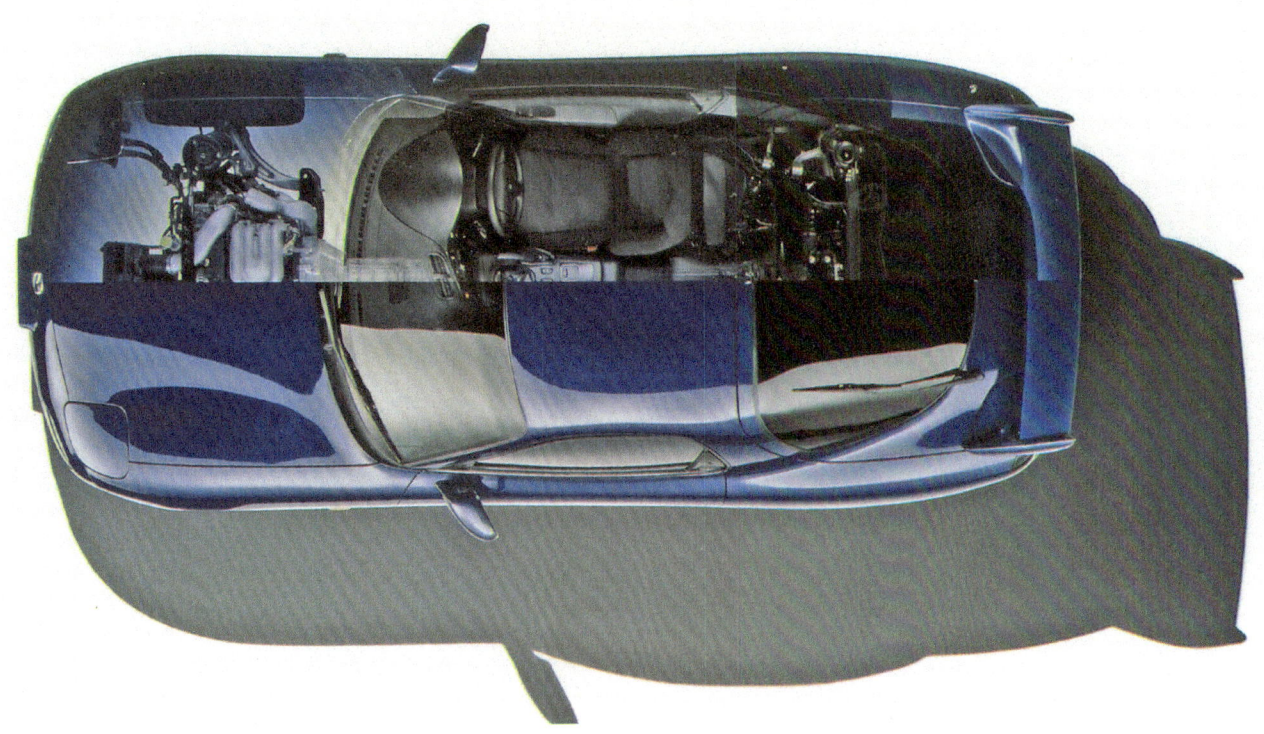

An interesting catalogue shot of the Type RS.

Cover from the 1999 catalogue. Top designer Koichi Hayashi was in charge of the 1999 MY facelift. An awful lot of work was done in the wind tunnel, trying to get a nice balance between the styling cues required to give the car its marque identity (the five-sided air intake), leading-edge aerodynamics and function.

The 'Touring Kit A-Spec' model by Mazdaspeed, seen at the 1999 Tokyo Auto Salon, an event for factory-approved and aftermarket tuners.

An advert that appeared in Japanese newspapers at the time of the 1999 Tokyo Show, featuring James Miller and the RX-EVOLV.

clockwise to allow the pointer to start at the six o'clock position, and the oil pressure gauge was replaced by a boost gauge.

To round off the changes, the 1999 RX-7 was given a minor facelift at the front end (comprising new-style signal light clusters and more aggressive-looking air intakes) and, for the R and RS, a new, purposeful rear spoiler with adjustable pitch (the original 1992 spoiler was still available as an option, by the way, but this fact was not widely publicized, probably because it was 25,000 yen cheaper than the latest version). A fresh range of colours now included Innocent Blue Mica, Highlight Silver Metallic, Brilliant Black, Chaste White and Vintage Red.

The 1999 model year

When sales of the new line-up started on 21 January 1999, prices ranged from 2,898,000 to 3,778,000 yen. The five-speed Type RB was the cheapest in the line, although the S-Package (comprising rear spoiler, ZR-rated tyres greater, now quoted at 231lbft at 5000rpm.

Further modifications to the suspension, centred around new front bump stops made of urethane and a different front anti-roll bar, enhanced the car's handling, while at the same time making the ride smoother.

Dual SRS airbags became standard, the driver's side one contained in a new leather-rimmed, three-spoke Nardi steering wheel. The seats on all but the RS (which was trimmed in Lux suede) acquired the same highly-textured fabric, the tachometer was moved anti-

The RX-EVOLV at the 1999 Tokyo Show. It eventually formed the basis for the all-new RX-8.

The new RX-7? Many of us thought so ...

The 280bhp Renesis rotary engine. The key to the future of the RE.

mounted on the familiar 8J five-spoke rims instead of the standard 225/50 VR16 items, a rear strut bar, foglamps, suede seats and a stereo radio/cassette) added 230,000 yen; the 265bhp RB could also be bought with automatic transmission, but the S-Package was not available on this four-speed model which also had 10bhp less power.

The Type R started at 3,470,000 yen, with the basic Type RS listed at 308,000 yen more. As noted earlier, both were powered by the 280bhp version of the 13B-REW engine (linked to a five-speed manual gearbox), but the RS came with a 17-inch wheel and tyre combination instead of 16-inch, albeit a similar-looking design. Both had front and rear strut bars, and a dark tint on the rear glass, but only the RS came with Bilstein shock absorbers, the larger brakes and foglamps; the Bose Premium Audio System option was available for the R and RS, priced at 200,000 yen.

Car Graphic tried the Type RS in early 1999, and observed that the 280bhp engine was exceptionally smooth with sharp response. The magazine felt, however, that the unit was not quite as torquey as before. Both 280bhp machines had twin-oil coolers as standard, incidentally.

Sam Mitani of *Road & Track* fame visited Japan, and tried an RX-7 whilst there. He said: "The top-of-the-line RX-7's twin-turbocharged two-rotor engine now pumps out a head-snapping 280bhp at 6500rpm (up from 255 on the last US model). And does this extra power ever make itself felt around a twisty road course!

"Drop the clutch at about 3500rpm and the RX-7 jumps off the line. Keep your right foot planted and, amid the hum of the spinning rotors, the car dramatically surges forward. Snap the shift lever to second gear and replay the scene. By the time you hit fourth, you're past the century mark.

"The extra power really makes its presence known during the exit of a turn. If you apply throttle abruptly, you'll leave the corner sideways. Turn-in response is immediate and crisp, the car displaying rock-solid stability with minimal body roll. The new RX-7 doesn't feel as firm as the last US version (notably on bumpy surfaces where ride quality is actually bearable), but to me it remains one of the best-handling cars in the world.

"After my test drive, for some reason I regretted driving the car. Why? Because I realized how much we all miss this exciting sports car. So allow me to get on my knees and say, 'I'm begging you, RX-7 ... come back to the US and let's give it another shot ... please.'"

At the same time as the new range was launched, Mazdaspeed announced the 'Touring Kit A-Spec' for the latest model. The main features included an aero-kit to make the car resemble a JGTC racer, which included a lowered front airdam, side skirts, a rear valance and a wacky rear spoiler. There was also a selective limited-slip differential, ultra-lightweight 18-inch five-spoke alloys, new brake pads, and a number of suspension revisions.

The 1999 Tokyo Show

By 1999, after six fiscal years of recording an operational loss, Mazda was once again profitable. At the Tokyo Show that year the RX-EVOLV concept car was displayed, powered by a new-generation Renesis rotary power unit. A joint press release issued by the Ford Motor Company stated: "The new Mazda RX-EVOLV concept sports car is being unveiled for the first time at a major international motor show on its home ground. Powered by a new rotary engine, the RX-EVOLV presents new technologies which put the message 'new ideas that stir your emotions' into action. RX-EVOLV is a sports car with an interior roomy enough for four adults to enjoy spirited driving without any compromise in the same body size as the RX-7. It extends Mazda's reputation for consistently building sports cars with the essence of fun."

Based on the MSP-RE first seen in the RX-01, the normally-aspirated, 280bhp, Renesis multi-sideport power unit (654cc x 2) developed 166lbft of torque at 8000rpm, and drove the rear wheels through a six-speed semi-automatic transmission. Maximum power was developed at a heady 9000rpm (the red-line was marked at 10,000rpm, incidentally). Despite this high level of performance, Mazda was confident that this latest incarnation of the Wankel would reduce fuel consumption by as much as 40% and be able to meet all regulations for the foreseeable future.

The RX-EVOLV was full of new ideas, such as a double-clamshell bonnet, front doors that moved forward before opening fully to give better access, with small 'suicide' doors for the rear (the pillarless design aiding entry and egress), micro-HID headlights, and an ID Access Card that even stored data on the driver's level of skill at the wheel, cutting engine power to 240bhp for the inexperienced.

Five-spoke, 20-inch magnesium alloys were employed. Lurking behind them were truly massive brakes, with six-pot calipers up front, and four-pot calipers for the rear; anti-lock braking, Dynamic Stability Control (DSC), and the so-called Active Cornering Brake (ACB) systems were built-in features.

The four-seater had a 2720mm (107.1in) wheelbase and an overall length of 4285mm (168.7in); height and width were 1350 and 1760mm (53.1 and 69.3in), respectively. It weighed in at just 1250kg (2750lb) which, combined with up to 280bhp, promised an excellent turn of speed.

The RX-7 was not forgotten at the Tokyo Show, however. This example was displayed alongside a red MX-5, both managing to attract a lot attention after the event opened to the public (this picture was taken on press day).

Fascia of the 2001 model year RX-7 (this is the Type RS), with its new gauges and steering wheel. The white dials are extremely effective, especially at night when they become dark and the calibrations glow bright red.

Below left: Cover of the special brochure produced for the limited edition Type RZ. It also appeared in national advertising (usually in motoring or men's magazines), which represents an awful lot of investment for just 175 models.

Another view of the Type RZ.

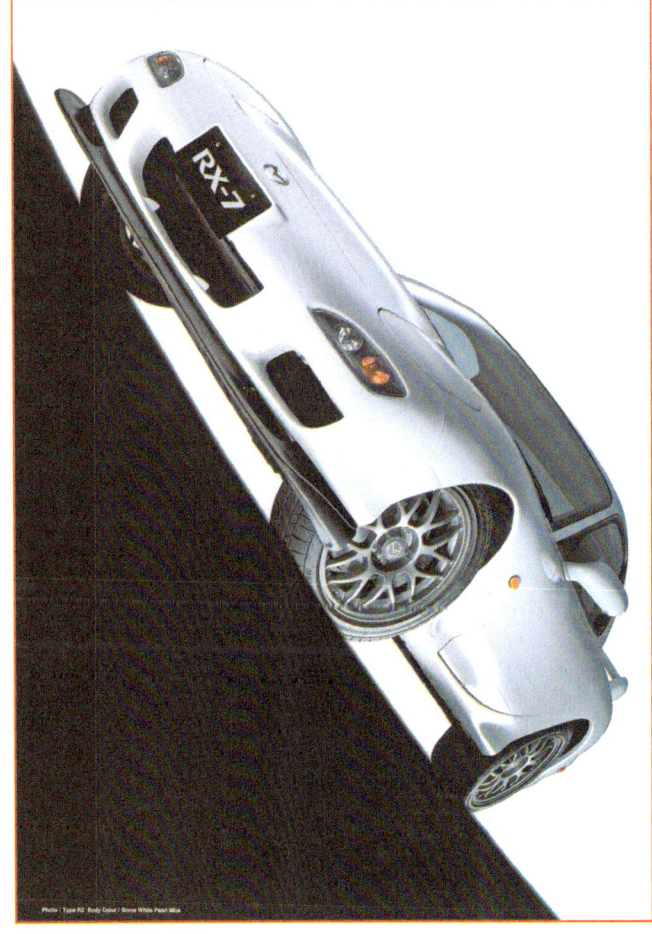

The author's five-speed RB S-Package model – dating from March 2002, it is one of the last built. There was supposed to have been a manual version of the Spirit R-Type RB, with its slightly more supple ride, but the grade was scrapped, hence the last-minute decision to go for this car instead.

A page from the October 2000 catalogue showing the heritage behind the RX-7. The car on the left is one of the latest Type RS models, seen here with the optional 17-inch BBS alloy wheels.

Entering the new millennium

Even as far back as 1992, people were predicting the end of the RX-7. That the model made it into the new millennium proves Mazda's faith in the RE, and determination to keep it in production.

Not surprisingly, given the recent changes, prices and grades were carried over for the 2000 model year. However, for the 2001 season, Mazda couldn't resist the chance to bring the car bang up-to-date, and introduce another limited edition version.

The 2001 model year was announced on 18 October 2000. Further refinements in the steering, suspension and brakes (the ABS now featured an electronically-controlled braking distribution, or EBD, system) were the main features, but also a clutch interlock mechanism was added (meaning the driver couldn't start the car without depressing the clutch first), and the former side-impact bars were joined by an additional one, mounted lower down.

A new knit rubber fabric was introduced for all models except the Type R and the cheapest RB (although the bolsters were finished in Lux suede), while the gauges – like on the latest MX-5 – were given black-on-white markings that glowed red when

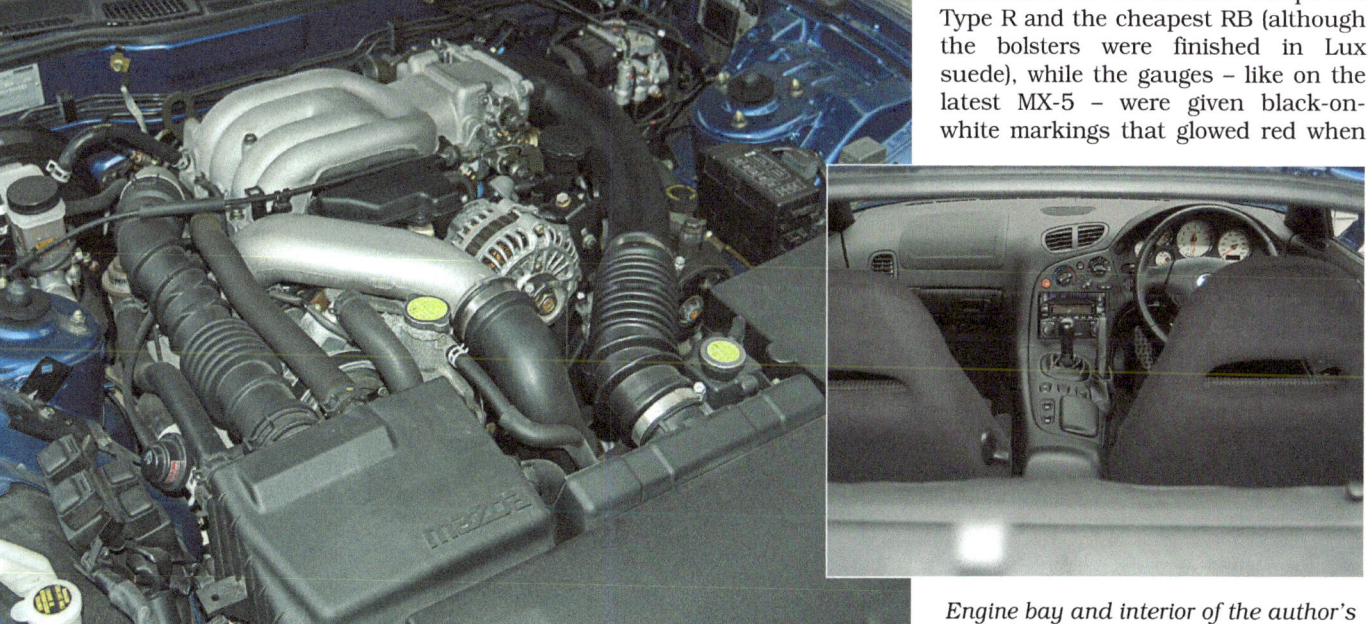

Engine bay and interior of the author's RX-7.

193

A Bathurst R in Sunburst Yellow, seen here as part of the 2001 Tokyo Show press preview. The rather unusual monorail design may give a clue to the location – Tokyo Bay NK Hall on the Tokyo Disneyland site.

The Mazdaspeed A-Spec model at the 2001 Tokyo Show, although it was superseded by the R-Spec a few months later.

THE ROTARY SPORTS TypeR BATHURST

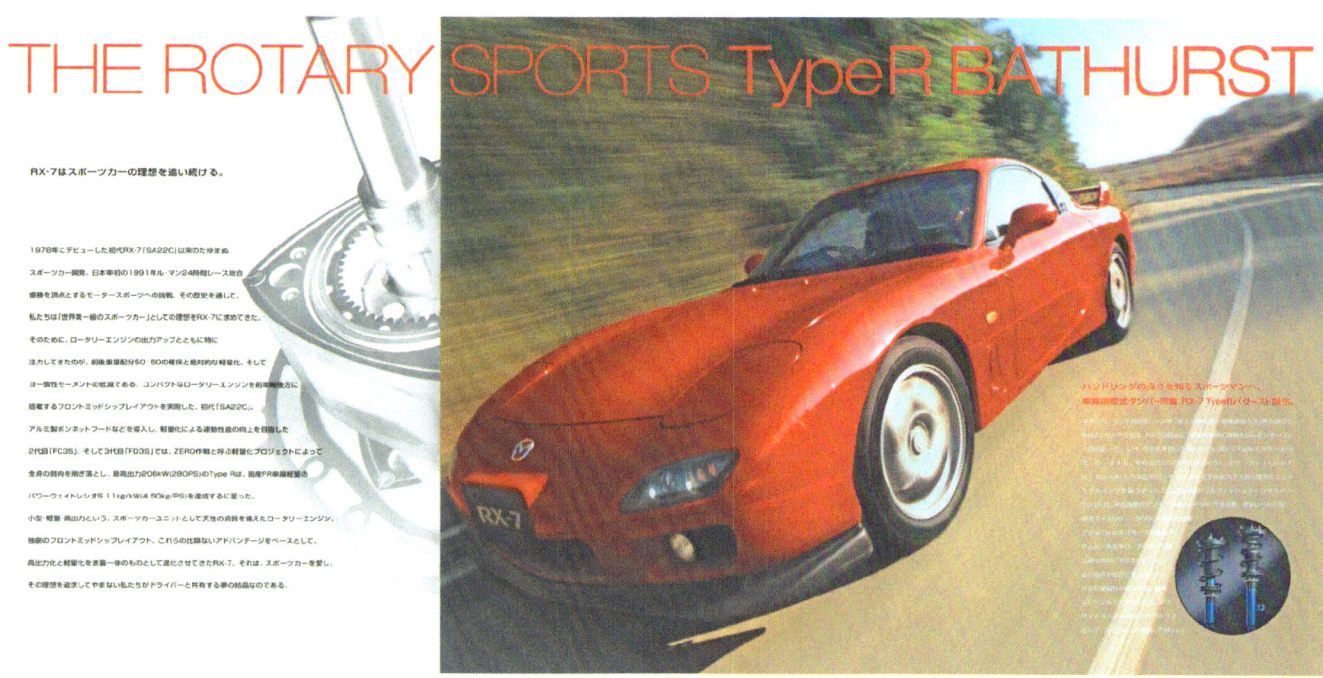

Promotional material for the Type R Bathurst, launched at the end of 2001.

the lights were switched on, along with chrome trim rings.

The Nardi steering wheel was of a new, more elegant design, and a five-speaker stereo radio returned as standard, a CD being added on the RS, the RB with S-Package, and the automatic model; the modular system allowed a cassette or MD player to be fitted quite easily. Optional equipment encompassed such items as mudflaps, side skirts, the rear spoiler, foglights, and a titanium gearknob, handbrake grip and pedal set.

Colour schemes now included Innocent Blue Mica, Vintage Red, Brilliant Black, Pure White and Sunlight Silver Metallic, the last two being new shades; trim was finished in a dark grey. With the same grades as before, prices ranged from 2,948,000 to 3,848,000 yen.

At the same time, the Type RZ appellation made a welcome return, though only 175 of the two-seaters were made available, priced at 3,998,000 yen apiece. Finished in a unique Snow White Pearl Mica colour with contrasting red Recaro bucket seats, a nice touch was the red stitching on the Nardi wheel and gearshift. It featured the same engine specifications, gearing, Bilstein shock absorbers and uprated braking system as the Type RS, but came with dark grey 8J x 17 BBS alloys up front (shod with 235/45 ZR-rated Bridgestone Potenzas) and 8.5J items at the rear, with 255/40 rubber; at 1270kg (2794lb), it was 10kg (22lb) lighter than the RS. Incidentally, the BBS alloys were available as an option on the Type RS, but finished in silver.

The RX-EVOLV provided the basis for the RX-8 prototype displayed at the 2001 Detroit Show. The body, designed by Shigeo Hirata under the direction of Yoichi Sato, carried over the leading features from the RX-EVOLV, such as the pillarless side frame and novel door arrangement, as well as the basic profile, although detailing was quite different. The interior, too, was toned down to something a little closer to a production model.

Mechanical specifications had been revised, but perhaps not by as much as most industry watchers had predicted. The Renesis engine (still with a 654cc x 2 capacity), developed a healthy 250bhp at 8500rpm, with 159lbft of torque being produced 1000rpm lower down the rev-range. Power was delivered to the rear wheels via a six-speed gearbox that allowed either manual or automatic changes. Like the RX-7 and MX-5, the RX-8 employed a Power Plant Frame (PPF) to enhance drivetrain smoothness and rigidity.

The wheel sizes were taken down to 19-inches, the five-spoke alloys being shod with 225/50 ZR rubber up front, and 245/45 at the back. Four-wheel ABS with DSC was retained, along with the enormous brake discs, with six-piston calipers at the front and four-pot items at the rear. Suspension was via double-wishbones all-round, and the power-assisted rack-and-pinion steering was electronically controlled.

Interestingly, Nissan displayed its new Z-car at the same event, helping to generate some fresh interest in sporting machinery. The RX-8 was not a new 7, but a completely new concept using rotary power, and one that could be marketed in all corners of the world. This was an important factor, as the 7 had long since disappeared from all but the home market.

At least the RX-7 was still alive in Japan, and, at the end of August 2001, Mazda announced a 500-off limited edition model – the Bathurst R. Based on the Type R, with its excellent power-to-weight ratio, it featured adjustable dampers, and carbonfibre-

The privately-run RE-Amemiya racing RX-7 that has consistently shocked some of the works cars in the JGTC. This picture was taken at the 2002 Tokyo Auto Salon.

style handbrake and gearlever, plus a number of cockpit trim pieces (including the dash centre panel, centre console, power window switch surround and storage compartment cover on the driver's side), in the same material to add to the sporty feel inside. Available in Pure White, Innocent Blue Mica and Sunburst Yellow (the latter unique to the limited edition model), and sporting custom decals, it was priced at 3,398,000 yen.

The 2002 model year range was the same as that for the 2001 season, the only difference being that the computer controlling the ABS system now had a 16-bit processor rather than the original 8-bit one. However, on 10 December 2001, the Type R Bathurst joined the existing line-up as a catalogue model, becoming available in the same five coachwork colours (namely Innocent Blue Mica, Pure White, Brilliant Black, Vintage Red and Sunlight Silver Metallic). Based on the Type R, it added foglights and adjustable shock absorbers to the spec list, and sold for the same price as the limited edition version launched four months earlier.

Continued on p201

The Mazdaspeed R-Spec Touring Kit developed by Hirotaka Tachibana and his team. The third generation RX-7 was the first RJC 'Car of the Year'. Amazingly, it received another award from the Japanese NPO ten years later for this factory-tuned variant. The author was lucky enough to ride alongside Takao Kijima on the RJC test day.

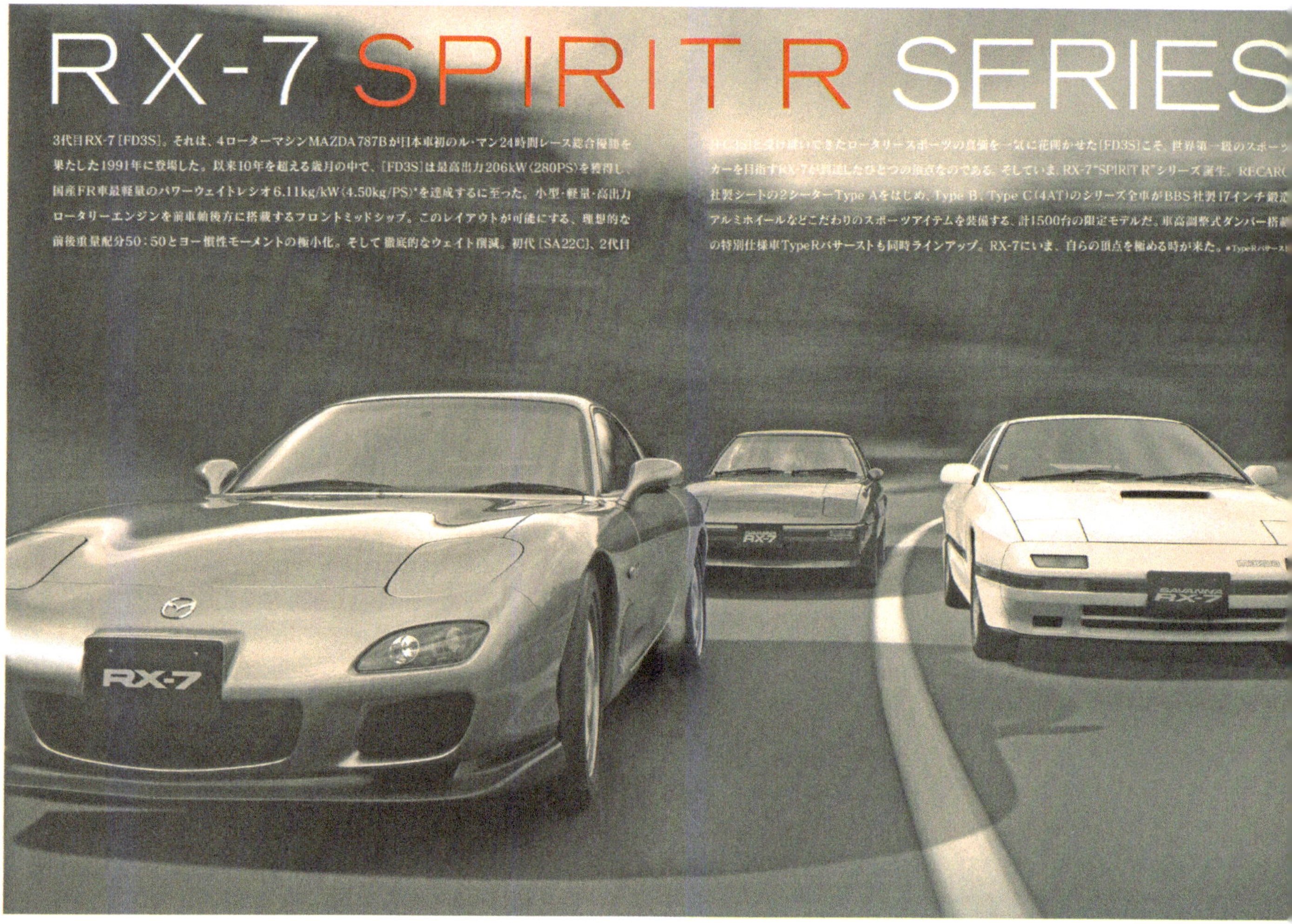

RX-7 SPIRIT R SERIES

3代目RX-7[FD3S]。それは、4ローターマシンMAZDA787Bが日本車初のル・マン24時間レース総合優勝を果たした1991年に登場した。以来10年を超える歳月の中で、[FD3S]は最高出力206kW(280PS)を獲得し、国産FR車最軽量のパワーウェイトレシオ6.11kg/kW(4.50kg/PS)*を達成するに至った。小型・軽量・高出力ロータリーエンジンを前車軸後方に搭載するフロントミッドシップ。このレイアウトが可能にする、理想的な前後重量配分50:50とヨー慣性モーメントの極小化。そして徹底的なウェイト低減。初代[SA22C]、2代目[FC3S]と受け継いできたロータリースポーツの真髄を一気に花開かせた[FD3S]こそ、世界第一級のスポーツカーを目指すRX-7が到達したひとつの頂点なのである。そしていま、RX-7"SPIRIT R"シリーズ誕生。RECARO社製シートの2シーターType Aをはじめ、Type B、Type C(4AT)のシリーズ全車がBBS社製17インチ鍛造アルミホイールなどこだわりのスポーツアイテムを装備する、計1500台の限定モデルだ。車高調整式ダンパー搭載の特別仕様車TypeRバサーストも同時ラインアップ。RX-7にいま、自らの頂点を極める時が来た。●TypeRバサースト

RX-7。それは、誰もが忘れられない、決して絶えることのない、スポーツカー。

Selected pages from the final RX-7 catalogue.

The last shipment of RX-7s at Chiba Port, the site of Mazda's PDI centre for the Kanto Bay area. Five Spirit Rs and a Type R Bathurst model can be seen in this shot, taken by the author in June 2002.

The last batch of RX-7s to go through the Chiba PDI centre, where the cars are checked over prior to shipment to the dealerships of Tokyo and the surrounding area.

One of the very last RX-7s, photographed by the author at an Enfini Chiba dealership in the summer of 2003. Initial sales were very brisk, but the last handful of cars (a total of 3903 were built in 2002), took some time to clear.

The end of a glorious era

In March 2002, several grades were dropped completely from the line-up, including the Type R, the Type RB S-Package, and the regular manual RB – the others were replaced by the Spirit R series in April. While the Spirit R Type A was a unique flagship model, the Spirit R Type B superseded the RS grade, and the Type C took the place of the automatic RB; the 3,398,000 yen Type R Bathurst was the only model to continue unchanged.

According to Kijima-san, the original idea was to build 700 Spirit R (or Final Version) models, but the figure was soon increased to 1000 units, and ultimately upped to 1500. The first one left the line in early April 2002 (for sales to start on 22 April), with the final car rolling out of Hiroshima four months later.

So what was the Spirit R? As already noted, there were three grades. All three models were equipped with various common interior and exterior features, such as BBS 17-inch alloy wheels, red brake calipers and front strut brace, 'Spirit R' badging on the front wings and tachometer, red stitching on the Nardi leather steering wheel, gearknob/gaiter (on manual cars, at least) and handbrake lever, and interior panels surrounding the driver finished with a special soft coating. In addition, each variant had a number of unique features.

The Type A was a 280bhp two-seater with a five-speed manual transmission and Recaro bucket seats. These lightweight seats were approximately 10kg (22lb) lighter than the regular pair, and came with a red cloth face and a natural finish on the shell. Braking was uprated by the use of drilled discs and high-performance stainless mesh brake hoses, and Bilstein shock absorbers were employed to enhance handling. The alloy wheels were finished in gunmetal grey on the Type A (silver on the Type B and Type C).

The Type B was a 280bhp 2+2 with a five-speed gearbox. Like the Type A, it was priced at 3,998,000 yen, and came with the uprated brakes and Bilstein dampers. All four seats were trimmed in red leather.

The Type C was another 2+2, but this time with the 255bhp engine matched up to a four-speed automatic transmission. Listed at 3,398,000 yen, it had standard brakes and suspension, but the BBS alloys and red leather seats of the Type B.

Body colours included Titanium Grey Metallic (an exclusive shade for the Spirit R series, as the Bathurst continued with Sunlight Silver Metallic as its fifth coachwork colour option), Innocent Blue Mica, Pure White, Brilliant Black and Vintage Red. It should be noted that Spirit R floormats (optional) had red edging rather than the traditional black.

RX-8 update

A final RX-8 prototype was displayed at the 2001 Tokyo Show. Shortly after, Mark Fields revealed it would go into production at the end of 2002, or early 2003 at the latest. Sure enough, just as the last RX-7s were disappearing from the showrooms, the RX-8 was launched on the home market in April 2003. Initial sales have been brisk, with prices ranging from 2,400,000 yen for the base model to 2,750,000 yen for the Type S or Type E.

Since then, the RX-8 has been launched in all the world's major markets, and it's fair to say it has been very well received. The Renesis engine was voted the 'International Engine of the Year', and the car it powers has already picked up numerous awards.

My initial mistake was to judge this latest rotary rocket as a replacement

Mark Fields (seen here with an RX-8 styling model), was Mazda's President at the time of the RX-8 announcement, although Lewis Booth had taken his place by the time the vehicle made it into the world's dealerships. Recently, Booth returned to Ford Europe, leaving Hisakazu Imaki in charge of the Hiroshima company.

for the 7. This is wrong. It should be viewed in the same way as the Jaguar XJ-S is, which superseded the legendary E-type – a fine car in its own right. Jaguar later brought back a more direct replacement for the XKE in the form of the XK8. One can only hope the same thing will happen at Mazda one day, and we will have a true successor for the RX-7 mantle.

It is sad to see the end of the RX-7 – a car that can bring a smile to the face of even the most demanding and enthusiastic of drivers. The author has a video of some of the top Japanese racers putting the 280bhp model through its paces, and not one of them failed to be impressed by the model's effortless turn of speed (a reason why a number of police forces use them for highway patrol), and handling poise. Few machines can deliver such sensory delights as an RX-7. The term 'Pure Sports' may as well have been invented for the last of the RX-7s. Without doubt, it will be a hard act to follow ...

Compared to the RX-EVOLV, the bonnet and lighting arrangements on the RX-8 were simplified, with the air intakes given the now-familiar, five-pointed Mazda styling signature.

The pillarless design makes a big difference to access for rear seat passengers, and also allows proper accommodation. Luggage space has not been forgotten either, making this a far more practical car than the RX-7.

Mazdaspeed displayed this RX-7 prototype with aluminium panels at the 2003 Tokyo Auto Salon. The striking paintwork certainly attracted attention, but, more importantly, the lightweight panels would be ideal in the years to come when restoration work is needed on the earlier FD models.

The final batch of three cars coming down the line.

Afterword by Takao Kijima

It is sad to reflect that after almost a quarter of a century of RX-7 production, it is no longer possible to see one of these legendary sports cars on the line at Hiroshima. I still have a strong desire to introduce a new generation RX-7, but, for the time being, all we can do is look back at the magnificent era of rotary-engined vehicles covered in this book.

When I joined Mazda in 1967, the rotary engine was still fairly new. Ten years later, despite its undoubted advantages, we all started to wonder if the RE would survive. Fortunately, when the RX-7 came along, the rotary was presented in such a wonderful package, the future of the RE was secured.

Nearly half a million people bought the first generation RX-7 before the second generation was introduced in 1985. I was heavily involved with the suspension on the new car, which was altogether faster and more luxurious. There was also a cabriolet version, but it was the lightweight Anfini series that probably signalled the way forward.

With the MX-5 LWS proving a great success, it was decided to make the third generation RX-7 into a true supercar. No expense was spared in producing a vehicle that could compete on equal terms with the world's best, and, launched in 1991 (the year in which Mazda won at Le Mans), it delighted motoring journalists and enthusiasts everywhere.

I became the RX-7 chief in 1992. Unfortunately, strict legislation killed off the definitive 'rotary rocket' in most countries in the mid-1990s, although it continued to be built for the home market until August 2002, by which time a total of 811,634 RX-7s had been sold.

The RX-7 will always have a special place in my heart, as I'm sure it does for many people. This book records every development relating to the RX-7 from its inception to the final 'Spirit R' model leaving the line, and is a fitting tribute to a wonderful car.

The last RX-7 built. The end of an era ...

The RX-7 of the future? The beautiful Mazda Senku on display at the 2005 Tokyo show.

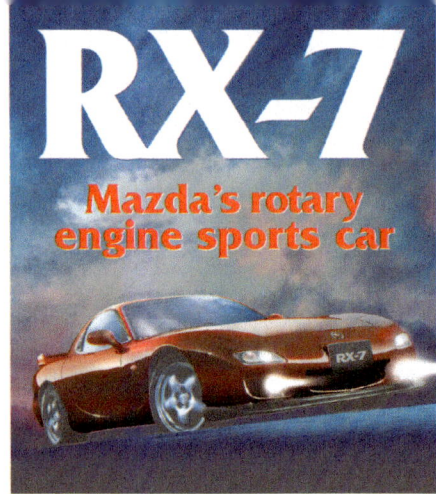

Appendix 1
RX-7 buyer's guide

Buying a used classic has never been easy. Even if the RX-7 you are considering looks like a bargain, it's still wise to be careful as genuine spares are relatively expensive. A lick of paint and a quick valet can give the impression of a pristine car, but it's the vehicle's mechanical condition that matters first and foremost. Panelwork isn't cheap either, so you need to know what's under that shiny top coat. A high asking price is unfortunately no guarantee, as most classic car owners have an inflated idea of what their prized possession is worth.

The advice, as always, is buy the best example you can afford, as it will save money in the long run. Join a Mazda club, and enlist members' help to make sure the car is good value before you part with any cash. Spending on club membership is an investment which will pay dividends in the long run – the chance to speak to fellow owners who've had similar problems, the route to cheaper spares, and a must nowadays for a lot of agreed value, classic car insurance policies.

Following are a few thoughts and some brief pointers on what to look for when buying an RX-7, with the bias being towards earlier cars which, after all, are the ones most likely to require attention.

Engine & transmission

Oil leaks from the front and rear crankshaft seals are not unknown, but worn rotor tip seals are by far the biggest bugbear, causing poor starting (the engine should start immediately), a lack of power and very heavy fuel consumption. Although the seals themselves are not particularly expensive, remember that they need fitting, and that's definitely a job for a specialist.

A good clue to the condition of an engine is to check on the nearside by the 'Mazda' insignia on the casting. Oil there points to a worn O-ring on the rotor housing. Incidentally, a puff of white smoke on start-up is not necessarily a problem as long as it clears straight away.

Water pump or viscous fan failure can also mean a major headache – serious overheating will doubtless result in a new engine being required. Also, check for constant water vapour from the exhaust, as this points to a broken seal between the cooling ports and the combustion chamber, which will ultimately cause the unit to overheat. The cooling system should always be kept topped up with a good quality anti-freeze.

Also be aware of problems with the unions used on the oil cooler on pre-1984 cars. They can crack, leading to a loss of lubricant and, on the Wankel unit, a useful coolant, as the oil actually does as much as 35% of the engine cooling. The oil should therefore be checked and changed on a regular basis to ensure its effectiveness.

Compression testing on the rotary engine is probably best left to the professionals, but there should be a minimum of 75psi, and ideally a reading of over 85. As for the oil pressure, look for around 60psi at 4000rpm once the powerplant has warmed through. Power delivery should be smooth throughout the rev-range, with no hesitation or obvious flat-spots.

Later REs, although highly-stressed in comparison to earlier units, should prove no less reliable if well maintained, regardless of whether they are turbocharged or not. Remember, though, turbochargers can be hideously expensive to replace or refurbish.

If the engine has been replaced, is it from the same country as the original? Specifications do change from market to market, and this could cause problems when getting spares in the future. In addition, there is no guarantee what mileage it has covered. Service intervals on early models were originally listed at 6250 miles (10,000km) for an oil change, and 12,500 (20,000km) for the filter and tune-up; there was no recommendation on chassis lubrication.

Genuine exhaust systems last well, but are notoriously expensive if they need replacing due to the emissions equipment fitted as standard. Cheaper alternatives are available, though it would probably pay dividends to invest in a stainless steel item if you intend to keep the car. The RX-7 has attracted the attention of many tuning concerns (in addition to Mazdaspeed, that is), so this could provide another option for the enthusiast, especially if one wants to release a little more power.

Later models should come with a full service history, of course, especially if a lot of money is changing hands. A book full of dealer stamps is worth its weight in gold – a car with a good service record could prove to be a better bet than one a bit cheaper but lacking paperwork.

For those people who find themselves mechanically-challenged, ultimately, the best advice one can offer is to consult an independent specialist or a local Mazda club representative – the engine is an expensive component to put right. However, once in good

condition, it should serve you well if you don't abuse it. Treat it with a modicum of mechanical sympathy when cold (ie. don't rev it too hard) and change the oil on a regular basis, and it will provide the owner with thousands of miles of enjoyment. There really is something quite special about the rotary unit, and most of the fears surrounding it are totally unfounded. Indeed, a *Road & Track* survey carried out in 1982 revealed a distinct lack of ailments. One reader noted: "Problems? You must be kidding! This is the most reliable new car I've ever owned." Having discovered that the majority of faults occurred on the very early examples shipped to the States, the magazine concluded: "It is clear that the RX-7 is considerably better than average in this regard ... For the most part, Mazda RX-7 owners view their cars as well made and trouble-free. And what of possible concern with rotary engine reliability? Virtually none of the owners in our survey group reported any engine-related mechanical problems."

Whether the car has a manual or automatic gearbox, shifts should be smooth, with no clunks in the drivetrain. However, as is so often the case with sporting machinery, the synchromesh on second gear can fail on high-mileage vehicles, mainly due to over-enthusiastic changes and forcing selections when the transmission oil is still cold. In addition, propshaft bearings are known to be a weak spot on first generation models.

Suspension, steering & braking system

The front struts tend to go off a little quicker than usual, while the rear shocks are quite expensive to replace for a vehicle of this type; the rear wheel bearings and radius arm rubbers at the back are another trouble spot. Check the steering for free play on early cars: although there is some adjustment available in the steering box, if it needs replacing, it can be very costly. In addition, front brake discs on earlier cars have acquired something of a bad reputation, having a tendency to crack in time if the owner drives with verve; the handbrake mechanism often seizes, too.

For those trying to run the car on a budget, many parts can be sourced from cheaper outlets, but components under this heading have a distinct bearing on safety, so avoid anything a mechanic wouldn't put on his own vehicle. Naturally, if it comes from a Mazda dealer, it's guaranteed to do the job properly, but will be much more expensive. Exercise a little common sense and caution – there is rarely such a thing as a true bargain!

From the second generation, chassis components started to get

There are a number of dedicated clubs and magazines catering for the RX-7. This meeting was held at Mazda America's HQ in Irvine, California, in September 2002 – it is an annual event. (Courtesy Ken Hoyle)

more and more complicated – the DTSS rear suspension is a perfect example of the progress made on the model's in-built technology. But features like this can prove expensive to restore. Buyer beware!

Most of the tyres employed by the RX-7 range are freely available, and can be bought quite cheaply if one is willing to shop around (as well as making sure they are the right size, ensure they are of the correct rating). Wheels are another matter, of course. They have a reputation for corroding on early cars, so should be in good condition to avoid a hefty bill for replacements. However, there is no shortage of people dealing in second-hand Mazda spares if money is tight. Wheels should be cleaned regularly, by the way, to avoid deterioration caused by brake dust.

Body & interior

Although more stringent measures were taken to preserve bodies, compared to most other manufacturers during the 1970s, like most cars from the period, the earlier sporty Mazdas suffer from the dreaded tin-worm. Look in all the usual places – the wheelarches (indeed, the wings in general), sills, suspension mounting points, door bottoms, front and rear valances, across the top of the windscreen and around the rear hatch.

As regards exterior trim, rust can occur behind the rubber on the original-style bumpers, and also behind the rubbing strips that run down the car's waistline. When fitted, check along the sunroof edges, too, as corrosion problems in this area can be hard to rectify (drain holes should be kept clear to avoid rust developing further). In addition, the early sunroofs have something of a reputation for leaking, so look for water damage on the headlining and carpets. If the marks are extensive, examine the floorpan with extra care!

From the second generation, the RX-7 came with a six-year anti-rust warranty. Therefore, on later cars, the most important thing to look for is signs of accident damage – ill-fitting doors, overspray on trim, etc., are always good indicators. Incidentally, lubrication of the headlight mechanism for all models is a must to ensure the longevity of the motors.

Early interiors were not particularly hard-wearing, and the driver's seat will almost certainly develop splits in the material in time. To replace the full trim could be costly, although there's no shortage of second-hand parts, especially in the States where so many cars were sold.

Some parts on the second generation can be a little expensive, so buying a good example to start with could save money in the long run; ie. avoid the temptation to try for a running restoration.

The best buy?

The *Road & Track* survey mentioned earlier in this section of the book found that 95% of owners said they would buy another RX-7, with only 2% dismissing it. It is a car that generates enthusiasm and loyalty, and in 1982, when the article was written, only three other vehicles had such strong support – the Porsche 911, the Alfa Romeo Giulia series, and the Honda Civic.

Viewed as a used car, as Colin Goodwin said in *Supercar Classics* after driving a 1982 example: "Minor quibbles aside, I can hardly believe that you can buy such a good car for so little money. To be truthful, I think I'd have one for its engine alone."

The spares situation is relatively good, with almost everything being available from the factory, even for the 1978 cars. With a newer model (or in trying to keep the service record intact), the added expense of going to a dealer will probably be insignificant, but it could hurt the enthusiast with a small budget.

Fortunately, there are a number of specialists who can keep running costs down (the low prices on the second-hand market have resulted in a lot of vehicles being scrapped because a decent restoration is simply not financially worthwhile). But it probably wouldn't hurt to speak to a few people in your local club first to establish what their reputation is like.

Early second generation cars will doubtless appeal to some tastes, and you can certainly get a lot of car for surprisingly little money. However, enthusiasts may opt for the Turbo at the expense of fuel consumption, or perhaps even an Anfini – if you can find one – for the ultimate. The soft-top versions, of course, offer a very special experience, but they are thin on the ground and tend to be much more expensive.

The third generation models are pure sports cars – a delight to drive on a fast, mountain road. There are far too few machines like this available today, but it could prove tiring if used on an everyday basis for commuting to and from work. And could you live with what amounts to a two-seater with very little luggage space? Naturally, prices are in a different stratosphere to those of the earlier RXs, so this has to be considered, too. It's all very well being able to buy it, but running costs are a different matter.

As *Autocar* pointed out: "Servicing is a job for a specialist and it's almost certainly costly. Very thirsty if provoked. Mechanical parts expensive as also is Group 20 insurance." However, on the plus side, the magazine noted: "Turbine-smooth rotary motor gives supercar performance and reasonable reliability. Superb build quality that includes aluminium. Exclusivity assured."

All RX-7 models have a unique character, and prices vary wildly depending on which one it is and where one looks. Find the right car to suit your needs (for instance, is it to be for everyday or weekend only use?), your personality and your wallet, then have it checked by someone familiar with the series.

Writing in 1981, the respected journalist Roger Bell stated: "Like the Datsun 240Z (but not the current 280ZX softie) the RX-7 is going to become one of those rare Japs that will be just as cherished in 20 years' time as it is now."

Today, more than 20 years after Bell jotted down that line, he has been proved right. Buy a good example, and you will not be disappointed.

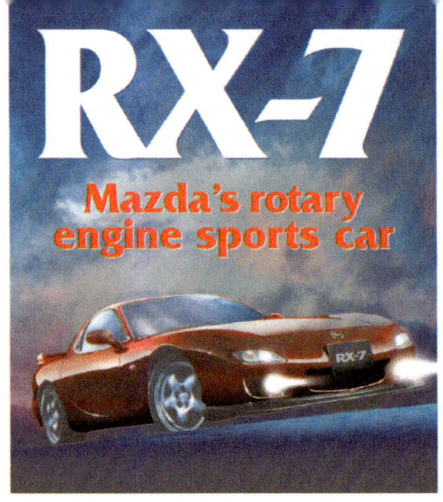

Appendix 2
Production figures

The figures below show annual production for each of the three generations, and the running total for the entire RX-7 series at the end of every calendar year.

Year	RX-7 production	Cumulative production
First Generation		
1978	72,692	72,692
1979	71,617	144,309
1980	56,317	200,626
1981	55,321	255,947
1982	59,686	315,633
1983	57,864	373,497
1984	63,959	437,456
1985	33,562	———
Second Generation		
1985	29,543	500,561
1986	72,760	573,321
1987	52,204	625,525
1988	34,592	660,117
1989	37,624	697,741
1990	29,411	727,152
1991	15,648	———
1992	245	———
Third Generation		
1991	975	743,775
1992	26,654	770,674
1993	6801	777,475
1994	5962	783,437
1995	5202	788,639
1996	4762	793,401
1997	3556	796,957
1998	1423	798,380
1999	4151	802,531
2000	2611	805,142
2001	2589	807,731
2002	3903	811,634
Total First Generation		471,018
Total Second Generation		272,027
Total Third Generation		68,589
Total RX-7 Production		**811,634**

Also from Veloce Publishing –

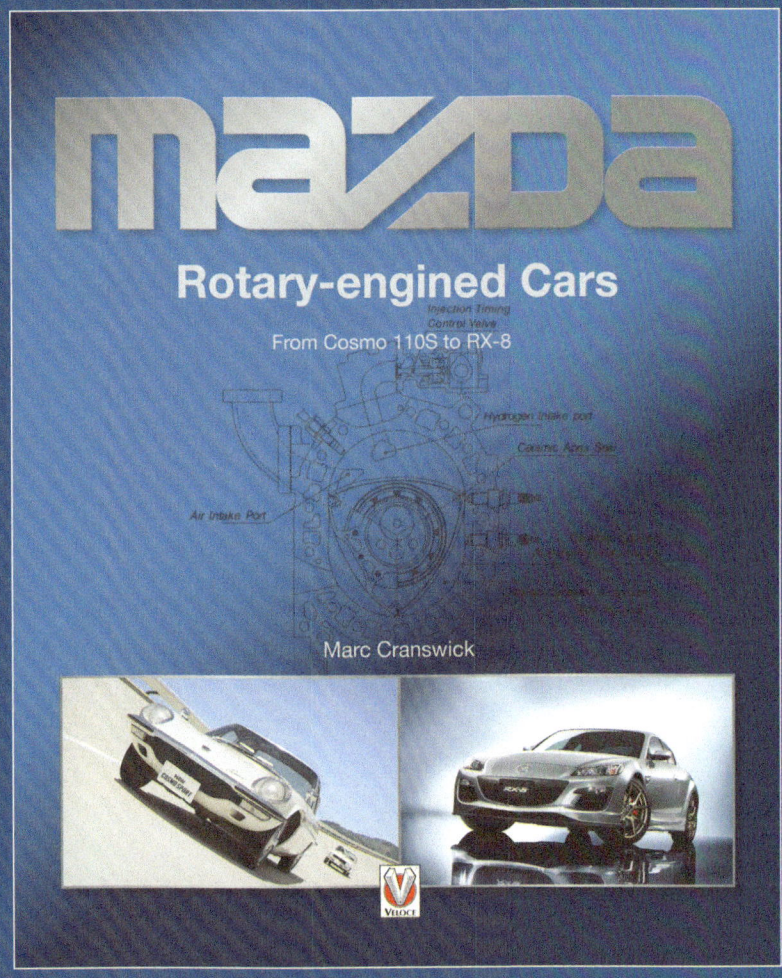

The complete history of Mazda's rotary engine-powered vehicles, from Cosmo 110S to RX-8. Charting the challenges, sporting triumphs, and critical reactions to a new wave of sports sedans, wagons, sports cars ... and trucks!

ISBN: 978-1-787117-71-6
Hardback • 25x20.7cm • 192 pages • 233 colour pictures

For prices and more info on Veloce titles, visit our website at www.veloce.co.uk • email: info@veloce.co.uk
• Tel: +44(0)1305 260068 • * prices subject to change, p&p extra

This is the definitive history of the first generation Mazda MX-5 – also known as the Miata or Eunos Roadster. A fully revised version of an old favourite, now focussing on the original NA series, this book covers all major markets, and includes stunning contemporary photography gathered from all over the world.

ISBN: 978-1-787117-77-8
Hardback • 25x20.7cm • 144 pages • 221 pictures

For prices and more info on Veloce titles, visit our website at www.veloce.co.uk • email: info@veloce.co.uk
• Tel: +44(0)1305 260068 • * prices subject to change, p&p extra

Enthusiast's Workshop Manual

Mazda
MX-5 Miata 1.8 1993 to 1999

Easy to use! Over 350 pages & over 1600 illustrations!
Hands-on maintenance and repair
Full step-by-step stripdown and rebuild

The only aftermarket workshop manual available for the MX-5! Phenomenally detailed book examining the car from bumper to bumper. Every detail of important repair and maintenance jobs is covered.

ISBN: 978-1-787114-20-3
Paperback • 27x21cm • 368 pages • 1600 colour pictures

For prices and more info on Veloce titles, visit our website at www.veloce.co.uk • email: info@veloce.co.uk
• Tel: +44(0)1305 260068 • * prices subject to change, p&p extra

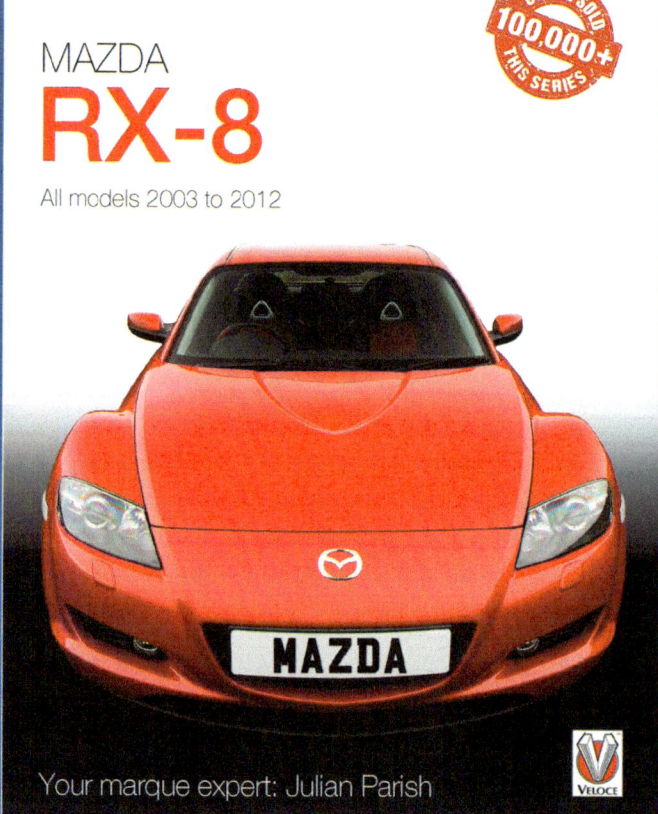

Having these books in your pocket is just like having a marque expert by your side. Benefit from the authors' years of Mazda ownership experience, learn how to spot a bad car quickly, and how to assess a promising one like a true professional. Get the right car at the right price!

ISBN: 978-1-845842-31-4
Paperback • 19.5x13.9cm • 64 pages
• 107 colour pictures

ISBN: 978-1-845848-67-5
Paperback • 19.5x13.9cm • 64 pages • 100 pictures

For prices and more info on Veloce titles, visit our website at www.veloce.co.uk • email: info@veloce.co.uk • Tel: +44(0)1305 260068 • * prices subject to change, p&p extra

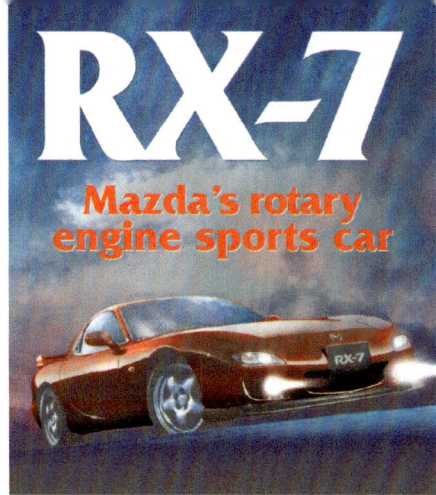

Index

Ablamis, Duane 184
Acropolis Rally 177, 178
Alfa Romeo 2, 16, 71, 99, 122, 130, 209
Allport, Neil 179
Andruet, Jean-Claude 178
Aoki, Hideo 7, 33, 46, 64, 68, 90-92, 102, 115, 140, 168, 171
Assenza, Tony 102
Audi 2, 151, 177-179
Austin (-Healey) 2, 27
AutoAlliance Int. Inc. 104
Autocar 53, 71, 75, 91, 99, 108, 151, 209
Avatar 8, 66, 67, 105

Bacon, Al 184
Baldwin, Jack 170, 171
Bathurst 157, 158, 161-163, 165, 180, 181, 186, 194-196, 200, 201
Bedard, Patrick 41
Bell, Roger 174, 209
Bellefleur, John 177
Bergstrom, 166
Bertone 11, 13, 76
Best Car 142
BF Goodrich 153, 155, 167, 178
'Biche' 178
Blick, Kevin 121
BMW 2, 15, 28, 51, 122, 173, 176, 181
Bohren, Walt 166, 167
Bonneville Salt Flats 181
Booth, Lewis 202
Boucles de Spa 178
Brands Hatch 2, 18
Bridgestone Supercar Champs. 184
British Leyland 16
British Motor Show (NEC) 49, 50, 151
British Rally Champs. 177
Bruce Garages 60
BTCC 53, 54, 172-174
Budweiser Sunriser Rally 180
Buffum, John 178-180
Buhrer, Werner 28
Burck, C.G. 17

Cadillac 100
California Custom Coach 67
Car & Driver 20, 28, 31, 41, 42, 59, 71, 95, 97, 102, 104, 115, 117, 148, 153, 181
Car Graphic 37, 69, 92, 103, 118, 143, 163, 189

Carlsson, Ingvar 178
Car Styling 28, 83, 142
Caterham 2, 127
CCR Racing 183
Chevrolet 47, 81, 101, 148, 171, 181
Chicago Show 100
Chin, Wu-Huang 132, 134
Circuit of Ireland 177
Citroen 16
Classic Cars 2, 47, 50
Classic & Sportscar 135, 152
Clement, Morris 176
Cobb, Price 184
Cole, Malcolm 59
Complete Car 162
Creative Car Craft 166
Crompton, Neil 181
Cruickshank, Gordon 108
Curtiss-Wright 16

Daily Express 157
Daimler-Benz (Mercedes) 15
Danielsson, Bror 177
Daytona 67, 166-169, 175, 181, 183, 184
DeMere, Mac 148
De Thoisy, Pierre 173
Detroit News 23
Detroit Show 5, 6, 195
Devendorf, Don 166
Dieudonne, Pierre 175
Dinkel, John 32, 42
Dodge 2, 101
Donington Park 174
Dooley, Al 66
Downing, Jim 166, 167, 170, 183
Duez, Marc 178
Dunham, Jack 171
Dykstra, Lee 183

Earls Court Show 121, 124, 155
Elford Eng. 59
Escort End. Series 177
Estes, Pete 23
Estrada, Joe 177
ETCC 175, 176
Euro. Rally Champs. 178

Farrell, Peter 153, 184
Fast Lane 76, 98
Ferrari 2, 67, 122, 127, 141
Fiat 2, 40, 51, 76
Fields, Mark 3, 202
Finger, John 176
FISA 5
Fisher, Stu 166
Ford 2, 8, 10, 12, 16, 48, 51, 54, 99, 104, 143, 163, 171, 190, 202
Ford, Maurice 48
Frankfurt Show 17
Freeth, Rodger 179
Freon, Franck 173
Frere, Paul 92, 113, 138
Frey, Peter 42
Frisselle, Brad 166
Froede, Dr Walter 15
Fujimoto, Akira 83
Fukuda, Shigenori 133
Fushida, Hiroshi 171, 173

Gachot, Bertrand 141
General Motors 10, 16, 23
Gillies, Mark 98
Giugiaro, Giorgetto 11

Goetze 15
Goodwin, Colin 209
Gormley, Kevin 177
Greer, Dick 184
Griffin, Larry 95
Grissom, Scott 177

Halsmer, Pete 181, 183, 184
Hanaoka, Shinpei 24
Hansford, Gregg 181
Harris, Bryan 177
Hayashi, Koichi 187
Hayden, R.E. 38
Hella 178
Herbert, Johnny 141
HKS 155
Hirata, Shigeo 195
Hitler, Adolf 15
Hoeppner, Ernest 15
Hogdal, John 176
Holden 30
Holman Moody 172
Honda (Acura) 18, 42, 71, 77, 94, 101, 112, 122, 142, 148
Honda, Soichiro 15
Honegger, Pierre 173
Horsley, Allan 181
Hoshijima, Hiroshi 38
Hoyle, Ken 168, 183, 208
Hutchins, Mark 173

IAD 132
Ikusawa, Tetsu 173
Imaki, Hisakazu 202
IMSA 8, 38, 76, 80, 166, 167, 170, 171, 181-184
Inomoto, Yoshihiro 6, 87, 99, 129
Ishida, Mr 31
Isuzu 10, 99

Jaguar 2, 20, 49, 55, 89, 122, 127, 130, 173, 176, 202
JAHFA 7
Japan Airlines (JAL) 16
JARI 81
JATCO 12, 68, 87
JGTC 180, 190, 196
Jones, Alan 60

Karr, Jeff 117
Kashiwagi, Akihiro 127
Katayama, Yoshimi 17, 31, 88, 166, 168
Kelsey, Richard 179
Kendall, Tom 171, 181
Kent, Dave 166, 167
Kent Racing 167, 169
Keppler, William 15
Kia 66
Kijima, Takao 7, 8, 88, 127, 152, 197, 204
Klinc, Jeff 166
Kobashi, Mr 160
Kobayakawa, Takaharu 6, 7, 40, 101, 103, 126, 127, 168
Kochi, Yasuhisa 127
Kott, Douglas 153
Kraushaar, Bob 178
Kunhe-Weiss, Heinz 176
Kuroda, Takashi 16

Laguna Seca 168, 183, 184
Lancia 2, 37, 63, 122
Le Mans 2, 4, 5, 8, 69, 124, 125, 139, 141, 152, 166, 168, 170-173, 175, 176, 183, 204
Lewis, Michael 184
Lewis, Willy 184
Lime Rock 171

215

Linge, Herbert 17
Long, Miho 7, 101, 152, 186
Longman, Richard 173
Lord, Chris 177
Lotus 2, 122, 148
Lovett, Peter 173, 175
LSR 8, 181

Maebayashi, Jiro 23, 87
Maeda, Matasaburo 26, 82
Maeda, Tamotsu 6, 101, 138
Mallory Park 172
Mandeville, Roger 76, 166, 167, 170, 181
Mankin, Tom 177
Marathon de la Route 17, 19, 166
Maserati 2, 32, 122
Matano, Tom 133
Matra 2, 37
Matsuda, Jujiro 9, 11
Matsuda, Kohei 24, 32, 33
Matsuda, Nobuya 11
Matsuda, Tsuneji 3, 9, 13, 15, 16
Matsuo, Yoshihiko 79
Mazdah, Ahura 10
Mazdaspeed 4, 124, 159, 171-174, 187, 190, 194, 197, 203, 207
Mech. Eng. Society (Japan) 19
Mees, Mike 184
Melander, Benny 178
MG 2, 110
Miami 184
Michelin 60, 153
Mid-Ohio 183, 184
Mikkola, Hannu 124
Millen, Rod 95, 153, 177-179
Miller, James 188
Mitani, Sam 153, 189
Mitsubishi 2, 18, 66, 99, 101, 125, 139, 147, 148, 151, 163
Mizuma, Takashi 127
Mizuochi, Masanori 6, 159, 160
Mnich, Matt 177
Mochizuki, Sumio 24, 26
Moffat, Allan 173
Monte Carlo Rally 177-179
Morgan 2, 71
Morikawa, Osamu 177
Moriyama, Hiroyoshi 127
Mosport 167, 184
Motor 49-51, 53, 79, 85, 97, 98, 174
Motor Fan 38, 43
Motor Magazine 51, 92, 140, 142
MotorSport 2, 4, 38, 52, 53, 59, 75, 92, 97, 104, 121, 125, 139, 141, 151, 153, 166, 173, 174, 184
Motor Trend 42, 66, 92, 101, 104, 143, 147, 148, 153, 155, 160, 161
Motospeed 60
Mouton, Michele 179
MRTE 178
Mueller, Lee 167
Muller, Fritz 176

Nakagawa, Hajime 177
Nerad, Jack 115
New Orleans 184
New Zealand, Rally of 177, 179
Nickerson, Charles 173
Nippon Oil Seal Co. 17
Nippon Piston Ring Co. 17
Nishi-Nippon 91
Nissan (Datsun & Infiniti) 6, 10-12, 16, 20, 23, 28-29, 32, 38-42, 45-48, 51, 58, 62, 65, 66, 70, 79-81, 91, 95, 99, 100, 112, 121, 123, 138, 142, 147, 148, 150, 152, 163, 164, 166, 181, 183, 195, 209

Nor'wester Rally 178

Oda, Shoji 127
Oda, Yasuji 80, 82, 83
Ohzeki, Hiroshi 85
Ono, Takashi 82
Oulton Park 2, 174

Palmer, Mr 176
Parks, Ed 166
Percy, Win 7, 54, 171-176
Performance Car 121
Peugeot 2, 173, 178
PFS 155, 184
Pike's Peak 179, 180
Pirelli 50, 59, 67, 69, 76, 118, 119, 124, 152, 153, 155
Playboy 73, 153, 177
Polish Rally 178
Pontiac 2, 71, 76
Porsche 2, 15-17, 20, 21, 27, 28, 31-33, 37, 39, 40, 42, 47, 51, 58, 62, 63, 75-77, 79, 81, 97, 99-101, 121, 122, 127, 131, 139, 148, 151, 167, 176, 181, 184, 209
Porsche, Dr Ferdinand 15
Praxl, Ewald 17

Quickor Eng. 54

RAC 2, 19, 173, 177, 178
RAC Rally 2, 177, 178
Racing Beat 167, 170, 181
Racing Services 172, 173
Rainbow, Bryan 178
RCOJ 159
Recaro 119, 152, 155, 159, 163, 195, 201
Redrup, Bob 60
Redrup, Mike 60
Reed, Robert 176, 177
Reliant 2, 51
Renault (-Alpine) 122, 151
Richardson, Clive 52
Riverside Int. Raceway 97
RJC 6, 7, 38, 79, 101, 140, 142, 197
Road & Track 28, 31, 32, 34, 40, 42, 47, 58, 61, 71, 76, 94, 95, 100, 101, 105, 106, 108, 114, 119, 147, 148, 152, 153, 161, 189, 208, 209
Road Atlanta 176, 184
Road Test 20, 148
Rolls-Royce 2, 16, 127
Rover 2, 31
Russell, Jim 126
Rusz, Joe 58

Saab 2, 181
San Antonio 183
Sato, Yoichi 127, 132, 133, 195
SCCA 8, 38, 59, 80, 166, 176-180, 184
Sears Point 170
Seattle Int. Raceway 94
Sebring 181
Sherman, Don 31, 42, 181
Shute, John 132
Sigma 172
Silverstone 2, 176
Simanaitis, Dennis 147
Skoda Rally 178
Sno-Drift Rally 179
Society Auto. Eng. 30
Soto, Ernesto 173
Spa-Francorchamps 19, 174
Start, Tom 177
St Yves, Dick 184
Sullivan, Danny 148

Sumitomo Bank 13, 23, 24
Supercar Classics 209
Susquehannock Trail 178
Suzuki 2, 165
Swedish Rally 177, 178

Tachibana, Hirotaka 101, 159, 197
Takeuchi, Hironori 180
Targa Florio 110, 113
Tatsutomi, Yasuo 173
Terada, Yojiro 88, 166, 171, 173, 176
Tippet, Hugo 176
Toivonen, Harri 178
Tokico 178
Tokyo Auto Salon 187, 196, 203
Tokyo Radio 11
Tokyo Show 8, 12, 17-19, 30, 45, 63, 88, 90, 105, 123, 140, 141, 152, 160-162, 164, 168, 171, 188, 190, 194, 201, 205
Topeka 183
Tourist Trophy 19, 176
Toyo Cork Kogyo 9
Toyo Kogyo 3, 9-13, 15, 17, 29, 33, 34, 36, 38, 66, 75
Toyota (Lexus) 10, 11, 16, 18, 23, 29, 33, 46, 48, 51, 66, 67, 73, 76, 80, 88, 90, 101, 102, 122, 125, 142, 153, 162-164, 168, 172, 174
Triumph 2, 29, 37, 48, 51, 173, 176, 178
TVR 51, 122
TWR 2, 54, 173, 174

Uchiyama, Akio 18, 26, 80
Uria, Peter 184
Vaccarella, Nino 113
Vallelunga 176
Van Nugteren, Nick 181
Vauxhall 173
Vial, Michel 178
Volkswagen 2, 15, 23

Wada, Yoshihiro 142
Waldegard, Bjorn 177
Walkinshaw, Tom 53, 54, 172-176
Wallace, Henry 163
Wambergue, Philippe 178
Wankel, Dr Felix 15, 109
Warmbold, Achim 177, 178
Watanabe, Moriyuki 24
Watts, Patrick 152
Weidler, Volker 141
West Palm Beach 184
Willow Springs 71, 148
Woolf, John 178
WRC 2, 8, 124, 177-179

Yamaguchi, Jack 30, 124
Yamamoto, Kenichi 16, 30, 33, 43, 75, 76, 79, 80, 92, 124, 132, 142, 173
Yamamoto, Nobuhiro 127
Yamasaki, Yoshiki 34, 36
Yorino, Takashi 88, 166, 173
Yoshioka, Noriaki 80
Yura, Takuya 173

Zaima, Hiroshi 21
Zolder 174-176
ZW Enterprises 173

The Mazda company and its products are mentioned throughout this book.